Living with Questions

DAVID E JENKINS

Living with Questions

Investigations into the theory and practice of belief in God

SCM PRESS LTD

334 00913 8

First published 1969
by SCM Press Ltd
56 Bloomsbury Street London WC1

© SCM Press Ltd 1969

Printed in Great Britain by
Billing & Sons Limited
Guildford & London

CONTENTS

ACKNOWLEDGMENTS

The original occasions of the papers collected in this book were as follows; the author thanks the publishers concerned for permission to include material which has previously appeared elsewhere.

Part One

1   A sermon preached at Pusey House, Oxford, in Michaelmas Term, 1956, in a series entitled 'God and the Universe'. In that series the sermon was entitled 'Signs of God in the Intellect of Man'.

2   An article specially written for inclusion in *The Honest to God Debate*, edited by John A. T. Robinson and David L. Edwards, published by the SCM Press, 1963.

3   An article written for *Learning for Living* (the journal of the Christian Education Movement), and published in 1963 as a commentary on the '*Honest to God* Debate'.

4   An article commissioned by the editor of the London Quarterly and Holborn Review for a symposium on 'The Doctrine of God', published in July 1964.

5   A university sermon at Leeds, March 1966.

6   One of the Bishop of Coventry's Lent Lectures in 1966, delivered in Coventry Cathedral to an audience invited by the Bishop from all the parishes in his diocese.

7   (i) A review written for *Frontier*, Winter 1967/68.
   (ii) An essay written at the request of the Archbishop of Canterbury for circulation among those attending the 1968 Lambeth Conference at which I was a consultant.
   (iii) A lecture given in Canterbury Cathedral, October 1968.

Part Two

1   Prepared and delivered as a paper in section R (Religion and Psychiatry) of the First International Congress of Social Psychiatry, St John's Wood, London, 1965.

Acknowledgments

2   A paper presented to a private conference at Nuffield
College, Oxford, in 1964 and involving psychiatrists, theologians and social scientists.

3   An address to the annual service of the Highgate Counselling Centre, Jackson's Lane Methodist Church, Highgate,
London, January 1965.

4   An open lecture under the auspices of the University of
Lancaster, 1965.

5   A lecture given at Durham University in November 1968
as a contribution to a week entitled 'Christian Viewpoint
1968' under the title 'The Christian and Other Faiths'.

6   An Easter meditation given in the BBC Third Programme
on Easter Day, 1969.

Part Three

1   A sermon preached at Pusey House, Oxford, in Michaelmas Term, 1964, in the series 'The Needs of the Church
Today'. The title in the series was 'Dynamic Doctrine'.

2   A talk given to the Annual Conference of the Modern
Churchman's Union at Oxford in 1966.

3   Extracted from the introduction to the section on 'Ethics
and the Christian Tradition' in a privately circulated *Hand-
book for Teachers of Christian Ethics in Theological Colleges*,
prepared under the auspices of the Central Council for the
Church's Ministry of the Church of England in 1964.

4   A version of a talk given to the Christian Frontier Council
in London in 1967.

5   A short paper prepared at the second consultation on
'Health and Healing' held at Tübingen in 1967 under the
auspices of the World Council of Churches and the Lutheran
World Federation.

6   Based on a talk given to a conference at Oxford of the
Fellowship of St Alban and St Sergius and held at Pusey
House in 1964.

The *Postscript* was specially written for this book.

INTRODUCTION

The Inquiry of Faith

God is either a gift or a delusion, the source of all gifts and
of the possibility that everything may be received as a gift, or
the phantasy of men who prefer to imagine that they receive
gifts rather than to acknowledge that they must face facts –
on their own.

I believe in God. It often puzzles me that I do; I am
often hard put to it to explain why I do, while my conduct
and attitudes not infrequently suggest both to others and to
my reflective self that I do not. But I do. I believe that life
is a gift, a response, a dialogue – a dialogue with more than
myself, more than others, more than the facts and the
beauties, the mysteries and the muddles, the terrors and the
trivialities of the universe. I believe that life is from God,
with God and to God, and sometimes I begin to experience
it so. Therefore I hold that this faith also is a gift, my given
starting point, my proffered attitude, my donated way of
proceeding.

But faith has now replaced 'God' as the possible and even
likely delusion, the delusion of my misinformed and mis-
directed attitudes and emotions. How can I know that this
is not so? In one mood and mode of approach to my living
I do not need to answer this question. In another mood and
mode I know that I cannot. In the former mode, faith is both
the given and the given attitude to (and relationship with)
the given – who is also the Giver. It is therefore like
knowledge and provides the human basis on which my living
is to preceed and within the context of which my living is to
be understood and directed. In speaking of my faith I am

speaking of how the world seems to me, of how I experience it, of how I know it. In this mode, when I speak of my faith in God I am not speaking of a separable attitude or disposition which is one among many in the bundle of attitudes, dispositions, intentions, emotions and so on which make up my dynamic self. For example, 'my faith in God' does not describe a disposition to hold that God exists and a consequent set of attempts to believe as if this were so which has to be fitted in with and, where possible, applied to, my other dispositions and intentions. There is nothing hypothetical, nothing of the 'as-if-this-were-so' in faith in the mode of which I am now speaking. Nor is there anything partial or separable about it. Faith describes the given context and direction of my living. My life is to do with God and my living in the world is to do with God. This is not hypothetical. This is how things are given and hypotheses arise from this. So the question, 'How do I know my faith is not an illusion?', does not, in this mode, arise – because it cannot. My faith is the given on the basis of which and within which I know. For him who has faith, God is not an illusion, he is not even a hypothesis. He is God.

But even the faithful faithful walk by faith and not by sight, and I am one of the frequently unfaithful faithful, one of those whose living has frequent inconsistency with the givens of his believing. Consequently, for myself, let alone for those who do not share my believing or who do not share it in my way, the mode in which faith is, or is as good as, knowledge, has to live alongside the mode in which faith clearly is not, or is not acceptable as, knowledge. Faith, in fact, may be a delusion and the 'knowledge' which faith gives and qualifies, and which is given in faith, may be both false and illusory. For God is not obvious, the faithful are not obviously right and the world is not obviously godly. How, then, can I know whether faith is a way of knowing or a form of illusion?

I must move constantly between not needing to know and knowing that I do not know and thus commit myself to the process of finding out. I experience faith as a gift and as a question. The very nature of the gift requires that I face the question. If it is truly a gift of the Giver, a real response to a

true God, then the questioning will enable the deeper
receiving of the gift and a deepening knowing of the Giver.
If there is no Giver, then there is no gift, and the questioning will expose the illusion. Nothing I can do can alter
the ultimate situation here. I can only seek to put myself in
the way of receiving an exposure of this situation. I must
investigate. I must respond, I must see – and let be whatever
I am brought to see.

But my 'faith in God' is not some general concept or
unscientific attitude. It is a particular kind of faith in a
particular kind of God. I am a Christian. My faith has
arisen from, and my faith is fed by, the people who have
found in Jesus Christ and the things concerning him the
focus of faith in God. My faith in God is some version,
however wretched, of Christian faith in the God and Father
of Jesus Christ. In the tradition of this faith there is a good
deal of content, a considerable amount of alleged information
and understanding about God, the world and men; the past,
the present and the future. Hence there is plenty of material
to be put to the question and to raise questions for my life,
my world, my relationships. It is from this material that I
derive substance for the inquiry and the inquiries of faith.
As a Christian, I have to live with the questions put to the
faith of myself and my community, i.e. with the question
which this faith puts to me, my fellows and our world.
Living with questions is the inquiry of faith, and the inquiry
of faith is the practice of the process whereby faith lives and
either grows or dies, is found to be either a gift or an
illusion. I have ceased to have any confidence in, and very
much respect for, *a priori* theology. Theologians seem to me
to have got into the habit of talking largely about what
theologians have talked about, and while this was something
in the world once, for the world now it is largely talk about
talk (about talk!). Hence I find it imperative to treat faith as
a gift to be acted upon. I must expose (what foolishness!)
myself and my faith in attempts to expound what may be the
truth of what is given in faith in the situation, to the situation,
and for the situations in which I and my fellows find
ourselves.

Clearly such exposés and expositions must reveal my folly and my failures of faith, but it may be also that, if there is a God, something of the reality of faith may also, by his gift, emerge. I cannot tell, but I must try, or rather, I must commit myself to a response, to a search and to an explanation. Because I experience faith as a gift, I must proceed in *faith*, that is, *confidently*, and state as clearly as I can what faith seems to imply in and for particular situations. Because I know something of my own folly and the precariousness of faith, I must also proceed *faithfully*, i.e. according to the nature of faith, which is, *tentatively*. I am expressing what, as far as I can see, may be true that, in the exposition, there may be a more general and public investigation of what the exposure is good for. I do not know. I dare to hope. I must expect much failure. But it may be that it will be good for something by way of human and godly living before man and before God – if there is a God and faith is a gift.

Therefore, I am stupid enough and bold enough to set about publishing the following occasional pieces of mine which are offered as examples of living with questions, of pursuing the inquiry of faith. I have tried to offer examples of facing the question of God and then facing the question of man and of Jesus Christ. These are Parts One and Two. The third section is meant as a group of examples of discussion of aids which are available for facing the questions. Finally, I have added an extended and hitherto unpublished and unused reflection on what seems to emerge of the authority of faith.

For I must confess that as of the time of writing this introduction I find the inquiry of faith to be a living matter of joy and thankfulness. The gift seems to be abundantly given and I should be perpetrating a cowardly and shameful lie if I were not bold enough publicly to praise and confess the Giver. Nonetheless and even so, the questions are not settled.

PART ONE

Concerning God

I | *There is no God*

'There is no God.' Is it only the fool who says there is no God? Surely the declaration of atheism has been made by some of the most sensitive, the most passionate and the most serious of men. Sometimes they have made it as a cry nearly of despair, sometimes as an exultant cry of freedom, sometimes as a sober statement of fact. 'There is no God.' How can there be – for consider the meaning of 'God'. God, St Anselm tells us, is *that than which nothing more perfect can be conceived*. God is the summit of all possible perfections and then a perfection beyond them. He is more than we can utter, more than we can conceive; the fulfilment, infinitely beyond our hopes, of our deepest longings; the reality, infinitely beyond our conceptions, towards which our highest thoughts are striving. He is the only being who alone is worthy of worship. God is not to be reverenced *because* he is the worthy embodiment of a quality of qualities which are recognizably supremely good. If God is to be worshipped *because* he is supremely good, this would make the supremely good transcend him; he would depend for his being God on being supremely good. But God is not transcended, nor does he depend. Therefore God must be supremely good – *and more*. What more? That more which makes him God, i.e. 'that than which nothing more perfect can be conceived'. God is not to be reverenced because he is the supreme end of all things. If God is to be worshipped *because* all things are supremely and finally fulfilled in him, this would make the fulfilment of all things transcend him and he would *depend* for his being God on the fulfilment of all things. But God is not transcended, nor does he depend. Therefore God must be the supreme end of all things – *and more*. What more? That more which makes

him alone – and in himself – and because of himself alone –
the sole being worthy of worship, the only truly worthy object
of our worship.

But here is the stumbling block, that 'more' which God
must be if he is to be God. For the point about all beings
known to us, about all objects of which we have experience or
of which we can form a conception, is that they are not in
themselves or because of themselves worthy of worship. To
exist as an object, or to have any being, *means* to have limiting
qualities by which the object is recognized, the being is perceived as existing. Or to put it more crudely and simply, you
do not know that any object is there unless it is pointed out as
being there by its qualities and properties. And when you say
an object or a being exists you mean it is 'there'. 'Being there'
means that it is there as 'an example of . . .', it exists 'because
of'. But we have seen that God, to be God, cannot be 'an
example of . . .' or exist 'because of . . .'. God, in fact, to be
God must be more than an object, more than a being. But if
God is more than a being, then he is not a being. You do not
get yourself anywhere by saying 'a being and more' – for
what sort of a being is that? But if he is not a being, then he
does not exist. That is to say, 'There is no God'.

I fear that you will long ago have decided that this is
merely a philosopher's discussion and not only have lost the
thread but decided that it is not worth following. Moreover,
as you know, or think you know, that I believe in God, you
are probably complacently sitting back and treating all this as
conjuror's patter while you wait for me to produce the expected rabbit out of the hat – to wit, my explanation of how,
after all, of course we may comfortably and assuredly believe
in God.

Be clear about this, then. If you have not at least sensed
the strength of the arguments for atheism, it is more than
probable that you have not really sensed what we mean when
we say we believe in God. For God must be whatever we like
to say – and more, or even, whatever we like to say – but he
is not (which is the same thing, logically speaking). No description of God is sufficient. But if no description is sufficient,
then it would seem that no description can be given. And if

4

no description can be given of God, how can we say God exists? To put the matter more philosophically, if God has to be defined, as we have seen, as whatever you like to say *and more*, then the notion of God's existence is logically self-contradictory. But this is not a mere philosopher's point. For this logical notion of self-contradiction in the idea of God's existence transcends and embraces all sorts of practical and theoretical difficulties which count against believing that God exists.

'There is no God.' A despairing cry: how can perfection exist when perfection means that which is beyond anything now known to exist, that which is beyond our strivings, that which our very strivings testify does *not* exist? 'There *is* no God.'

'There is no God.' An exultant cry: we are not shut in by any conception, any scheme or any pattern already existing. The world is wide open to infinite and undetermined possibi-. lities. Patterns are to be made and ends built up. We are not shut up in that which already exists. We are free. 'There is no *God.*'

'There is no God.' A sober statement of fact: we must be content with what we can observe, measure and see. It is true that men strive and men seek aims 'beyond' themselves. But we cannot extrapolate ourselves out of the theoretically observable universe or project ourselves beyond the theoretically comprehensible psychosomatic organisms that we are. There can be no evidence for that which goes beyond the evidence. 'There is *no* God.'

In short, worship is a mistake and perfection is a logical construction which never has existed and never will exist save as something in the minds of men. All that we have said in the first part of this sermon about the notion of 'more than' which is implicit in the idea of God, all the notion of transcendence, of a perfection of perfection which cannot ultimately be spoken of but which alone is worshipful – all this is a mere construction in the minds of men who have misinterpreted their experience on the basis of their ignorance and their undeveloped mental faculties. It may be that reverence is an innate human capacity, but it does not, properly understood, point man beyond himself *to* any supreme object of worship. Neither logic nor fact support such a conclusion as often as it has been drawn. 'God' is a mental construction.

It may be so – I think it is very important to see that there are plausible grounds for holding that it may be so. There is no logical step, no proof, from the fact that men *conceive* of God to the fact that God *exists*. The only thing that the observable fact that a very large number of men worship God goes to prove is that a very large number of men indulge in a practice called worship.

But there are two questions which we can ask *ourselves* – *not* as outside observers of the phenomena 'men other than ourselves believing in God' and 'men other than ourselves worshipping' – but as people who are ourselves part of the evidence which we observe.

The first is this. Can we really do without that to which such notions as perfection, transcendence and worshipfulness point?

Not merely, 'Can we do without as pieces of mental furniture?' Very likely we can. Certainly we can for good stretches of time. But can we rigorously and absolutely exclude from every element of our being, activity and thought all suggestion that there is 'more than' the sum total of other selves like us, the sum total of natural phenomena like those known to us, the sum total of the dialectic of history as it is described to us by the secular historian and so on? Will it '*do*' to say that transcendence and perfection are mere extrapolations, a sort of $n+1$ of things ordinarily known to us where the '1' stands for something precisely like the 'n's' or for a mental operation on our part? Or is there in worship an activity of response as well as, or even rather than, an activity of creation and self-projection? Can we *believe* that perfection, that the dimension of transcendence wherein lies the worshipful, *is* a mere notion?

Another way to put this point would be this. In the first part of my sermon I tried to describe what the intellect means by 'God' and to go on to show that this notion is probably *logically* self-contradictory. Some people would therefore say that this notion of God is *unthinkable*, i.e. ought not to be thought of, but rejected. How many people would want to say that even if this notion is *logically* contradictory, what is *'unthinkable'* is that they should give it up? What leads them to this? An experience of God or an ignorance of logic?

I have time to refer only to my second question – which is, perhaps, the reverse of the first. It is: Why does atheism have to be justified, and why does doubt about God's existence have such penetrating and anguished quality? Is it because God is not a being like other beings, *not* in the sense that he does not exist, but rather in the sense that he is the one being whose existence cannot be a matter of indifference? That is, is it because he is the one being upon whom all beings depend? It might be, therefore, that one of the signs of God in the intellect of man is precisely the peculiarly intensive quality of the doubt that arises about his existence and the need rather to assert atheism than to treat the whole issue of his existence as 'not a proper question'.

These signs, however, real as I believe them to be, are not proofs but pointers, not substantiations but signs whose true significance can be evoked only by the witness of the Christian church and the proclaiming of the word of God. None the less, they remain as constantly fretting signs that we are made by the transcendent God for the transcendent God and that our folly is to say 'There is no God', while our joy and peace comes as in worship we confess him as 'he who is' and as 'God of gods and Lord of lords'.

2 | Concerning Theism

I assume that the '*Honest to God* debate' is sufficiently shown to be an urgently necessary one by the response which the original book has evoked. The evidence of my own contacts and those of many of my friends is sufficient to convince me that the approach of the book has encouraged many people to feel able to look again, with a very real possibility of discovery, at questions concerning God, the meaning and context of life, and the practice and possibility of religion. Persons who have felt encouraged and set free by the example of the book to renew their quest into these matters include both some who have hitherto 'written off' all talk of God and all practice of religion and some who have succeeded in clinging with more or less difficulty and desperation to a 'Faith' and the practices of a Faith which they have not dared to investigate deeply because they have more than half suspected that under investigation the 'Faith' will collapse. Thus the book consti-tutes an occasion of liberation and advance, whatever occasions of stumbling it may also be in danger of offering.

This being so, merely negative criticism would be a disaster and a faithless and disobedient throwing away of the oppor-tunities opened up. But genuinely to further this discussion, full and careful use must be made of the resources at our disposal. At some stage in the continuing search for, and witness to, the truth about God and the world, a careful and extended contribution needs to be made which will show that one main strand in traditional Christian theism has always been concerned to deny or at least to be very cautious about precisely those features of 'theism' (e.g. being misled by the concept of God as *a* being or *a* person) which the Bishop rails against. There is an immense amount of material in the

Fathers, both Western and Eastern, which, taken along with
the insights of the great mystical writers and masters of the
spiritual life, should remind us first very sharply and then
very profitably of the scandalous poverty of much current
'theism'. The true extent of the scandal is peculiarly well
shown by the fact that not only does the theism against which
the Bishop protests seem to very many people to be recognizably the theism of the Christian church (and the only possible
theism – hence the need and justification for atheism), but
also the Bishop actually seems to be trapped in this belief
himself. His attempt to be honest to God is so dishonest to the
God of, for example, Athanasius or the fourth century
Cappadocian writers or of Thomas Aquinas, let alone
Augustine or, again, to the God of the author of the *Cloud of
Unknowing* or, say, to the God who is worshipped in and
through the shape of the Orthodox Liturgy, that it is clearly
high time that we were confronted by an explosive reminder
of the need to 'get our theism right'. It must, however, not be
taken for granted that we can do this by forgetting all the
traditional language because we superficially focus attention
on its imagery and ignore its insights. Certainly the Bishop is
in no position to be our guide here, as he is plainly ignorant
of, or indifferent to, what has been said and what has been
meant by what has been said. But this, in so far as it is true,
must be taken not as a satisfactory criticism or refutation of
what the Bishop has said, but as a challenge to those who are
more familiar with those insights to bring them to bear on the
situation which the Bishop indicates and exemplifies.

As I have neither time nor space here and now to take up
my own challenge I wish, as a contribution to the continuing
debate and as a prelude to the type of enterprise I have asked
for, to try to show that it is extremely unlikely that the way
forward will lead to a restatement of Christian belief which is
in any way 'the end of theism' or the giving up of the notion
of God as personal. It may be that I am committed to arguing
in this way not by the points to which I shall later draw
attention but entirely by my own personal predilections. For
while I very greatly sympathize with and believe that I share
in the Bishop's bewilderment, agnosticism and protests, I

would not, I think, spontaneously or even on consideration, state the position from which I face and attack these bewilderments as he does. When he says (and again I find myself in agreement) that often in debates between Christians and Humanists his 'sympathies are on the humanist's side' he goes on to say: 'This is not in the least because my faith or commitment is in doubt' (p. 8). The difficulty I find with this statement is that, for me, 'faith' implies 'faith in', and 'commitment' implies 'commitment to'. I do not think this is just a question of language – or, alternatively, if it is, it is a point to be followed up because, in one sense, the whole discussion is about language – about how we should talk and have grounds for talking about 'ultimate realities'. I feel a similar disquiet when he says (p. 27): 'I have never really doubted the fundamental truth of the Christian faith – though I have constantly found myself questioning its expression.' I am unable to be at all clear what it is that the Bishop has never really doubted. I do not think one could be altogether blamed for being inclined to deduce that what the Bishop has never doubted is that somehow or other his own 'attitude' or 'feeling' or 'commitment' is 'right'. If this suspicion were at all justified then one might not be very far from having to conclude that the one thing that the Bishop, is deep down, clear about is that he cannot be basically wrong – although it is not really clear what is the nature of this 'not-wrongness'.

Now this is almost certainly not only unfair but also verging on the unkind. None the less, it may serve to bring out the point that whatever the difficulties about objective language in talk about God there are also very grave ones in subjective language. The only way I can describe my own attitude, to and in, the doubtings and difficulties to which the Bishop so rightly and with such evident sincerity directs our attention seems to be this. Even in moments of complete intellectual – and still worse, moral – bafflement, or when I feel wholehearted assent to a 'Humanist' case apparently over against a 'Christian' one, I am still unable to doubt my faith *in God*, and if I could in any way direct or control my commitment I would wish it to be commitment *to God*. Indeed I think I would go so far as to say that I do not really care about the truth, fundamental or otherwise, of the 'Christian faith'. I am only concerned with whatever the Christian faith is in so far as it helps on the question of God, his being, his nature and the possibility of relationship to him. I am, it is true, thus far only describing my attitude, and it may quite plausibly be argued that this attitude is (*a*) subjectively immature and (*b*) objectively wrong. But the fact that it is possible to attack it on, say, Freudian or existentialist grounds under (*a*) is not the same thing as proving (*b*) – unless one holds that the only possible theory of knowledge (as a whole, not merely knowledge of God) is the extreme existentialist position or that Freudian insights define and exhaust reality. I may perhaps, therefore, be allowed to maintain for the purposes of the argument that my attitude has built into it an objective reference to God, although I should add that 'God' operates not so much as the name of an object but much more like a proper name. (I understand faith in or commitment to persons or causes. I do not understand, or perhaps rather do not accept, the notion of faith in or commitment to an object. That certainly is idolatry – or insanity.)

If I try to maintain such a position, including that my attitude is a 'proper' attitude (i.e. is related to truth, to the way things really are), I clearly lay myself open to plain and straightforward contradiction powerfully urged. 'You say that you are unable to doubt your commitment to a *personal God.* That may be your psychological state but it is a regrettable one (or at least a delusion if that is not necessarily regrettable). There is no God.' I have in fact demonstrated just what Tillich says (quoted by Robinson, p. 57): 'The first step to atheism is always a theology which drags God down to the level of doubtful things.' This may be so, but I very much fear that there is a real sense in which the existence of God *is* doubtful (i.e. capable of being doubted), that atheism will always seem a real existential possibility, and that this remains so even if you attempt to restate the doctrine of God in terms of 'ultimate concern' and the like. In this connection a remark of the Bishop's is very instructive (p. 29): 'God is, by definition, ultimate reality. And one cannot argue whether

ultimate reality *exists.*' We have, I think, detected some very
determinedly anti-traditional-metaphysic thinkers trying to
get away with a concealed and possibly inverted version of
the traditional ontological argument. (This is the argument
that the *idea* of God includes the idea of existing and so God
must exist. The mistake in this has usually been supposed to
be that while the *idea* of God may include the *idea* of existing
the fact that people have *ideas* of a certain sort is, of itself, no
evidence at all that anything corresponding to the ideas
really exists.) Of course you cannot argue whether ultimate
reality exists. You can only ask whether pretentious phrases
like 'ultimate reality' are wanted at all and, *a fortiori*, whether
there is any case for bringing the word 'God' within smelling
distance of the argument. Moreover the 'ultimate reality' or
'ultimate concern' of Robinson and of Tillich (in the
quotations Robinson uses) is no more an obvious, self-evident
or demonstrably necessary feature of the world or of our
experiences in the world than God is.

Thus Robinson continues the passage I have just referred
to (p. 29): '. . . one cannot argue whether ultimate reality
exists. One can only ask what ultimate reality is like. . . .' It is
quite clear that the answer he wishes to maintain as the true
answer to *that* question is by no means self-evident, and if it is
not self-evident it is, of course, doubtful and deniable (like the
God of the theism he is wondering whether to repudiate). For
example, on p. 49 he writes: 'To believe in God as love
means to believe that in pure personal relationship we
encounter, not merely what ought to be, but what is, the
deepest, veriest truth about the structure of reality. This, in
face of all the evidence, is a tremendous act of faith. But it is
not the feat of persuading oneself of the existence of a super-
Being beyond this world endowed with personal qualities.
Belief in God is the trust, the well-nigh incredible trust, that
to give ourselves to the uttermost in love is not to be con-
founded but to be "accepted", that Love is the ground of our
being, to which ultimately we "come home".' 'In face of all
the evidence', 'the well-nigh incredible trust' and so on make
it quite clear that talk about the existence of ultimate reality
not being arguable is irrelevant bluff. 'Ultimate reality' is a

trivial and meaningless phrase until you begin to characterize 'it', and the character the Bishop (and Tillich) want to give 'it' is something over and above 'it' where 'it' is just plain matter of fact reality (the 'stuff' that is 'all the evidence'). They say, in fact, that 'it' is to be described in 'personal categories', and that 'Love is the ground of our being'. Since *all* human conduct is manifestly not loving, and it is very doubtful in what sense any of the processes of the physical universe could ordinarily be so described, it begins to appear that 'ultimate reality' is logically very much like a phrase describing an 'object' which is 'other than' the objects we actually encounter, even if it is thought of as 'underlying' rather than 'being above' the phenomenal world.

The fact that this 'Ground' is 'something' which is other than the stuff of our ordinary life and existence even if it is in that ordinary stuff that 'it' is encountered is made clear enough at numerous points, despite repeated statements which try to equate the two. Compare for example the quotation above where 'Love' suddenly gets a capital letter and we are said to be 'accepted' and 'come home', even if only in inverted commas (i.e. it is at least *as if* we were in a personal relationship with the Other – why not then a (carefully guarded) conception of a personal God?) Further, we are warned that 'the eternal *Thou* is not to be equated with the finite *Thou*, nor God with man or nature' (p. 53), just after we have been told (correctly on the basis of the first epistle of John) that the statement that 'God is love' is not reversible, i.e. God is the subject and love is the predicate. But all this is surely to say that as a matter of logic we are justified in maintaining what, as Christians, we do about the universe and life in the universe because God exists and because he is love. What Tillich and Robinson following him are talking about is *how* we (or some of us modern 'we's') come or may come to maintain what we do, but this is different from *what* we maintain.

But the logical difficulties of theism are not even clarified, let alone removed by their procedure. Indeed, a good deal of the language seems in danger of being less clear and, thereby, possibly more dishonest than some more traditional

statements. Take, for example, the extended quotation from
Tillich on p. 81, where the talk is of grace. Grace is carefully
referred to as 'it' but 'it' behaves in a very personal way (and,
indeed, since the 'happenings' involved are said not to be at
our command it looks very much as if grace 'comes in from
outside' – at any rate from outside us). The situation referred
to is 'as though a voice were saying "You are accepted" '.
Now 'seeming to be addressed' and still more 'accepting the
fact that we are accepted' sounds like descriptions of a
personal relationship with a being who is at least personal
and we may perhaps believe that this *is* what is being pointed
to, as later on the term 'Ground' gets a capital 'G' which
suggests that perhaps it is being treated as very like a proper
name. Again, statements like 'we all know that we are bound
eternally and inescapably to the Ground of our being' (cited
on p. 80) are just not true save where 'we all' means 'all we
who believe in an eternal personal God who will not let us
go'. If, for example, 'we all' meant 'I and my friends', then
there would be some who would hold that any 'I' is simply a
temporary and temporal collocation of matter who could
only be spoken of as 'bound eternally and inescapably to the
Ground of our being', in so far as it is true that matter or
energy cannot be created or destroyed. (A very doubtful
proposition, I believe.)

I should maintain, therefore, that the traditional theistic
talk about a personal God is no more (although admittedly
no less) *logically* difficult than is the talk about 'ultimate
reality' and 'ultimate concern' which is urged upon us. For
as used the term 'ultimate reality' no more refers to some
self-evident existence than does the name 'God'. One can
refuse or be unable to believe in God and one can refuse or
be unable to believe that 'ultimate reality' has the character
asserted.

Further, *if* ultimate reality does have the character asserted
of 'it', then it looks very much as if it remains true that there
exists a personal God who is other than and more than the
stuff and phenomena of our life, however true it must be that
he is to be encountered only in and through this stuff.

Hence the task to which the Bishop of Woolwich's book

and the response to it summon us is that of re-deepening our
theism by drawing much more fully on the rich and deep
truths of the Christian tradition, always with a full conscious-
ness of the difficulties and demands which modern insights
make upon us (although by no means all these demands are
in essence new; I suspect that the only thing which has
always counted decisively against the difficulty of believing in
God is that as a matter of fact he exists and makes himself
known).

In connection with this task I would like to add two brief
postscripts. First, it is by no means self-evident that images of
depth are richer or more satisfactory than images of height –
and that especially in the area of personal relationships and
personal development. Here is a matter for urgent discussion
between psychologists and theologians. How far does 'depth'
imagery correlate with desires to escape from reality as it is
manifested in persons, to 'return to the womb' and to get
away from the stretching demands of integration in relation
with, and with reference to, others? And how far does 'height'
stand for the demand always to go further than every outgoing
experience wherein the self is expressed on behalf of other
selves? Ought we to understand that over and above going
'deeper into ourselves' our *real* end (? ultimate concern) is to
reach out and, so to speak, up far beyond ourselves to a
fulfilment which embraces all persons? It might perhaps be
true that the problem of transcendence is the problem of the
fulfilment of human personality in a fullness of personality
that embraces all personal possibilities in a Transcendent
which (who) is fully personal. To this end the best symbolism
might be the challenge of height symbolism. Perhaps it may
turn out that the doctrine of the Trinity (the transcendent
'personalness' of God which is more than 'persons' and yet
the perfection of unified personality) is not all that irrelevant
psychologically, metaphysically or theologically.

And secondly, if the conviction that ultimate reality is love
does require us to continue to believe in a personal God (or
does depend for its truth on the existence of a personal God –
whichever way we happen to or always have to come to the
truth), then it may very well turn out that the material

which the Bishop brings to bear in his fourth chapter on the question of christology is again to be used to re-enliven rather than replace the traditional understanding of the person of Jesus.

For example, on p. 74 Robinson writes: 'It is in Jesus, and Jesus alone, that there is nothing of self to be seen, but solely the ultimate, unconditional love of God. It is as he emptied himself utterly of himself that he became the carrier of "the name which is above every name", the revealer of the Father's glory – for that name and that glory is simply Love.' But Love is the ultimate reality of the universe who is God. If one were wanting to relate this directly to the traditional way of stating Christian doctrine (based on the Greek language of the third and fourth Christian centuries) one could point out that 'ultimate reality' could legitimately be tied up with the Greek word *hypostasis* ('that which stands under', 'what in each individual case is really there'). One would want to make this tie up because *hypostasis* is the traditional word for the 'persons' of the Trinity and for the 'person' of Jesus Christ. But since this ultimate reality is rightly thought of as personal (i.e. *is* – really – Love) and since Jesus is 'solely the ultimate, unconditional love of God', is it not legitimate to say that the *hypostasis* who is Jesus (i.e. the *reality* of the person who is called 'Jesus') is, as the creed says, 'of one substance with the Father' (i.e. a real expression of the reality which/ who is God)? For Jesus is the perfect, particular, personal expression of the underlying personal reality of the universe. Further, as the Bishop indicates in his talk of 'emptied himself utterly of himself', we are now in a position to have a much richer understanding of the traditional doctrine of the divine self-emptying in Jesus. For if love is 'existence for others', then to be 'really Love' (an 'hypostasis' who is 'of one sub- stance' with the Father) is identical with existing wholly for others and emptying oneself of one's own self-existence to that end, so that the human personal existence of Jesus *is* the divine existence in the terms of our limited and creaturely existence.

This is not just theological word-play or logic-chopping, but is closely related to the matter of a 'tremendous act of

faith' or 'the well-nigh incredible trust' of which the Bishop
(on p. 49) speaks with some enthusiasm, but which rather
troubles me. Certainly I believe that the decision on what
ultimate reality is really like demands what is always an act of
faith, i.e. you decide to 'back' and indeed to 'put your trust
in' some part of the evidence that is lying about as the crucial
clue to the whole (which human concern is really ultimate,
which facet of reality – things as they hit me and others – is
directly and decisively related to ultimate reality, etc.). This
is a similar decision whether you decide that it is physical
explanation which is ultimate or Love or what you will. But
acts of faith and trust are not to be commended for being
'tremendous' or 'well-nigh incredible'. To be anything other
than irresponsible escapism they must have grounds. And one
very powerful ground for deciding that ultimate reality is
Love is belief in God, and one of the most powerful grounds
for believing in God is Jesus, especially Jesus as both the
climax of a long tradition of belief in God and the source of
such a tradition. Hence 'who Jesus really is' is directly linked
with 'what is the nature of ultimate reality'.

Of course there are very great difficulties in all this. In
particular I am personally convinced that the Bishop's
strictures about traditional christology in practice being
alarmingly and misleadingly monophysite (i.e. treating Jesus
as God absorbing and in effect removing human nature) are
far more generally true than his strictures on the practice of
theism (which are true enough). But I wished simply to give a
brief indication in the area of christology of my general thesis
which is that the way forward to do justice to the insights and
challenges perceived and conveyed by such as Tillich,
Bonhoeffer and, in their steps, the Bishop of Woolwich, lies in
taking very seriously, far more seriously than is current
practice over an alarmingly large area of the church, the
insights and assertions of the continuing Christian tradition.
For our primary concern is surely not that 'they', whoever
they are, should agree with 'us', whoever 'we' are, but that
'we' and 'they' should together be taken beyond our present
partial insights and errors nearer to the wholeness of understanding which is truth.

To this end, total surrender to what are alleged to be the 'necessary' ways for modern thinking is likely to be as stultifying and misleading as is abject and unreflective clinging to older statements and ways of thinking treated as mere formulae. But in so far as they represent an understanding of God and ultimate reality which our fathers wrested from their own encounters with life and with God we surely neglect them at our peril. I believe that the Bishop is wholly right to seek to shock the church into really awakening to the fact that the way we look at the world we live in must be radically different from the views acceptable to those who lived before us. But if there is any sense in talking about God at all, we can scarcely suppose that we shall know what we may *truthfully* say if we neglect what others have, under the pressure of their ultimate concerns, learnt to say of the God who was ultimate reality to them.

3 | *Where is God?*

Where is God? This is a question which those who believe in
God are at first inclined to say should not be asked. And then
they feel that some sort of answer must be given and so go on
to give a series of unsatisfactory, confusing and contradictory
answers. The question ought not to be asked because God is
not an object or like an object. He is 'the Other', the 'altogether more than', the 'transcendent'. And whatever that
sort of thing means it certainly means that he cannot be
located, i.e. placed in time and space and therefore you must
not ask 'where?', for that demands an answer 'here' or 'not
here but there' and both 'here' and 'there' are equally space-
time (i.e. appropriate to object) words.

But although the question cannot be asked it must be
answered. For a God who is neither here nor there is nowhere.
And as the writer of the letter to the Hebrews puts it, 'anyone
who comes to God must believe that he exists and that he
rewards those that search for him' (Heb. 11.6, NEB). Even if
God is not an object it must be possible in some real sense to
'come up against him' and to receive something from this
encounter. But that is to say that my meeting with God is an
objective experience, i.e. that 'God' is not simply a name or a
word which refers to, or which I give to, my experiences when
they take on a certain pattern and have a certain emotive
tone. But what is the difference between objective experience
and experience of an object? Moreover, I or any other
believer am certainly located in space and time when I have
these experiences. So we must apparently say that God is
encountered 'here' and 'here' and 'there', i.e. that he is
object-like. But because we know that he is 'transcendent' (i.e.
much 'more than', including more than an object), that he is

not object-like, we then go on to say that to speak of him as 'here' or 'there' is only part of the answer which is an untrue answer if we do not at the same time say that he is *not* 'here' or 'there' (where 'here' and 'there' are still simple locating or pointing words) *but* he is 'beyond' or 'up' or 'down' or 'over there' where 'there' is a very mysterious sort of 'there' which is over against (different from, in sharp contrast to) all other 'there's' (or 'here's'!). But the point to notice about this last move is this. We have felt ourselves obliged to use object-like language and then to make some move to counteract this object-likeness. But the move we make is still object-like. For absence is as much an object-like notion as presence. That which is present is so because it is 'not there but here' while that which is absent is so because it is 'not here but there' and the reversal of the order of 'here' and 'there' makes no difference to the fact that we are talking about objects.

Now you may say that this is all very well and very obvious. We have always known that talking about God is a tricky and difficult operation. But talk we must and talk we will. Let us by all means have a due awareness of the difficulties and limitations and then get on with the well-proved methods of talking about God and bother, not about the theoretical difficulties, but about practical effectiveness. But the warning and challenge which the Bishop of Woolwich, drawing on Bonhoeffer and Tillich, has, with the help of modern publicity, so explosively put before us traditional practitioners of traditional theism is this. The technique which we have evolved or rather inherited for dealing with these difficulties of talk about God is based on a set of pre-suppositions and a pattern of thought about the world which is now outmoded. Therefore we are trapped in our traditional ways of thinking and talking with the result that our talking about 'God' even among ourselves ('the believers') is dangerously often not about the true and living God at all and certainly fails to convey sense and truth about God to those who are not of 'us' ('unbelievers' – often such because the way 'we' go on is utterly and rightly incomprehensible and unacceptable to them).

The point is this. Christianity, in the sense of the commonly

received pattern of thought entered into and passed on by the
continuing body of the church form, say, the end of the New
Testament period to today, has in practice worked out an
answer to the question 'Where is God?'. And it is an answer
which for us now is both false and dangerous. Put briefly and
crudely it amounts to saying 'God is to be found in the gaps'.
God is the 'higher than the highest' who explains whatever
cannot be explained and deals with whatever cannot be dealt
with. That is to say, he is to be found in the gaps which
human reason cannot fill up or in the inadequacies with
which human resources cannot cope. In biblical times the
gaps were very wide, but now they are much narrower and
always narrowing. We do not now need God to explain a
thunderstorm, that is taken care of by meteorology, but we *do*
need him to 'explain' the universe. We do not need God to
deal with disease, this is a matter of medical care and research,
but we *do* need him to deal with sin and death. But the effect
of this way of thinking and teaching is to confine God to the
'ultimate questions' and thus, so to speak, to push him to the
very edge of our universe and our concerns or outside them
altogether. For 'ultimate questions' of this sort seem to very
many people to be quite plainly unanswerable at best and at
worst meaningless. Meteorological explanation is a sort of
explanation we can understand; it serves to clarify certain
limited issues and it gives us knowledge that may be of use.
Ultimate explanation is, almost by definition, incomprehensible, does not clarify but mystifies and it is very difficult to
see what use it has. Death, however distressing, is still a
universal natural fact and not a problem, while so-called 'sin'
is much more likely to be dealt with by controlled and careful
studies of neuroses and social, economic and political
maladjustments than by some mythology about cosmic 'Falls'
and 'Atonements'.

Moreover, the God who is portrayed in all this way of
thinking is hardly godlike. To 'fill in the gaps' is more the job
of a celestial super-handyman than a reflection of the worshipful perfection and fulfilment of all that is valuable and
worthwhile and real. To require the payment of a penalty
exacted in respect of a guilt for which a man is doubtfully

responsible before it is possible to enter into a right relationship, is more like the act of a tyrannical demi-god than the
attitude and concern of One whose nature is said to be love.
To bestow rewards upon 'faithful servants' and penalties upon
rebels may seem much more in keeping with the character of
a magnified and super-human emperor whose criterion of
value is subservience to himself rather than the perfecting of
all things in full accordance with holiness, righteousness and
love. So 'the God of the Christians' seems to be a Being in
whom it is neither possible nor desirable to believe, a
metaphysical ineptitude and a moral scandal.

Those of us who would passionately protest against so
scandalous a caricature must face the fact that a very great
deal of Christian talk and Christian 'going-on' does present
and heighten such a picture. Christian worship seems to be an
odd activity of those who choose to belong to a religious
rather than to any other club. Services must often look like a
displeasing mixture of placating a Being who if he requires
this sort of thing is not very nice to know, pestering him on
subjects we would be much better advised to get on with
ourselves (pray for peace and avoid politics!) and pleasing
him with hymns and rituals which suggest that knowing him
can hardly be an exciting, still less an infinite, adventure if he
finds such dreariness acceptable. On morals, too, the one
thing that his followers seem to be quite clear about is that
living according to his will involves a great list of 'Thou shalt
not's'. God in fact has shrunk from being a potent mythical
figure to being a hobby (an idol?) of the religious, and as the
religious do not want to face life as it really is, their God
(made in their own image) is anti-life.

But anyone who believes himself to have had the least
glimpse of the God who is witnessed to, worshipped and
known in the true heart and real depth of the tradition of
biblical and Christian theism will know that this is a mon-
strous perversion. But it is not a non-existent perversion. By
giving in practice a wrong answer to the question 'Where is
God?', we have encouraged the building up of a wrong image
of the answer to the question 'Who is God?'. And it is their
desire to break through to the true and living God which has

moved Bonhoeffer to talk of religionless Christianity, Tillich to attack a supranatural picture of God and Bishop Robinson to ask. 'The End of Theism?' Those who need to try to get at the essence of their protests and their positive contributions (such as they are) in as short a compass as possible should get hold of Daniel Jenkins' book *Beyond Religion* (SCM Press, 1962) and then follow up Bonhoeffer and Tillich from references given there as they have time. As usual, protests tend to be as exaggerated as the distortions against which they react and we must look for the contribution of traditional theism properly understood and interpreted to the whole debate. But at least we must be clear that even if the answers offered are neither for the most part clear, nor always satisfactory when they are clear, yet the questions and challenges are entirely valid.

The present stage of the debate seems to be something like this. Very many people would agree or be inclined to agree, or at least be ready to understand what other people are saying when *they* maintain, that when we reflect upon our experience of the world and especially on our experiences with and of other people we perceive or sense or feel the need of, a 'dimension' which is somehow deeper than, extends further than and is even in some way other than the face-value of the experiences and the obvious constituent parts of these experiences. One feels a compulsion to reject the notion that there is no mystery in or to the world. Even if on some grounds it seems reasonable, none the less it somehow does not seem right to accept the view that scientific explanation is the only sort of explanation which is appropriate to the world. There is worthwhileness to be perceived in the possibilities and demands of personal relations which seems at one and the same time to be of the very essence of these relations and yet also a challenge which demands more than is yet given or experienced and even, perhaps, points beyond the relationships as at present enjoyed to a fulfilment which is far richer than anything so far attained. These and similar features of our experience are taken as experiences of and intimations of 'depth', of the 'inwardness' of our life, of clues to the 'ultimate reality' which underlies all our living, if only we

seek to live fully and deeply enough, and of hints about our
'ultimate concerns'.

Talk of 'depth', 'ultimate concerns' and the like can
become as much jargon as any theological formulae, but their
use represents a real and significant attempt both to get
away from the inadequacy and incredibility of the language
of the 'God of the gaps' and to find ways of directing men's
minds and spirits to those areas of living and perceiving in
which God is to be found and can be known. For God is
either the fullness of fullness, the value of all the valuable, the
wholeness of wholeness, the life of life, or he is nothing. It is
the conviction of those who are seeking to develop this line
of approach, as it is the conviction of those wedded to more
traditional ways of talking, that the ultimate source, end and
underlying reality of the universe is love, that is to say, that
we are right to find our highest values in the loving relationships of persons and that the ultimate way things are is
consistent with this and will, indeed, give fulfilment to these
relationships. The conviction is, too, that it is this reality of
personal love which was increasingly encountered in the
developing religious life of Israel with all the demands and
promises of righteousness and holiness which a fully personal
love is gradually seen to involve. Further, it is believed that
this love was wholly fittingly expressed and lived out in the
life of Jesus who was the man who lived completely for
others and completely for God. There is reluctance to say that
God himself is personal (which I myself think will in the end
prove mistaken) because of the evident dangers and frustrations that have followed from treating him as a super-natural
person (someone 'up there' and 'over there' who is then
rightly edged out of the universe because he becomes
manifestly too small and petty to be relevant, let alone God).
But the whole concern is to enable men to see and know and
respond to just that reality and possibility and offer of loving
which was of the essence of the life of Jesus and which we
believe is the fulfilment and purport of the whole biblical
revelation as it is the meaning and purpose of all things.

Not very many people nowadays can be brought directly
or at first to 'see God in this or that'. But if they can be

helped to attend, truly attend to their own deepest concerns, the concerns which are theirs as persons, and to seek to live and to love in ways which are striving to be truly living and deeply loving then the belief is that they will come face to face with that which (or I would prefer to say him who) is God. He is then known not as a remote and scarcely credible 'addition' to a clearly homogeneous and self-contained universe, but as the depth and mystery who is the richness of and enrichment of our very being as living personal creatures in the magnificence and complexity of the universe.

There is very much to be worked out here and much to be worked back into this understanding from the true depths of Christian spirituality and mysticism, but surely this is a way to recapture the magnificence, the glory, the transcendence and yet the intimate closeness and depth of concern of him whom the Bible calls Lord of Lords and yet who is known in the stillness of a man's wrestling with his own calling and future or in the broken humility of a man forsaken on a cross.

4 | *Whither the Doctrine of God Now?*

This paper does not get nearly far enough. But I do not believe we have yet gone deep enough in diagnosing the situation with regard to the doctrine of God. Until this is done we cannot see anything clearly about where the doctrine of God should go. Hence this paper is intended as a contribution to the future development of the doctrine of God by being an attempt to diagnose the present situation more clearly.

The question has been raised as to whether we are or ought to be in sight of the end of theism. Theism would come to an end if one of two mutually exclusive sets of conditions obtained. The first possibility is that there is no God and that everyone comes to realize this. Theism is thus known to be void, ceases to exercise any hold and fades completely away. The second possibility is that the Christian symbol of the Last Day stands for that which will be realized in the eventual experience of all men. In that 'event' men would 'in the End' see God with an immediacy which is best described as 'face to face' and theism would be shattered not because it was voided but because it was fulfilled. The point is that theism does not exist in its own right. It is either totally superstition or a body of belief, understanding and practice which in some form or other is required by the intermediate and interim nature of our situation and our experience. Theism is either mistaken about reality or else properly expectant about reality. In neither case is it completely and straightforwardly descriptive of reality.

Our present debate, however, is immediately occasioned by

some who, while intending to remain Christians, wish to deny
the continuing validity of some clear and exhaustive distinction between the positions of theism and atheism as just
touched on. In raising the question 'The End of Theism?',
Bishop Robinson clearly did not think he was pointing to
either of the possibilities referred to above. Rather he was
suggesting that the symbol of a transcendent and personal
God which was the essence of theism had indeed now turned
out to be superstitious. That is, this symbol not only did not
correspond in any understandable or life-enhancing way with
reality, but was positively misleading and mythological about
reality. Thus, if modern 'believers' are to continue to keep
hold of those features about reality for which the symbols of
theism had once stood and if others are to be helped to come
to grips with those aspects, it is necessary to recognize the end
of theism. We must face the possibility of abandoning the
symbols of theism associated with and focused upon that of
the personal and transcendent God and find other ways of
talking and organizing our experience. None the less, this is
not a programme for atheism. It is aiming at some third
thing which would rescue theism from superstition and atheism
from unbelief. Reluctant believers and enthusiastic unbelievers,
however, tend to refuse to accept this and hold that the
programme does look, logically, like a programme for
atheism.

For reasons which will, I hope, appear, I agree with this
diagnosis. For theism to come to an end in this world would
only leave everyone as atheists. But it will merely encourage
everyone to become or remain atheists if theistic believers do
not face up to the reasons which prompted that sort of an
attempt to find a third way (between theism and atheism) of
which Robinson has given us an example. In this connection
there are two sets of considerations, the first to do with the
climate of thought in which theism is to be entertained as a
live option and the second to do with the manner in which a
theistic position has in fact been occupied and maintained
over a very large range of recent and general Christian
thought and practice.

With regard to the climate of thought, I wish to focus on

what seems to me to be the crucial point for the development of theology by talking of 'Post-Copernican Man'. I choose this symbol from Kant's preface to the second edition of his *Critique of Pure Reason* and I do so because I believe that Kant rightly perceived the inwardness and the implications of the revolution in thought which modern man was producing and which was producing modern man.

Kant was concerned 'to introduce a complete revolution in the procedure of metaphysics, after the example of the Geometricians and the Natural Philosophers'. He proposed 'to do just what Copernicus did in attempting to explain the celestial movements. When he found that he could make no progress by assuming that all the heavenly bodies revolved around the spectator he reversed the process and tried the experiment of assuming that the spectator revolved while the stars remained at rest.' In this Copernicus was typical of the various experimentalists who had 'learned that reason only perceives that which it produces after its own design, that it must not be content to follow, as it were, in the leading-strings of nature but must . . . compel nature to reply to its questions'. Kant saw that this revolution in thought about the world (the replacement of the objective knower with his divine gift of reason by the subjective observer with the human capacity for experiment) required a revolution in thought about thought. Men did not gain their knowledge by the pure and *a priori* use of a reason which had the intrinsic capacity of penetrating through the appearances of pheno-mena to the ultimate realities. It was no longer one's under-standing of reality which determined one's articulation and assessment of the observed appearances. Rather one's observation and articulation of the appearances was on the way to becoming that which determined one's understanding of reality.

It is necessary to say 'on the way to becoming' when we are at Kant's stage and part in the revolution because, as is well known, Kant himself held that while the speculative reason could not go beyond its own categories and the phenomena, practical reason took one validly into the sphere of reality in which talk about God, Free Will and Goodness was proper, necessary and truthful. Here Kant remains a believer in transcendental reality, to the knowledge of which he held that the practical reason could build a rational bridge.

Post-Copernican Man in his maturity has not allowed Kant's revolution in philosophy to stem the whole revolution and preserve the transcendent realities in the manner Kant himself intended. He has carried through the revolution in thinking about the world and in thinking about thought to the completion of a revolution in the understanding of understanding itself and of knowledge. The result is that the first question which must be faced in any serious and relevant attempt to maintain, develop, re-state or even re-establish a doctrine of God is not 'Is there a God?' or 'What is meant by "God"?' but 'What is it to know?'. For the answer to that question implies and presupposes an answer to the question 'What can be known?', i.e. 'What can, with reasonable confidence, be held to be real?' or, even, 'What is real and how is it real?'. The spirit in which Post-Copernican Man explicitly or implicitly answers such questions is well reflected, for example, in the definition which Professor D. R. Newth gives (in his contribution to *Science in its Context*, ed. J. Brierley) of science as 'the process by which men create knowledge in which they can place a high and often measurable degree of confidence'. Knowledge is that which is produced by the use of the experimental method when men 'compel nature to reply to . . . questions' (*vide* Kant cit. *supra*). Such knowledge is firm and can be confidently used, although it is never 'final' in more than a strictly limited sense. As Heisenberg says (*The Physicist's Conception of Nature*, pp. 27f.): 'In the exact sciences the word "final" obviously means that there are always self-contained, mathematically representable, systems of concepts and laws applicable to certain realms of experience, in which realms they are always valid. . . . Obviously, however, we cannot expect these concepts and laws to be suitable for the subsequent description of new realms of experience.' A little later he remarks: 'The exact sciences also start from the assumption that in the end it will always be possible to understand nature, even in every new field of experience, but that we may make no *a priori* assumptions about the meaning of the word "understand".'

Knowledge is a strictly human achievement which is strictly limited and relative, but which is none the less extremely potent within its limits, not least because these limits are precisely known. For Post-Copernican Man knowledge is the articulated understanding of observable and measurable realities so far achieved. There is more to know by the same and developed techniques. As such knowledge is gained it will change our understanding of what has hitherto been known. Truth is relative and it becomes truth as it is discovered, established, put to the test, articulated and used as the basis for further discovery, further relative but relevant truth. You cannot 'go beyond' the knowledge you have save by building on what you have got in strict continuity with it. Experience, experiment and techniques for testing by application in understanding and action are the tests of knowledge and thereby of reality.

The symbol 'Post-Copernican Man' as representing the attitude to knowledge and reality not very precisely indicated above is, I believe, a more useful representation for our purpose in considering theism than the vaguer 'modern man', for the symbolism draws attention to the fact that the crisis for belief is, at its centre, epistemological – to do with knowing and what is knowable. Further, anyone who embodies or expresses the qualities and approach symbolized by Post-Copernican Man has today an unquestioned authority, an authority which is believed to be self-evident. Any other approach will not be heeded unless it can give a very good account of itself in terms which at least overlap those of the Post-Copernican Man and which can establish their own claim to relevant meaningfulness. This is why Robinson attempted a version of what I have called the third way. Theism (belief in and talk about a transcendent and personal God) goes beyond the knowable facts. Theism is therefore not knowledge concerned with reality. Once it was symbolism referring mythologically to features of reality but now, on Post-Copernican principles it is, seen to be superstition and must therefore come to an end. The features of reality the symbols of theism used to refer to must be found now more firmly located in 'real' reality, i.e. that which is now known and judged to be knowable. Hence the programme to re-express theism in terms of depth, concern, encounter and relationships.

But, understandable as such a programme is, it is not really a programme to replace outmoded symbols. The trouble about symbols is only symptomatic of the real trouble which is that about knowledge and reality. For the programme is an attempt to come to terms with Post-Copernican Man on his terms and these do not envisage the possibility of there being a reality which can only, and must always, be pointed to by symbols. That which is real is that which is known and that which is known is that which has been described. There is always more to know, but we shall know this when we are able to describe more. Knowledge and reality remain relative terms. Hence if theism is to become acceptable to Post-Copernican Man it must become atheism, i.e. it must surrender to him, for he has no terms for anything other than relative reality and relative truth. Whatever the symbols of theism stood for, they stood for something that was in logic (and, the theist contends, in reality) different from anything which falls within the logical possibilities of Post-Copernican Man's terms. For the theist, the significance of God's presence, immanence, availability is always derived from his otherness and his absoluteness. This is a matter not of mythology, but of logic. Part of the confusion in *Honest to God* and in much of the current debate is the failure to recognize this. Anyone concerned with the future of the doctrine of God must face up to the starkness of the clash involved here. Concentrating on symbols can simply disguise the fact that the full development of the approach of Post-Copernican Man to the world is literally godless. Symbolism is certainly a question for the doctrine of God but only after, or at least as part of, the answer to the question as to how a doctrine of God is to be maintained and commended in a world where the acceptedly authoritative man is godless.

I have spent half of this article seeking to define more clearly what seems to me to be the essential nature of the

challenge now presented to theism and to make clear how
stark and definite a challenge it is, because I am myself sure
that the future of theism, the direction for the development of
the doctrine of God, is to be found in facing up with accuracy
and rigour to the challenge of the situation. This is a theological conclusion derived from my present understanding
of the doctrine of God and it is reached as follows.

Any doctrine of God which is in continuity with the theism
of the Bible and of Christian tradition must be clear about at
least the following. *First*, the word 'God' refers to, or, better,
names *a* reality who/which is other than the sum total of
the realities which constitute the observable (or theoretically
observable) universe.

The being named 'God' is not simply different *from* other
beings or realities. He is different *in* being and reality. That is
the logical point indicated by the caution which has to be
used in referring to him as *a* being. That is also why he can
be referred to only in symbols, analogies, etc. To use the
name 'God' and to believe that one is using it meaningfully
is to assert that the reality of the world is not exhausted by
the realities in the world and that symbols of the type 'out
there', 'beyond this', 'on another level' or the like (logically
like, that is) are inescapable if we are to attempt to do justice
to the reality in which we are involved. It is also why the
conflict between Post-Copernican Man and the theist is
logical with the certainty that one position or other in its
ultimate conclusion about the world is false, rather than
mythological with the hope that a third way would resolve
the conflict. The debate is not about talk but about the way
things really are. Thus the radical otherness of God (in a
logical, ontological and existential sense) is a theistic axiom.

Secondly, however, the theist in the biblical and Christian
tradition holds that this is no absolute bar to the knowledge
of God because God relates himself to the world and to man.
The symbols which refer to this relationship are primarily
'Creation' and 'Revelation'. The symbol of Creation stands
for the assertion of the fact as a fact that the existence of
realities other than God is ultimately dependent upon God.
Therefore, it is conceivably in the nature of things that these

other realities in their own reality may reflect God or be usable as a means of communication about God or even of God. The symbol of Revelation stands for the assertion of the fact that God so relates himself to the world that he evokes knowledge of himself in and in connection with particular persons and events.

Now this belief in and assertion about God as reality who is both other and at the same time related as Creator and Revealer seems to have been almost completely thrown on the defensive by a full and open confrontation with Post-Copernican Man. In this defensiveness theism is false to its own premises and experience. This brings us to the second set of considerations related to the future of the Doctrine of God – those to do with the manner in which Christian theism has very largely been practised and the doctrine of God taught as men have moved into the Post-Copernican era. There has been a widespread failure either to teach sufficiently radically about, or take practical notice of, the fact that theism does not exist in its own right. It has been unconsciously assumed that on the basis of a taken-for-granted authority of the Bible and/or the church, talk about God would remain both meaningful and relevant in its own right. But religious symbols which are taken for granted and left to have force in their own right and by their own weight become idols. The very name of God is only too easily taken in vain and the repeated sin of religious men is to rely on their religion (their concepts and their rules) rather than on the God to whom the symbols pointed and with whom the religion was validly concerned. Symbols are inescapably necessary in theism. But they operate only as stultifying idols unless they are used in a manner which is not self-contained but open. God is radically other. Therefore, the truth about him or the reality of him cannot be contained in or be equivalent to any particular set of symbols, symbolic acts or significant encounters. All such may be means of knowing God but are not to be equated with God.

But God is related and present as Creator and Revealer. Hence the universe is always furnished with potential symbols, and the possibilities of symbolic acts and opportunities for encounter which can kindle and have kindled the knowledge of God. Hence when theism is threatened and much (or even all) of the symbolism seems to be going dead, the believer in the God with whom the theistic tradition has to do will look for a renewal of theism. (He knows that, as there is God, theism cannot either fade away or be done without.) This renewal he will look for by seeking a greater openness to God. And *this* he will seek by a greater openness to the real (and not the supposed, muted or turned aside) challenge of the situation. For the God who is other is known in the intermediate and interim manner of theism through his presence and relatedness. And because God is real and is concerned with reality, he is not to be found in our illusions about the situation, but he is to be found as we seek to come to the closest grips we can with the objective reality of the situation.

It is here that the true concern of the theist meets up with the maturity of Post-Copernican Man. For Post-Copernican Man is determined to put everything to the test of experience and experiment and to proceed inductively from the knowledge he has to the building up of further knowledge. In fact, he is taking the givenness of what the theist would call the created universe absolutely seriously and in its own right. His ideal is to be open to observed and verified facts and thereby to dispel illusion and unclarity and to work in the light thus gained. This ideal represents an absolute commitment to pursuing the truth of the matter which is wholly proper to the givenness of a created universe, the data of which demand the respect which rejects all *a priori* treatment. The theist who believes that 'created' is a proper adjective to apply to the universe must not and cannot go back on this achievement of Post-Copernican Man in which he is more mature than theists have generally shown themselves to be.

What the theist knows is that there is also God to be known and that ultimately it is this knowledge which is both primary (God is the proper context of everything) and ultimate (God is the proper fulfilment of everything). He cannot, however, blame Post-Copernican Man for refusing to allow that he (the theist) has anything that can be called knowledge about 'God' if he neither behaves as if he has knowledge (i.e., does not approach given reality on the basis of a real – because competent and practical – understanding of something real) nor can give any reasonably plausible account of the source or bearing of his knowledge. The questions which Post-Copernican Man puts to the theist are 'How do you know God?' and 'How would you suggest to me that "knowledge of God" is knowledge?'. These questions require answers based on experience (How was the body of knowledge built up and how is it passed on?) and related to possibilities of experimental living.

In facing this challenge of the situation, I would suggest, we are required to work our way towards a post-Copernican natural theology, an account of revealed truth which is always sensitive to origins on the one hand and practical relevance on the other, and the development of a spiritual discipline and discipleship which is clearly an experimental attempt to make sense of our modern life in the light of our theistic understanding and to make sense of our theistic understanding in the light of our modern life. In other words, there is no way forward in the doctrine of God save on the broadest of fronts and by combining a number of enterprises.

It may be thought that, on my usage, 'Post-Copernican natural theology' is a contradiction in terms, but I do not believe this is so. As a theist, I maintain the view that the universe is rightly characterized as 'created'. The experimental and inductive approach of Post-Copernican Man is the mature approach to the givenness of the created universe. If the theistic approach is in accord with the reality of things, then careful, sensitive and prolonged investigation of the methods, results and presuppositions of the post-Copernican approach must yield material for a natural theology. It must be possible to find material to make a case for the 'theistic hypothesis', although it will never be possible to establish it finally. (This is where the other two aspects of the enterprise mentioned above come in.)

Among the areas for search may be included: epistemology itself (Logical Positivism is by no means as complete or satisfactory as some of its first proponents supposed or as some *avant-garde* but possibly behind the times theologians now suppose. Also pure existentialism may perhaps without much difficulty be shown to lead to 'the Absurd'); freedom and morality (particularly the former where it may fairly speedily become evident that man cannot be established or maintained as human on strictly post-Copernican principles. But in either field the insight of Kant that here lies a bridge to the transcendent needs to be vigorously explored); psychology and sociology (The more we know about individual and group features which affect and produce persons and personality, the more we may be able to see features in which self-contained descriptive and reductionist accounts of what personality is or what persons may be or may become are self-evidently unsatisfactory and incomplete). There is also the need to investigate and re-assess those ranges of human experience which Post-Copernican Man tries to undervalue or ignore in relation to knowledge and which have their revenge in producing a modern literature which is largely pessimistic, uncertain and unclear in contrast to Post-Copernican Man's certainty, clarity and optimism. But this again must be investigated in its own right and not be prostituted and distorted by being prematurely forced into ready-made theological categories (i.e. guilt, sin and the like). The natural theology must be built up from what is observed in the natural as it is given to us.

But this search for a post-Copernican natural theology would never be undertaken, nor would it have any hope of success, if it were not the case that there existed a reliable tradition of revealed knowledge of God and a constant community of current experience recognizably continuous with the experience of those who were the means of producing the tradition. God is to be known in and through the realities of the situation, but God is not the same thing as the situation, the otherness remains a reality. Natural theology can aim at showing that there is a possibility of God in the situation. But to look for a possibility of God one must have some idea of what 'God' could mean and this comes from a sensitive and lively confrontation with the tradition in which one begins to separate the symbols from the logic, and the

mythology from the experience. It is to this end that the
tradition, whether in the Bible or in doctrinal formulations or
in the worshipping and praying practice of Christians, is to be
studied and sifted with particular regard to origins (the
situations which gave rise to the tradition) and relevance (the
way situations were held to be affected by that which was
formulated into tradition). (Here particular attention will
have to be given to the data of and about the historical Jesus.
I would venture the prophecy that more can reasonably be
known in this field than the present prevailing fashions in
exegesis will allow, overwhelmed as they are by a probably
unsound existentialist epistemology. There may well be
sufficient facts of a 'hard' [by post-Copernican standards] sort
about Jesus to go quite a long way in legitimately raising the
question as to whether the reality of the world is contained in
and exhausted by the realities in the world.)

But that which convinces the theist that there is a God and
that the challenge of Post-Copernican Man is a challenge to
learn more of God and not a summons to fight a rearguard
action on God's (doubtful) behalf are the occasions, whether
individual or corporate, whether vivid or faintly and evasively
remembered, when the challenge of the situation and the
givenness of the tradition are kindled into an awareness which
makes practical, comforting and illuminating sense of both by
giving what must be described as the knowledge of a Presence
and a Power. Hence it is that no doctrine of God can go
forward unless it is clearly related to a spiritual discipline
and discipleship which is experiential and experimental in
relation both to the tradition and to the current situation.

Thus the future of the development of the doctrine of God
must lie in sustained attempts to give an account of the ways
in which confrontation of the situation, exploration of the
tradition and personal discipleship yield knowledge of God
and what the content and bearing of this knowledge is. Such
attempts must emerge from and be backed up by a Christian
community which is plainly living experimentally and openly.
The challenge of Post-Copernican Man has decisively
reminded us that Christian theology and Christian living must
be conducted together.

5 | God Today

If one is asked to talk about God today in the context of a series on the general topic of why we should believe and what the roads to belief are, then one must clearly face up to the current tendency to maintain that all God-talk is finished. This being so, perhaps the approach to the subject should be to tackle first the question 'How can I find a use for God-talk?' and then go on to ask, 'Why should I in fact use such language?'. It will be necessary to go back to more or less these questions, but it is first necessary to be quite clear about one thing. That is, that there is only one decisive reason for believing in God, namely because *God is*. I am aware of the difficulties of the existential use of the verb 'to be', but I remain unrepentant about my formulation of this reason. The only satisfactory reason for believing in God must be because in the last analysis, the attitude, commitment and content of believing is the proper response to what is there, to what is given. We must not be turned aside by the difficulties of using object-like language about God. The basic question remains whether in believing in God we are responding to He who is, to Truth as it is given, to Reality as it is *there*. It is very necessary in this whole area to strive after simplicity which enables us to see with singleness of eye into what the whole debate is really about.

To use God-language for any other reason than that it is held to describe or at least to point to the truth as it really is and reality as it truly is, is both blasphemous and pathological. It is blasphemous because it is simply the practice of idolatry to use God-language because one is conscious of the need for a cosmic anodyne or because one must have a prop and basis for morality or a sop for one's soul in its loneliness. Such a use of language is simply making use of the idea of God to fill an alleged human gap. If God truly exists as God, then to make use of God for human ends is clearly blasphemous. But such usage is also pathological. For its object is to escape from reality, to erect a fantasy which conceals from us the way things really are. The refusal to come to terms with reality is at best immaturity and at worst madness. If, therefore, we are all atheists now, then for God's sake we must be atheists, or at any rate if there is no God then we must be atheists for men's sake. I am clear, therefore, that there is only one valid answer to the question 'Why believe?'. Because God *is* and he lets it be known that he is.

On the other hand, such a reason clearly does not get us very far. We have also to consider the questions which in practice will often be much more pressing, 'How believe?' and 'What does it mean to believe?'. Let us therefore turn to the question of how we may believe. There are many ways of coming to believe, many pointers to the possibility of believing, many ways of evoking and sustaining belief. The few examples which I am about to give are not arranged in any order of weight. I am quite clear that different pointers, experiences, arguments are 'weighty' for different people. That is to say, there are many different ways which get differing people on to God, and it is not possible to say that one argument or experience is necessarily more decisive or satisfactory than another. But the following four ways or areas do seem to me to be of particular significance and, often, helpfulness.

The first I would call the open study of man, both the study of human kind and of individual persons. There is a very strong case for maintaining that, in whatever way we are studying man, we will always find that in the end we need what might be called one more dimension than is contained in the normal structure of our method of study for doing full justice to all that is involved in the human situation. Biology might look as if it should find its firm and only basis in the reduction of its concepts to that which can be finally measurable in terms, say, of physico-chemical reactions. But it is clear that ecology is as important as analysis and that human ecology raises acute problems of the possibility of exhaustive analysis. Similarly, we know that psychology is liable to be divided between those who see their aim as producing results of research which can be tabulated and turned into graphs and those who are aware that such analysis is only one side of the observational study of the dynamics of personality and human relationships. Many people may feel that graphs are far more scientifically respectable, but science is based on observation, and it is not scientific, i.e. not in accordance with the total range of observations possible and necessary, to suppose that the effects of the human psyche can be exhaustively reduced to the type of tables which record the reaction time of rats. Likewise, in the field of sociology, when one proceeds to matters such as criminology and actual prescriptions for dealing with social ills and maladjustments, it rapidly becomes clear that value judgments cannot be left out of account, and that however important proper scientific and impersonal analysis is, total reductionism is just a mistake.

This feature of the situation with regard to what might be called the human sciences is reflected also in logic. Here we are up against what may reasonably be called the mystery of the 'I'. Hume himself was not really satisfied with his reductionist version of the self. Current philosophical writing is once again tending to lend support to the view that logical analysis does not remove all mysteries from the understanding of the human situation. (An excellent example of this is to be found in Mr Strawson's philosophical lecture for 1962 to the British Academy entitled 'Freedom and Resentment'.) And there is much else which makes it clear enough that we cannot say that philosophy has done away with the dimension of mystery in human existence in such areas as 'self' and questions like the problem of free will and determinism. In philosophy in the still broader sense, it is quite clear that there is a rediscovery of the need for facing up to what I have described as the additional dimension which confronts us when we try to take into account all that is involved in human existence. I believe that an excellent example of this is to be found in the work of Heidegger, who, for all his anti-metaphysical endeavours, clearly finds it necessary to have a special way of talking about the essence of humanness which lands him in exactly the same logical problems in his own terms, as more old-fashioned ways of thinking find in their terms, over the notion of transcendence. The open study of man gives plenty of evidence of the need for facing up to a 'breaking out' from what we might call our normal dimensions, a necessity to go beyond our ordinary descriptive categories, in fact a possibility of transcendence.

The second significant area for the possibility of believing is that which I would call the 'exploration of commitment'. Here it is a question of exposing oneself to what is truly involved in being in relationship to other human beings and to what it is to be oneself. In such an exploration one finds that one seems to be faced occasionally with great heights and with immense possibilities and worthwhileness. At other times there is the facing of the depths and the threats of nothingness and destruction. Here the very depth of the threat seems to reflect the high significance of that which is threatened. Moreover, in such an exploration and in such a facing of heights and depths we may find resources on which we had never bargained or of which we had never thought. Possibilities are discovered of powers beyond our own powers, in fact what the religious man calls grace. This may arise as we see the need for resources that are beyond our own and glimpse the possibilities of such resources. Here again, in this whole exploration of commitment we are confronted with the possible existence of mystery and we are led to hope that the world is not 'flat'. That is to say, that measurable and predictable things do not rule over the affairs of men or at any rate need not rule or, perhaps, must not rule. We are therefore encouraged to ask in a meaningful way the question, Who then does rule? Might it be true, as Augustine said, that God made us for himself and that our hearts are restless until we find our rest in him? Might it make sense to learn that he who rules is the Lord God?

The two areas we have considered so far which may lead, provoke or persuade us to believe lie in the mystery of the world and the heights and depths of commitment and are of a general nature. We turn now to something more particular, namely the way in which it is possible to be led to, and sustained in, believing through the community and practice of believers. Here we have the possibility of sharing in the response of worship and knowing, however dimly and fleetingly, that it is indeed a response. Here, too, we have the opportunity of learning for ourselves and with the help of the experience of others the response of prayer. Although this is often a difficult affair and never a guaranteed affair, there are none the less many experimental data and many ways of practice through which we may discover our particular way of entering that practice of the presence of God which has been the strength of so many in so many different situations. Then, and in connection with the community of believers, we may also investigate the response of doctrine and discover that once the doctrinal propositions of past ages are set free from a fossilizing respect which treats them as unquestionable oracles, their content can once again become living. We may learn that they are the formulation and crystallization of what men have been led to discover about God and that when they are broken open by the questions which our experiences oblige us to put, then they once more become the source of discoveries about the same God. A further way of coming to and entering more deeply into belief, in sharing the life of the community of believers, is to be found as we seek to work out and to express the practice which is demanded by the understanding of God which it is alleged has been given to believers. In fact, we may well come to believe, and we shall certainly only continue to believe, as we share, however tentatively, in the enquiry of faith which is the experimental living out of the experience of the community of the people of God.

Finally, I must pass from the community of believers to one more source for the evocation of belief in, and knowledge of, God. This source is very particular indeed – it is Jesus Christ. This is the man of Nazareth who unquestionably lived and unquestionably lived as the man for God. The pattern of this living has led many to see him as also the man for others. His disciples believed that he was also discovered to be God for man, but this last point is already a doctrinal formulation, so we will leave it. At least we must agree that Jesus Christ is part of the givenness of history and that the pattern of his living is part of the data we have to consider when we are looking for the possibilities of believing. The relevance of Jesus Christ to the other areas possibly evocative of belief which I have mentioned would seem to be this. We may agree that man does not look as if he fits into any frame produced by any science or system of thinking, but we may well feel that this does not help us to believe in God, for there is one frame in which man exists, to wit, the universe as it is known to science, and, to put it crudely, the size of this both on the macrocosmic and on the microcosmic scale surely crushes out all grounds for believing in God. But is this so? The knowledge of this vast scale of existence has been discovered by man himself and we have also the opportunity of considering the givenness of Jesus Christ; we have the claimed knowledge of God that led up to him; we have the community and practice that follows from him. Why should size count more than all this, especially when we consider what we come up against when we explore commitment? Does it not still remain a proper and possible question to ask 'Who rules?'? Is it Jesus who is Lord, who rules for God, perhaps as God? Or is it the nuclear physicist or the astronomer who without question determines for us our understanding of reality? For the life of me I cannot see why we should automatically attribute the lordship to the measurers of size. Anyway, we are able to make an investigation. We can throw in our lot with the community who is seeking to live out and to live into faith in God through Jesus Christ. Certainly there is no decisive reason to conclude that God is dead. There are many pointers to how we may believe in God, many ways which may lead us to discover that God is.

But in closing I must say something about the question – what does it mean to believe in God? The first answer is that we do not know. To believe in God is to be committed to an ever open exploration, to be open to the possibility of being able to meet a never ending demand. In fact to believe in God is to know that we are called to enter into everlasting life, infinite possibilities. But we must ask, in practice, what does it mean? And still we must say, 'You will have to search and see'. But, perhaps this much may be said, to believe in God means to be learning that we are not surrounded by, or heading for, indifference. We are surrounded by, set in, and destined for responsive and responsible love. Therefore, to believe in God means, among other things, hopefully learning the practice of prayer in always new ways. It means hoping always for creative possibilities that may break out of and transcend every situation. It means getting together with other believers in God in a common loyalty with them to explore what this means in understanding and practice. It means also getting together with any human being who is your neighbour to explore without weariness the infinite possibilities which lie in being human. God is, and therefore indifference does not rule. God is for man, as Jesus Christ makes clear, therefore there is always hope.

Belief in God today is what it always has been. A commitment to a way of living based on response to a way of giving – to the way in which God gives himself to us in Jesus Christ, through our fellow believers, through that of God in every man and in the possibilities of the universe. Moreover, belief in God is experimental living and it is experiencing living. It is not being sure of a set of sentences nor of a set of facts which tell us that God exists. For if God is God then he must establish himself. If he is not God then there is nothing whatever to be done about it. But I am bound to bear witness to you that he is God – the living God who is active today to smash all the idols of religion in which men seek to start him up, and active today to meet and fulfil all the needs and possibilities of truly human living, in this world and beyond it.

6 | *The Suffering of God*

This is not an easy subject. I find that I need to go slowly
and to meditate, think through, something which is relevant
to this immense and terrifying subject of which we may
scarcely dare to speak, the suffering of God. I fear I cannot
make it any easier because I myself have not got far enough.
I am quite clear that, in the end, all subjects to do with God
are profoundly simple, and I have no doubt that there are
many who know far more about this subject than I do. But
while I feel I may well be confused, I see no need to be
worried. God in the end is not confusing, nor are we called
upon to understand things which are in one sense beyond our
intellectual capabilities. We are called upon to enter into the
depths of the mysteries of God, and this God gives us grace to
do.

Our subject, then, is the suffering of God. Nowadays one
cannot enter upon any subject to do with God by taking
anything for granted. Therefore, the first question to ask is,
Who are we talking about? Here we have a paradox. I am
quite clear whom we are talking about, but I am not clear
about him. Further, I am clear that he goes far beyond any
understanding I can have at the moment. None the less, I am
quite clear *whom* I am talking about. This is why I find I have
to regard all attempts to talk about God as prayerful under-
takings. I cannot possibly talk about him about whom I am
called to talk unless he assists me.

I am talking, then, about the God and Father of our Lord
Jesus Christ. I am talking about the God of Abraham, of
Isaac and of Jacob. I am talking about the God of Moses, of
Jeremiah, of Peter, of Paul and of John, and of countless
others, known and unknown through the ages. In fact, I am

talking about the Lord God who is involved with his people. People believe in God because people believe in God. And no amount of propaganda, complaint or commendation will cause people to believe in God unless God is there, keeping a people who believe in him. And therefore it is the case that people believe in God, because people believe in God. And there always will be a people who believe in God, because God has made it quite clear that he will keep a people for himself, and he will keep such a people despite all that we can do to run away from him.

It is quite clear that the church is used by God in his making himself known to us, and yet that the church is the greatest obstacle to believing in God. For people look at us of the church and cannot conclude that we believe in God, because of our way of living. Yet God keeps a people who believe in him and who seek to follow him. Therefore we are talking about the Lord God who is involved with his people. We are talking about the Lord, the Almighty One, the One who dwelleth on high, who inhabiteth eternity, who is profounder than the deepest depths, who is met with in the human heart, in the situations, the catastrophes and the joys of human living, in the history of the people of Israel, in the life of the church and, I do not doubt, who is met with in the lives of many people outside the church, outside the people of Israel, who do not yet know who it is with whom they are meeting.

We are therefore talking about the One who is met, the One who is known as Jeremiah knew him when he went down to Egypt in despair, but none the less knew God. We speak of the One whom the Psalmist knew, both in the heights of his hopes and in the depths of his fears. We are talking about the One who was looked for when Abraham went out not knowing whither he went, the One who was sought after when on the cross Jesus said, 'My God, my God, why hast thou forsaken me?'. We are talking therefore about the Holy and Righteous One who has made himself known as the One who cares. The One who cares, who is the Lord God who is involved with his people. And we know that he is in one way wholly other than us, wholly different from us.

This is made quite clear above all in worship. Worship is a recognition that the holiness of God, the Godness of God, the very way in which God cares, is so much beyond us that all we can do is to fall down, whether metaphorically or literally if it helps us, and have nothing to say and have nothing to do but simply to be in his presence as the Holy, the Worshipful, the Righteous One, who is other than us.

He is known also as the Holy and Righteous and Transcendent One who is trustworthy. This is a thing which has been borne in upon the followers of God, those who have been called to know that they are his people through all the ups and downs of their lives, through all the muddle and chaos and frustration, as well as through all the joy and excitement and hope. If we would only let the Bible speak for itself and just read it in simplicity, we would see that men do not believe in God because this gives them the answer to the problem of evil or because this shows what pattern things fit into. They believe in God because they discover him in their hopes and in their fears, constantly being renewed when they thought they were crushed; constantly being taken to higher hopes when they thought they had achieved all there was to be achieved; and what they have discovered about the Holy One who is involved with his people, is that he is wholly steadfast, trustworthy, the God who has a steadfast purpose which is expressed through the demand which he makes upon his people to follow him. Moreover, in discovering the holiness and the righteousness and the otherness of God, and in discovering his trustworthiness, men have discovered that he is a caring God, that his steadfastness is expressed above all in love. We are talking, therefore, about the Lord who is steadfast, purposeful, demanding, promising love. We are talking of the Lord who is our God, the Lord who is my God, just as he was the God of Abraham and the God of Isaac and the God of Jacob; the God of David, the God of Peter, the God of Paul, the God of Jesus.

As we can see from the Bible, there was built up a certainty of faith. It was a certainty and yet it was faith. It was a certainty because it was knowledge and experience and encounter, but it was faith because things never worked out in

the way in which you might have expected if there was this
God. As you see the whole knowledge of God developing in
the Bible, you find that this very *certainty* of faith created the
problem of faith. Men were clear that there is the Lord who is
God, and the Lord who is holy, righteous, loving. He is
indeed Lord, so much the Lord that he is to be thought of as
the Creator. There would be nothing if he were not there to
see that there is something. He is Lord of everything in the
sense that everything depends for its very existence upon him.
He is also the ruler of history, so men believe. So much the
Lord God that he controls for his purposes everything that
could come out of, and was coming out of, the processes of
history, and the processes of the universe. This was a faith
which may have been built up at a time when people did not
know that the universe is as vast as it is now, but it was a
universe which was quite as frightening, quite as mysterious,
quite as uncertain, and had so many immeasurable quantities
in it, that it must have seemed to those people quite as vast
as the universe now seems to us, and they had no doubt that
the Lord God was the Creator and Ruler of this whole
universe and of all history in it, and that he was indeed
righteous, holy, loving.

But this, of course, caused the very problem of faith. For
God is unquestionably Lord; he is undoubtedly holy, and
therefore determined to have only that which is in accordance
with his holiness and righteousness. He is also unquestionably
loving, caring for his people and determined to bring his
purposes out of history, out of the universe for his people.
How *could* such a Lord who was indeed Lord have a world as
it then was, as it now is? Consider the cry of 'O Lord, how
long?' 'If you are indeed Lord, why do all these ungodly
things happen? If you are indeed Lord, holy, righteous and
loving, what is all this unholiness, all this unrighteousness, all
this frustration and fear and trembling and frustration and
death and nothingness? O Lord, how long before you make it
clear, that you are indeed Lord and God?' 'Where is now
thy God?'

Out of this clash between the certainty of faith and the
problem of faith, there arose the expectation of the coming of

the kingdom of God, and the expectation of the coming of the Messiah, who will bring in the kingdom of God. The pattern of this is very simple. God is God and he does reign and therefore he will reign. As he is God, he is bound to do something which will take away all those things in his world and in his history and in his people which contradict his holiness and his righteousness and his love and reign as Lord God in his kingdom. But when is the kingdom coming? Where is the Messiah? When is God going to do something that makes it clear that he is God? We cannot avoid this certainty and this problem of faith. We are committed to this expectancy which arises out of the fact that God is God, and yet is an agonized expectancy, because the things in the world are not in accordance, so often and so many times, with the Godness of God. Surely we can have no illusions nowadays. There are innumerable things in the lives of each of us and certainly in the world at large, which count against the existence of a God who is Lord and Love, who is almighty and holy, who is undefeatable and righteous. And so in the midst of this sort of world, this certainty of faith and this problem of faith arises.

As you come to the end of the Old Testament period and beyond it, into the period that lies between the Old Testament and the New, there crystallizes the hope of the coming of the kingdom, when God will make it clear that he is indeed God, and the hope also of the coming of the Messiah, the One whom God has sent to make it clear that he is God. And who is it that came? Jesus. That is what has caused the Christian religion, that is why the church exists. There were a few men who were looking for the coming of the kingdom of God, who were expecting the Lord's Anointed, and they were persuaded, in a way which transformed them, that Jesus of Nazareth is the Lord's Anointed. It was this Jesus who lived a life for the very God about whom Jesus spoke and for whom Jesus lived. It was this Jesus who believed it was his mission to announce the coming of the kingdom of God. 'The kingdom of heaven is at hand. Repent, and believe the Gospel.' The Christ was this Jesus who lived an impressive pattern of life which we now interpret as a life for others, but which was first a life for

God and a life for others *because* it was a life for this God.
This Jesus believed himself to be called to announce and
inaugurate and bring in the kingdom of *this* God. In living
his life for *this* God and in living his life for others he set
himself to death, even the death of the cross. I am not now
talking about stories that have been coloured up by years and
years of piety – which might have been interpreted rightly
and which might have been interpreted wrongly. I am simply
talking about the bare outlines which make it clear that we
have to do with a man who so lived for God that that
impression has never been forgotten. Also he so lived for man
that *that* impression has never been forgotten. And he lived
out this life for man and this life for God as he went on his
way and died on the cross which has never been forgotten,
although it has often been sentimentalized.

So this man Jesus, serving this God, announcing this
kingdom, died this death, even the death of the cross, and
therefore once again it looked as though God was going to
make it clear that he was God but he did not. 'We thought it
should have been he that would have redeemed Israel' – but
now we go a-fishing. Get back to the routine and making the
best of life and carrying on with the odds and ends. But –
there wasn't a '*but*'. It wasn't 'We thought it should have
been *but*.' There was a *yes*, for there was what we call the
Resurrection. There was the undoubted conviction, the
undoubted knowledge, the undoubted certainty, that God has
raised him up. 'This Jesus whom you crucified, God has made
both Lord and Christ.' This Jesus is this God's Lord and
Christ, and therefore in the midst of the frustrations and
uncertainties of this world, in the very light of the doing to
death of this Jesus, we are clear that the kingdom of God is
declared and defined by Jesus Christ. Such was the message
of the first apostles and such is the apostolic message today.
Jesus *is* what God does to make it clear that he is God. Jesus
is the shape of the kingdom of God. This Jesus Christ is how
God gets things done. This is how God establishes his
purposes of holiness and righteousness and love. This Jesus
indeed is how God establishes himself.

'O Lord, how long?' When is the certainty of faith going to

get an answer to the problem of faith? When the Lord sends
the Messiah and the Messiah is Jesus. This is how God
establishes himself. And it is not until we get to this point that
we even dare speak of the suffering of God. For it becomes
clear that the pattern of Jesus is the pattern of God. For it is
in and through Jesus that God establishes himself and his
kingdom, and when we seek to follow in the steps of the
doubting Thomas and say 'My Lord and My God', then we
are beginning to enter into the significance of the pattern of
the living and dying and perpetual resurrection living of
Jesus. This is the Lord. This is the way God establishes his
Lordship. This is God, God involved for the sake of his
people, this is God indeed, the very truth of the pattern of the
life and the character of God, the Almighty. And so we are
called to acknowledge Jesus Christ the Son of God, who is the
'perfect image of the Father'. Here we come up against all
the complicated things which appear in the creed, complications like the doctrine of the Trinity, which is much too
difficult for us to believe today because we have not got the
patience or courage to think like people used to think. We
have, for instance, the phrase 'of one substance with the
Father'. Most unfortunate metaphysical language! We must
cut it out. It cannot be understood. So cut it out! Yet it
speaks of the Son who is of one substance with the Father, the
very presentation of the very reality of God himself. If you
want reality, if you want to know what is behind it all and in
it all and through it all, look at Jesus and you will come up
against the very substance of it. 'Of one substance with the
Father, God Almighty.' When you see the life of Jesus, you
see the pattern of the life of God.

At this point I would like to lapse into Greek if I have not
spoken Greek already! You can see what are called his
'energies', the way in which God expresses himself and comes
to us. You cannot, of course, see what is called his very
Being, because God is far too great a mystery for us to
penetrate to the very heart of his Being and there is always
something hidden. But we can see the reality of God towards
us in Jesus, the very pattern of his essential activity, even if
we cannot penetrate to the inmost essence, to the very last

depth. But what we can know is that God is through and through consistent and therefore what we are able to see of him in Jesus is wholly consistent with the whole pattern of his Being. The very pattern who is Jesus is the pattern of the Father, God Almighty. Jesus is the very Son of God, of one substance with the Father. That is to say, he is the pattern of the life and the being and the consistency of God. This is why we both may speak and must speak of the suffering of God. For in the pattern of Jesus we have the pattern of the life of God, and the pattern of Jesus is the pattern of suffering.

Now here it is very necessary to stress that the pattern of God must be seen in the *humanity* of Jesus. Let us have no nonsense about the suffering of Jesus on the cross which suggests that he knew that he was God and therefore he knew that it would come all right and therefore that there was something unreal about the desolation and about the suffering. There is a much greater mystery than that. In trying to discuss this mystery it is impossible to be anything but tentative. But we can at least try to consider what is involved. It is the human Jesus who is the pattern of God and we must put on one side any sentimental talk which somehow suggests that we have God masquerading in human suffering.

A way theologians tried for approaching this mystery is known as 'the emptying'. The Greek term is 'kenosis'. *Kenosis* – emptying? In approaching any mysteries it is useful to have words the meaning of which is not obvious. We hear many words about suffering and so on, and we think we know. We hear the word Love, and we think we know. Surely we do not. It would be much better, it sometimes seems to me, if half the words we used about Christianity were words the meaning of which we could not suppose we knew, so that we had to think every time until we had given them meaning in the light of Jesus. So there is this mystery of the 'emptying'. It is the pattern of the human Jesus who is the pattern of God. Nothing must detract from Jesus' humanness. Nothing must detract from the ordinary realism of the life and of the passion and of the cross. Many people, alas, suffer deeply, suffer sordidly, suffer in a way in which there is nothing ennobled to be seen. I do not believe that there would be anything visibly ennobling in the suffering and in the dying of Jesus. He died all right – right up to the reality of 'My God, my God, why hast thou forsaken me?'.

This is the pattern of God. So we have to believe if we follow out the shape of the understanding of Jesus which lies against the background of the Old Testament and is proclaimed in the New. This is the pattern of the God who is involved with his people, who is involved, so great is the mystery, *as* one of his people. Here is identification. Here is God, the God who cares and is therefore involved with his people. Identification to the point of being *one* of his people, and therefore God on both sides.

God on God's side. This does not stop his being God. I have stressed the human-ness at the moment, but we must not lose the Godness. We will come back to that. God on both sides of what, because of our sin, is the division between God and man. God on God's side and God also on man's side. God on our side. God on the separated sinner's side. I cannot explain this any more here, but I think this is what is behind 'My God, my God, why hast thou forsaken me?'. I believe that God so identifies himself with us because he is love that he is enabled in the expression of his power and purpose and personality, which is love, to undergo for our sakes what we must call, I think, almost a split personality. That is to say, we have God who is God in his holiness and God who is One with man in his sinfulness. This is something of what lies behind the mystery of 'My God, my God, why hast thou forsaken me?'.

Here we are on the edge of some very baffling mysteries which seem to me to be none the less close to the heart of the Gospel. In the man Jesus, we see God, the way in which, towards us, God has his way of being God. That is to say, this is the way God brings about his pattern and his purposes, and so in the man Jesus we see the involvement of God, and therefore it is literally true to speak of the suffering of God. This is the great and mighty wonder. This is how transcendent love, infinite love, almighty love, unchanging and unchangeable love, brings about his purposes. This is the power of God – this suffering and involvement and dying of Jesus.

C

And here we have something which requires facing
personally, although I do not see anyone facing it except by
the help of the grace of this same God and even then, by his
graciousness, only being led gradually into it, because only
gradually can we bear it. We have to face a very great
judgment – the suffering of God. The way in which God has
made it clear how he expresses the power which lies in his
being God is a very great judgment upon us. 'The kings of
the Gentiles lord it over them.' They have authority, they
know what power is. They know how to put people in their
place and show them what counts and what is authority, 'but
it shall not be so among you'. For how does God get things
done? The man Jesus. And therefore I believe that we must
stand under the judgment of the suffering God on all our
ways of doing things, whether it be outside the church, or
inside the church. You could equally well do research on the
power structure in the Church of England as you could on
the power structure in the Cabinet and so on. You could
equally well, no doubt, analyse out the activities of a cathedral
council, or of a local church council, and find how people
manoeuvre, and how they seek to put themselves in such a
position that they can put their views over on other people.
But the way in which God gets things done is through the
man Jesus, and we are therefore under the judgment of the
suffering God – under the judgment of the suffering God to
learn gradually to walk his way and to do things in the way
in which he gets things done, because it is the way of suffering
and self-giving love, which cannot be defeated because it
never sets up new obstacles.

We may have to use negative power, which is a power
which is not the power of love, for, in this life, we are trapped
in our 'fallen' situation up to a point. Yet if we do have to
use negative power, we may get what we want done, but we
also set up all sorts of other obstacles all round which are
carrying on their little bits of frustration and negativity and
fighting. It is only as we begin to walk in the way of the
cross, the way of self-giving love, that all the negative powers,
all the anti-things, all the against things, all the un-loving and
unlovely things are gradually absorbed. There is no doubt in

my mind, that to walk the way of the cross is the only
practical way of getting things done in accordance with love.
We are therefore under the judgment of the suffering God in
all that we do, and above all in the way in which we seek to
'run' the church.

But there is an even greater judgment than this and, as I
know I cannot face it, I hesitate to speak of it. I believe that
it surely must be true that we are shown, in the pattern of
Jesus, that God suffers with all his children. This is the
fundamental answer to the problem of evil. There is no
answer, but there is a way to live in it and through it. It
must be the case that God suffers with all his children. For if
Jesus is the pattern of God, if Jesus is consistent with the
whole pattern of God which is consistent through and
through, then it is surely true that God has made it clear to
us that his divine sympathy is truly a godly, a God-like
suffering with all who suffer. We are therefore under the
judgment that every hurt we do to any creature in this world
is shared by God. We are therefore under the judgment that
every hurt we permit, when we might have stood in the way
of it, we permit to happen also to God. 'Inasmuch as ye do it
not to the least of these my little ones, you do it *not* unto me.'
The conclusion seems inescapable that this is literally true.
This is a terrifying judgment, and we could not even say 'God
forgive me', unless we already knew, because of the very
pattern of God in Jesus Christ, that he does forgive us. We
may face up to this because God forgives us through and in
his very suffering, and therefore we must dare to speak of the
suffering of God. The suffering of God in the dreadful pictures
from Vietnam; the suffering of God in Oxfam posters; the
suffering of God to be seen in hospitals, to be seen in neglected homes, to be seen all round. This we may dare to speak
of. Here is God involved for his people in this terrible but
saving judgment.

This judgment is in fact the hope of the world, the light of
the world, the salvation of the world, the very Gospel. For
although it is right to insist that we see the suffering of God
in the humanity of Jesus, this must also be balanced by the
point that it is *God* who is involved for his people. It is his

transcendent power which is united with the suffering and with the threatened fragility of actual living. It is God, and this is so, because God is Love. Love is the very stuff of God and it is the infinite resource, the limitless power, the inexhaustible purpose, the ineffable holiness, the undefeatable righteousness of God who is Love, who is involved in this way. We must never lose our grip upon the transcendence of God, upon the otherness of God, however much we are led to see into the very humanity and the very suffering of God. And therefore we know that in this world belief in God is possible. How could we believe in a God who had not been crucified? What is he doing letting these things happen? I think the answer is, he is suffering. God is involved and this is how we face, this is how we endure, this is how we are transformed in and through the problem of evil and of suffering and of the monstrosity of so much of it. This is how we know that out of this very world and in this very world, God brings his purposes. For God is, and God is involved, and God is Love and above all this is God.

To talk of the sufferings of God is not to deny the *impassibility* of God. At least, it is not to deny what the doctrine of the impassibility of God has always stood for. Impassibility literally means un-sufferingness – not being able to suffer. But we must be careful about being bound by literal meanings. It stands for the fact that you cannot in any way take away the Godness of God. A right translation for the impassibility of God might be: 'God cannot be put off being God.' Nothing that can be done or can happen can put God off being God. He is God, he is God the changeless; he is God the unchangeable; he is God the wholly perfect and the wholly infinite and the wholly independent of everything else. Nothing makes any difference to God's being God. But God is Love, and therefore God can and God does enter into the suffering of the world. This does not put him off being God.

We, of course, cannot be open to the sufferings of the world, as the cross shows that God is open to the sufferings of the world. We could not bear it for one moment, but God can bear it, because he is God, and he is Love, and it has not put him off being God. It is the very expression of his being God. God can give himself away in being God, in the expression and pursuit of his purposes and this is how, in relation to his creatures, he is himself. He enters into the suffering of the world. Therefore I believe it to be literally true that Jesus is God and that we may and we must rightly speak of the sufferings of God, but I believe also that we must be quite clear that it is God who suffers – the one true, almighty, transcendent, holy and righteous God.

As we see God in the suffering and dying of his Son, in the humanity and the true human-ness and the realistic human being, Jesus, so we must believe in the self-same God who is the Almighty Father, not just immanent in suffering, by no means exhausted in suffering. We are concerned with the suffering of the transcendent God. The whole of God, if I may put it so, is in Jesus, but we must not suppose that Jesus alone is a sufficient symbol for all that God is. We must also have the understanding of God the Almighty, God the Transcendent, God the Father. God is Love. God therefore is God in and through his suffering, but it is God who suffers, and this involved and suffering love is the expression of transcendent and triumphant power. This surely is the decisive and the transforming Good News. This is the Gospel, the Gospel of Good Friday and the Gospel of Easter Day; the Gospel of the Cross and the Resurrection. God is, God is Almighty and God is Love and God is to be seen in Jesus. And the Almighty God, who is transcendent love, is for *you*, he suffers with you, he suffers in you and he suffers for you.

God was in Christ, reconciling the word to himself, and the way of the cross is the practical and undefeatable way of purposeful and redeeming love. Therefore we know, as Paul also knew, that there is nothing, nothing in death or in life, in the realm of spirits or superhuman powers, in the world as it is, or in the world as it shall be, when science has discovered more and more things – in the forces of the universe, however they are measured, however they are plumbed, in heights or in depths, nothing in all creation that can 'separate us from the love of God in Christ Jesus our Lord'.

7 | *How Dead is God?*

1 *Thoughts on the 'Death of God' Controversy*

I suspect that there is nothing much wrong with God. A great deal of the church and a very great deal of theology would seem, however, to be in a pretty sickly condition. This is how it seems to me after studying William Hamilton's *New Essence of Christianity*, wading through Thomas Altizer's *Gospel of Christian Atheism* and reading Thomas Ogletree's *Death of God Controversy* and skimming a good deal more.

The last book mentioned does give a very reasonable survey of the initial writings of Hamilton, van Buren and Altizer, which were, perhaps, the pacemakers of this very American controversy. There is also a useful introductory chapter on 'A Setting for Radical Theology'. But I fear the book is rather solemn in style and, on the whole, dull. So it will be boring to those already in the know and will scarcely give the flavour of the controversy to those who are not. After all, much of what Altizer says is so silly, much of what van Buren says is so theologically and philosophically weak, and all of what Hamilton says is so inconclusive, that there must be more to it than what the arguments (or 'argument') boil down to when judiciously summarized and arranged by so competent a person as Ogletree.

More is to be found by sympathetically probing behind the explosiveness of Altizer, the questioning of van Buren about how words have meaning (even if he has rather belatedly woken up to this one) and the very attractive and searching honest bewilderment of Hamilton. The last's *New Essence* is a very provocative and evocative book which we would do well to get right under our skin so that we can share in the humility and anguish of his search.

As with many of the writers in this literature, Hamilton equates theology with Protestant theology and Protestant theology with Barthianism; and Barth has let him down. The wholly sufficient (because divine) and wholly unsupported (equally because divine) Word of God which rescued Barth and a multitude of his followers from the relativism and insipidity of liberalism does not seem divine to Hamilton and his like, but dishonest, irrelevant and even complacent.

Thus what was radical objectivity for Barthians (God is because he is and lets it be so known, and for no other reason) becomes radical scepticism. There are no reasons and we do not know that God is – so he isn't. We live in the time of the absence of God and God is dead. Clearly, none of these writers have ever had joy in worship or prayer, or ever felt in contact with glory through their relations with the church and the Christian tradition.

The God whose death Altizer discusses is so 'sick' that if atheism means his death then it is indeed a gospel. But this God is a sort of perverted cosmic Emperor whose worship would be best described in terms of the slogan 'Down, crawl, salute, promote'. It is very important indeed to understand why Altizer holds, as he so clearly and firmly does, that this is the God of the biblical and Christian tradition. I believe that much of the practice of Christian teaching, worship and morality does tend to support such a view of God. But it is absolute nonsense to claim that such a view of, and attitude to, God is either typical of or truly consistent with the biblical and Christian tradition.

This is why I personally feel that the 'Death of God' controversy is chiefly symptomatic of the deadliness of much of the church and most of theology. Anyone who doubts this should read Hamilton's moving section on 'Beyond the Death of God' in his chapter 'Belief in a Time of the Death of God'. Curiously, he seems to imagine that what he says there about Christians today finding that God is 'there when we do not want him . . . and he is not there when we do want him' is

something new, symptomatic of our living in a new time of
the absence of God. In this he reflects many of his co-con-
troversialists. Theology begins with Barth and that has
collapsed. Knowledge of any earlier tradition is either absent
or alarmingly superficial. Neither Hamilton nor van Buren
could get more than very low marks for their knowledge of
creative Christian thought and spirituality about Christ and
the Trinity. This is further evidence of the way their Christian
tradition and practice has let them down.

This ignorance of the past is combined even, as far as I
can see, in the later Hamilton, with an arrogance about the
present and the future and a very curious *in*sensitiveness to
modern currents of thought outside the narrow world of
theology and philosophy. If everything is provisional, then so
are current fashions of thinking, and to absolutize them in the
assertive way of a van Buren or an Altizer would seem to be a
very unreasonable and unfeeling procedure.

Moreover, Altizer, at any rate, is very old-fashioned. He is,
in fact, drunk with his own version of a *macédoine* of Blake,
Hegel and Nietzsche. His book consists of an amazing string of
assertions drawn from, influenced by, or based on these very
problematic and highly dated writers. Every page provides
ample opportunity for searching critical questioning by anyone
who has any training in nineteenth-century ideas or philosophical logic. And this is supposed to be the sort of thing
which is an appropriate response to the situation of men in
the modern technological and scientific age! Any scientists or
technologists who fall for this will be indulging in an escapism
which is even more pronounced than the current fashion for
pseudo-Zen.

But we must not mistake the importance of the argument
because of the incompetence of the arguers. God may not be
dead but the current practice and practices of Christianity
are far too often deadly. The 'Death of God' controversy
must be seen, studied and received as a God-given challenge
to face up far more realistically than we normally do, either
in our congregations or in our theological faculties and
theological colleges, to the realities both of the modern world
and of the biblical and Christian tradition.

ii   *The Debate about God*

The Debate about God has taken on its present form because, by the grace of God, Western atheism has at last penetrated the church. A few theologians and even some men in positions of ecclesiastical authority have suddenly found themselves paying attention primarily to the realities of modern Western life instead of to the preoccupations of ecclesiastical organizing, institutional religion, and traditional theological debates. This has led them to wake up to a fact which has been a commonplace of Western intellectual life, everywhere else than among ecclesiastics, for several generations at least. The taken-for-granted way of looking at the world which holds widest sway and earns most prestige has no place in it for God.

The Copernican revolution has been completed. The observer (originally the man with the telescope) is both part of and the centre of his observations, and these observations are our decisive source of knowledge. So man is inevitably at the centre of his world. All that he knows are his observations and what he makes of his observations. The scientific observer is the only judge we have of what objectively exists, that is of what there is *outside* the observer. This does not make man the centre of *the* universe. Far from it. Observation suggests a vastness of worlds of which it does not make sense to speak of a 'centre' at all. But it does make man the centre of *his* universe. What he makes of the world, in so far as he can make anything of it, depends on him.

Before the pastorally minded take refuge from the intellectuals with the simple folk and before those whose life and experience are rooted in Africa or the East produce their often legitimate criticisms of 'the West', there are certain aspects of this debate which, admittedly, originates in the Western intellectual climate, which all who desire to take Christianity and the Bible seriously need to consider. These are the aspects which enable us, indeed require us, to see that Western atheism has much to teach us both about the liveliness of the world and about the deadliness of the church, and thence about God.

The debate about God, I have suggested, takes its present form because some thinkers within the church have become acutely aware that the prevailing way of looking at the world has no place in it for God. This way of looking at the world is very closely associated with the rise of science and the development of applied science. The observer must be at the centre of the development of the scientific method, just as the experimenter and the man of application must be at the centre of the development of techniques and technology. This is not a sinful attempt at the capture by arrogant man of that central place in the universe which by rights belongs to God. It is simply the inevitable practical consequence, or perhaps rather, the basic practical presupposition, of the method. The way to such practical mastery over the human environment as is possible (and who knows what the limits of this possibility are?) is through this observer-centred and experimentally tested method. Far more, for example, has been achieved by this scientific approach in dealing with the actual incidence of disease and misery than has ever been done or even claimed to have been done by prayer and miracle. Clearly there can be no going back on science. Even if it were practically possible it is humanly undesirable. The only hope of dealing with the practical problems of humanity, even if it is not an absolutely assured hope, must include the continuing develop-ment and application of the scientific method and scientific methods. Humanly speaking science is clearly essential, however much it may be held to fail, on its own, to be sufficient. And theologically speaking there can be no going back on science. To turn aside from the mastery which science offers over the human environment is to deny the biblical doctrine that man is created in the image of God and meant to have dominion. This dominion, no doubt, is biblically seen as within the purpose of God, but none the less it is dominion. And the practical way to the exercise of this dominion has come and is coming through science.

The fact that there are grounds in the present situation for judging that man's very existence is also threatened by some of the possible results of the dominion which science has been the means of his receiving, in no way blunts the point of the argument. Historically speaking, the way to the possibilities of dominion has opened up through the development of science. Christians who believe in a creator who is also Lord of history are bound, therefore, to take the historical development of scientific method in itself as of the most profound significance. When, therefore, the development of this whole approach to the world in fact (even if not in theoretical necessity) is closely associated with the development of an atheistic climate of thought, this also has to be taken very seriously. And this is what those who have initiated the present debate about God have at last begun to do.

The case for taking atheism seriously is reinforced when one further considers how, historically speaking, the development of science and the attendant development of atheism has worked towards the liberation of man. To rely upon your observations and upon the tested application of the results of your observations is to rely upon yourself and to find that it works. Of course, 'it' does not 'work' in the heavenly, cosmic, or eternal spheres. But where are the powerful observations which convince about the very existence of such spheres? Oriental fatalism or Western resignation to the providence and grace of God are all very well when nothing else can be done and man is seen as a nothingness who is part of the all or a miserable sinner dependent for any crumb of comfort or hope on an omnipotent deity over against him. But something else can be done, has been done, and is being done. If man is seen simply as man who observes, measures, organizes, and acts, he may not then reach as far as God, wherever that may be, but he does reach far more widely into his environment and far more deeply into himself than has ever been done or dreamed of before. And in this and out of this there is much actual fulfilment which can be seen, shared, and promoted, and which looks much more like some version of 'life abundant' than mere promises of the hypothetical hereafter.

It is true, once again, that there is another side to the picture. One can produce sufficiently minatory evidence from

the workings of so-called Marxist societies or from the
neuroticism of many Western patterns of life to show what
can go wrong with all this. But this does not alter the power-
fulness of so much that has gone right. Further, the discovery
of the possibilities of reliance upon oneself, of what it is like
to be man getting on with things, rather than man succumb-
ing to things or bowing down to inscrutability, has had an
explosively liberating effect. It was not the Christian religion
as institutionalized, presented to, and observed by them,
which brought life, activity, and purpose to such as Nietzsche,
Marx, Russell, their like and their disciples, but the liberation
from religious clutter by the discovery of atheism and the
facing up to the responsibilities and possibilities of being a
man in atheistic and open circumstances. If there is anything
godly in opening up men to the possibilities in themselves and
in their environment, then many nineteenth and twentieth-
century atheists would seem to show more signs of practical
godliness than many of their contemporary ecclesiastics
struggling to preserve the institutional existence and traditional
practices of the church.

Observer-centred science and an atheism which accepts the
apparent inevitability of working from the observer and with
the observer alone seem of late (? from the seventeenth
century onwards) and at any rate until very recently, to
have been the main life-stream and liberator of the liveliness
of man. So, at any rate, it has seemed to the recent debaters
about God within the church, as it has seemed to the majority
outside the church for very much longer. Thus, in the face of
all this, the debaters have found themselves forced to raise
and face the questions 'What does God count for?' and
'What counts for God?'.

Believers in God who have advanced to any true mono-
theism have always understood 'God' as standing for, and
God himself as being, the fundamental basis and greatest
dimension of all that is or can be (the ground and fulfilment
of our being and all being). Biblical believers in God have
understood him to be concerned with, and involved in, the
world and history for the sake of the salvation and wholeness
of man. Is it not therefore possible that a godliness which is

truly and wholly in the tradition of biblical theism should
have to take absolutely seriously this historical transference of
the 'centre of gravity' for the understanding and enjoyment of
the world from God in the heavens to man on the earth?
Might this not further mean that such a godliness should find
itself very hesitant to speak very much if at all, at least for a
time, of 'God' and find its current tasks and fulfilments in
seeking to extend the depth and the range of the understanding and development of the human possibilities in and
of the world? Both questions are surely at least legitimately
debatable, in a debate legitimated both by the pragmatic
weight of current evidence and by the theological weight of
the biblical traditions concerning the creative activity and
involvement of God and by the theme of the creation of man
in the image of God.

There is, moreover, further current evidence to lend
pragmatic weight to the legitimacy of the debate. It lies in
the sphere of the question of authority and it leads on to a
consideration of certain current and fairly long-standing
contrasts between the liveliness of the world and the deadliness of the church. I have argued that men within the church
have been reasonably forced to face the questions 'What
counts for God?' and 'What does God count for?'. These
questions have been posed with a particularly probing
acuteness because what I have called 'the Copernican
revolution' is, among other things, a revolution in the practical
understanding of the nature of authority, that is, in the
acceptance and understanding of 'what counts', of 'what has
weight'. Within an observer-centred and observation-tested
approach to things the Bible as such does not 'count for' God,
any more than does the church as such. In a precisely similar
way, for example, the fact that there is a long tradition, much
of it committed to writing, about the activities of heavenly
beings which purports to give an account of the movements
of stars and planets in no way, as such, now has any weight
with regard to our understanding of astronomy and astro-
physics. The fact that a written tradition was authoritative
because it expressed beliefs that were taken authoritatively is
not now, as such, evidence that such a tradition ought to be

taken as authoritative. The question is: What does it now
count for in terms of, and in relation to, that which can be
observed, tested, experienced? Neither antiquity nor intensity,
nor extensiveness of belief are, as such, of decisive weight
without further current evidence. And the case is the same
with regard to societies and institutions, such as the church,
which appear to be dedicated to the furtherance of some
particular world-view or a claimed authoritative approach to
the alleged realities of the world.

Indeed—and this is the crux—societies and institutions
dedicated to the preservation of a particular world-view are
generally held, and with a great deal of reason, to be the
enemies and opposers of true authoritativeness and the
upholders of false, limiting, and damaging authority. For
what these institutions tend to do, as manifested in the
behaviour both of their leaders and of their rank and file, is
to refuse to face openly and freely any evidence produced by
observation and experiment which seems to count against
what they hold to be the essential versions of their cherished
world-view. Thus, such institutions, and the church is the
most notorious of them, do not as such count for the truth
and authoritativeness of the views which they claim and pro-
claim as the reason for their very existence. Rather the
church's claim to authority has been exercised in such a way
as to make her essentially a 'non-authority', concerned with
herself and with her own views rather than with truth. It has
been atheism and not Christianity, at any rate in its
institutional forms, which has been seen as practising openness to evidence and to experiment. And it is openness to the
persuasion of evidence, and readiness to rethink one's
understanding and to reorganize one's practical approaches in
the light of evidence which is the source of authority in the
understanding of those fully exposed to the Copernican
revolution, which has given us modern science and technology.

Once again, one could put another side to the case. It
would be possible to attempt to stave off the full force of this
attack on the dogmatic authority of the church by pointing
to the evidence for holding that the 'open' atheism of Nietzsche
made no little contribution to the dogma of the Nazis, and

that Marxist dogma in one form or another can be one of the
most anti-liberal and anti-human forces in the world today.
The work of Bertrand Russell, also, is not free from some odd
dogmatisms. But failures in the practice of openness to
evidence surely do not constitute arguments against the
method of openness. How could any Christian who believes in
God as creator or God's Son as incarnate legitimately wish to
defend any use of authoritarianism to ignore or deny evidence
by pointing out that atheists fall into the same perversions as
the church? What has full authority is that practice and
approach which is open to observation, experiment, and
appropriate revision, both of understanding and of action.
The question is whether there *ought* to be any other
authoritativeness than this, whatever authoritarian attempts
may be made by theists or atheists. Atheists may be prone to
fall into errors of dogmatism in practice not unlike those to be
perceived in the practice of theism. All this represents false
authority. But can theists practise the same truly authoritative
openness as atheists and remain, authoritatively, theists? That
is, what, if anything, counts for God when the false authoritativeness of the theist is finally seen for what it is?

This is where we are brought squarely up against the
contrast which I have been referring to as that between the
liveliness of the world and the deadliness of the church. The
Gospels themselves contain a reference on the subject of 'what
counts', of 'what has weight' – the famous 'by their fruits ye
shall know them'. The upshot of the 'Copernican revolution'
in the matter of authority would seem to be that authority
follows from the production of fruit (authority is *a posteriori*)
and that this approach to authority has displaced the *a priori*
one, authority based on alleged prior rights to make authoritative claims and assertions. Thus to be taken as authoritative
and to remain authoritative, fruit must be produced. The
scientific approach to the problems and possibilities of the
world and of man has shown immense fruit. The refusal to
accept any authority just because it has been authoritative
and the refusal to be shut up in any dogmatisms about God,
man, and the world, which have often, in recent generations,
taken the form of atheism, have likewise shown great fruit in

newness of thinking, freedom of activity, and liberation of energy and purpose. In other words, the fruits of newness, openness, possibility, and liveliness have been abundantly displayed by activities in the world and with the realities of the world. The world is a very lively place and those who give serious and disciplined attention to it are able to make a considerable contribution to the possibilities of living. But the church, over a very large area of her concerns and activities, has for some time been on the defensive. And to be on the defensive is to be deadly.

The liveliness of the world has been seen as producing a series of encroachments upon, and underminings of, the authority of the church. Both the church and the world outside the church have agreed in interpreting this as, so to speak, undermining the position of God. The world on its own has found the church a false authority, and this has confirmed it in its judgment that a valid world-view has no place in it for the God whom the church attempts to set forth. The church has seen the liveliness of the world as an attack upon herself and as arrogance against God. Hence, within the church we see much suspicion and ignorance of the liveliness of the world and much energy given to defending the church and the church's place in this or that aspect of society, to reorganizing the church and even to reuniting the church. And all this is allegedly and ostensibly part of the necessary defence of God in a godless world. But this is nonsense. A God who requires defending is hopeless as God and useless to man. His existence is not even debatable, it is merely contemptible.

There are, further, two other strands to the deadliness of the church in addition to the deadliness of defensiveness. The first is that the church looks to the past while the world looks to the future. Ecclesiastical apologists call this loyalty to tradition, theologians can and must rightly work at the problem of loyalty to the revelation received in history, but most people experience the situation as stagnation. For example, the world is faced with assimilating discoveries which affect the understanding of the basis of life and raise immense questions about the very control and shape of life.

The church occupies itself with shuffling a few of the component parts of a baptismal service which is rooted in an anthropology defined by the circumstances and knowledge of fifteen hundred years ago at least. One of the clearest things to emerge from the reactions to the debate about God as conducted in Great Britain and the United States is the extent to which both worship and theology, as at present experienced in the church, are dead things even for many who continue to struggle to practise one and to learn from the other. In the United States this deadliness of the church has been misdiagnosed by some as the death of God. While most of the philosophy and theology contained in the 'Death of God' literature seems to be second-rate or worse, it is very necessary to reflect on how absolutely deadly must have been the experience which the writers of this literature must have had both in the worshipping and in the theological traditions of their churches. For example, the God whose death is proclaimed in Thomas Altizer's *The Gospel of Christian Atheism* is a very sick God indeed. But someone must have given him this idea of God. The evidence suggests that it comes from a sick church.

This sickness, which is truly to be called a 'deadliness', for it is killing to the true knowledge of God, to the true liveliness of the world, and to the true freedom of man, has a third strand beyond those of defensiveness and of living *in* the past (rather than *in* the present *out of* the past *for* the future). It is the deadliness of preoccupation with self-induced questions and issues and a consequent failure to be sufficiently alive to those moral issues which really pierce to the heart of those who are sensitive to the pressures of human affairs. The really human and important issues are found and experienced in and through the world, not in and through the church, issues such as race and equality, peace and economic justice, hunger and hope for the future. And when these issues are experienced in their living human demand and agony, what help is found in the actual practice and experience of the churches for facing them, living with them, and fighting for answers to them? Very often, at least in the West, it is the world which seems morally lively and not the church.

Now, this assessment of the background to the Debate is itself debatable. But one thing is clear beyond debate. It would be crass stupidity, born probably of cowardice and faithlessness, to write off the Debate as the unfortunate product of the ill-considered actions of a few persons who have irresponsibly expressed the immaturity of their own faith. It should also be beyond dispute that the Debate is about more than 'our images of God' and is asking for more than a refurbishing of traditional language to enable the church to be more 'with it' (although the incarnation suggests that God does have some concern to be 'with it' as far as man is concerned). The Debate is, in fact, a sign of the times, and it is up to the leaders of the church to make a responsible and, if God wills, a prophetic discernment of the significance of this sign.

The argument of this essay suggests that some insights may be found by following up, among others, the line of thought which links the liveliness of the world, the emergence of the independence of man, and the change in the nature of authority in such a way that the deadliness of the church is exposed and challenged to the point where there is an immense renewal in the knowledge of God.

In any gathering which is truly representative of a church which is world-wide there will be those who will hardly recognize in their own local situation many signs of the liveliness of the world or of the independence of man referred to in this paper. There may even be those whose local situations show few signs of changes in the nature of authority. But all such, while contributing some balance to the discussion of the Debate, must still ask themselves whether they can expect their situations to remain as untouched as they still may be by the immense effects of the originally Western scientific world-view. And as well as asking this question as a sheer matter of practical prediction, they must also go on to ask whether, either humanly or theologically, they have any right to hope that these developments should leave their corner of the world more or less untouched. For one of the main issues which the Debate raises, and which certainly requires prophetic discernment rather than piecemeal disgruntlement on the part of the church, is the whole question of the attitude to, and assessment of, science and technology. Is it or is it not a necessary consequence of biblical theism that science and technology as such and in themselves should be unreservedly welcomed? What does it mean to have claimed all along that the world is created and that the God who 'made' the world is so concerned with man that he was willing at some stage in the historical process to become one? Ought it not to mean that the world, properly handled, can be a very lively place indeed and that man is to be expected to find himself in the role of having to make something of the world? Do science and technology show that God has lost all initiative to man, or are they to be discerned as man's entering into the next stage in that created and creative process of which the Bible dared in a mythological but inspired way to speak long before there was much evidence available of any dominion open to man? Was it mere Hebrew mythology and arrogance to believe that the Lord of heaven and earth was specially concerned with insignificant and sinful man, or is it a vital insight into the truth and the very seed of the Gospel?

In fact, it may be argued that it is Western atheism, which is an intellectual growth rooted very firmly in the Western cultural tradition, which has done far more in recent generations to move both man and the world in the direction of that stature which they are intended to have in the purposes of God than has the church. But how can one possibly argue this of an atheism which denies God by finding him a mythological irrelevance? One can do so by seeing this atheism as a necessary judgment upon a church which has, in too many ways, reduced God to a mythological irrelevance. This, I believe, is what is to be discerned by considering what I have called the deadliness of the church. God, as the church too often appears to consider him and treat him, is just not big enough to deal with the liveliness of the world and the independence of man and is constantly in need of the support of a false authoritarianism. But the living God cannot be so and is not so. It is the pressure of God's world which is now forcing the church to have done with the medieval mummified God of the church and to recognize that such an idol is dead beyond debate. The divine worldly pressures are forcing the church back through tradition, beyond the Bible and deeper than any mere ecclesiastical experience to the living God who thrust Abraham out of a settled existence, did not allow Moses to settle into domesticity, worked through the destruction of the city and kingdom of his own people, and finally displayed himself as a suffering and crucified man of no great worldly significance but of total humanity and profound divinity. This is a God who makes his own authority and cannot be institutionalized. The first message of the Debate about God is to the church. And when the church has heard this message and taken it to heart, then she can speak to the world and for the world.

This speaking to and for the world is of the utmost urgency. For there is every reason to debate also the future of the world, of science and of technology, and of man. But the church cannot speak effectively of the God who redeems, and of Jesus Christ who gives indestructible hope, while she appears mainly as a survival of a world which is historically and definitely past, once and for all. She must first be reopened to the true scope and dimensions of God and of his world, not least to God through his world. Then she will be able to speak with conviction and true authority of an openness which is far greater than any which atheism can either know or practise, of an openness which is not an openness to a merely indefinite future, an openness of relativeness, or an openness of absurdity, but of an openness which has its beginning and its fulfilling in a God without limit who is life without limit.

III *The Ferment of Faith: Christian Faith in God*

Why believe in God? Until surprisingly recently the instinctive answer of believers in God to this question would have tended to be – 'Because everyone does, it's *natural* to believe in God'.

When a little reflection on this answer threw a bit of doubt on it, then the next move would have been to agree that there are atheists, but that they are the odd men out, the eccentrics and unbalanced radicals of civilized and cultural thinking. But if one wasn't quite convinced by this it was always possible to shore up this taken-for-granted belief in God as the natural attitude of all truly reasonable and normal men by moving on to the assertion: 'And, in any case, come to think of it, it's reasonable to believe in God. There must be some cause for the existence of things, some basis for goodness, some purpose to which everything tends.' So – if the question came up 'Why believe in God?', the answer was 'Because it is natural and reasonable and, surely, inevitable when you come to think about it'.

In 1963, owing to a series of accidents which included illness and some nearly fortuitous publicity, the Bishop of Woolwich finally made it public knowledge that this sort of answer to questions about God is quite unrealistic and unacceptable as a beginning and end to the matter. Belief in God is not natural in the sense that the vast majority of men obviously display it, enjoy it and admit it. The way men reason about the world for the purposes of science and technology does not require any talk about God at all, indeed rigorously excludes such talk, so that 'reasonable men' seem to be much more likely to be atheists than believers in God. And far from belief in God being inevitable, a large number of people, including many of the most sensitive and humane, seem to find it impossible. Belief in God has clearly ceased to be an automatic or obviously necessary part of our culture, our civilized approach to life, our human under-standing. 'Why believe in God?' 'Why, indeed, unless you cannot outgrow a nostalgia for inherited religion or an immaturity which refuses to face the fact that stories about the heavenly Father are nothing but stories and that man is on his own?'

John Robinson was, as a matter of fact, simply discussing a situation which had been developing for well over two hundred years and which had long been commonplace to every educated man who has not been ecclesiastically

drugged,* but he had the courage and humility to reflect this
situation in a peculiarly personal and, indeed, ordinary way.
This allowed, or even compelled, people to admit that this too
was their situation. To many this seemed peculiarly wicked,
not least because it was so peculiarly threatening. How dare
the Bishop publicly face what they could not bring themselves
privately to admit, viz. that the world no longer believed in
God, and while the church continued officially to speak of
him this talk carried very little conviction even in the hearts
and minds and lives of many of her members? A real ferment
of faith has been reflected, and to some extent caused, by and
in this debate about God.

There must be no doubt that this is a splendid thing. For
by this debate and through this ferment we Christians are
being challenged to faith in God and recalled to faith in God.
We are being deprived of any opportunity to rest in a
culturally inherited belief about the world, or a traditional
conformity with what we have supposed the church can
guarantee to us. That is to say that we cannot convincingly
answer the question 'Why believe in God?' either by replying
'Because it is the natural/reasonable/civilized thing to do' or
by the reply 'Because the church tells us to'. Further, the
failure of 'the church' to operate as an authority for God, or
the authority for God, is tied up with the inadequacy of the
first answer. The church no longer works as a taken-for-
granted authority for God because the church, as an institution, is tied up with just that type of society which took it for
granted that belief in God is natural/reasonable/civilized. And
that type of society belongs to the past. Its sorts of authority
are no longer authoritative. The church was one of those
authorities, consequently its authority, as an institution of
society, is just as *passé* as all the rest. This is a very important
point which people seem to find extremely difficult to
comprehend. It is not, however, difficult to *understand*, it is
simply difficult, for church people at any rate, to *accept*. It
must therefore be pondered on at great length until it can be

* See 'Whither the Doctrine of God Now', pp. 26ff. above and *Guide to
the Debate about God* (Lutterworth Press, 1966).

faced, for until it is faced we shall not be set free for Christian faith in God today.

Perhaps we may become clearer about the actualities and the opportunities of our present situation if we consider the description not infrequently offered of our present plight, that we live in a 'post-Christian age'. This is to suggest that some period of the past was an age, era and society which, as an age, era and society, accepted Jesus Christ as the Word and Son of God and was identified through and through with this acceptance. The age took it for granted that God was God. Society assumed and acted on the assumption that Christianity was the basis and guide of behaviour, the era was based on the presupposition that the worship of the church indicated the true goal and end of man. But an assumption of this sort is historical nonsense and biblical blasphemy, lent some plausibility by the historical fact that for a considerable period, in what might be called Christendom, the church was one of 'the powers that be' (a faint reflection of this lingers on with us in such facts as that the Archbishop of Canterbury has a precedence well up in the 'top ten' of the Realm!).

In fact there never has been a Christian age. The Christian era and the Christian society will not arrive until the Kingdom of God has fully and finally come and everything is at its end, its fulfilment, in the God and Father of our Lord Jesus Christ. The only place where the Kingdom of God can be unambiguously identified on earth and in history is in the person of Jesus himself. To identify even implicitly some stage in history, culture and civilization as a 'Christian age' (which can be measured and therefore be past) is to treat Jesus Christ as nothing but a historical accident, to accept Christianity as nothing but a cultural phenomenon, to identify the God and Father of Jesus and of Christianity as the mythological focus-figure of a particular way of looking at the world. Hence talk of a 'post-Christian age' is symptomatic of the absence of Christian faith in God. It shows that men have not been exercising or enjoying faith in God but have been conforming to a cultural habit and a historical fashion which is now very nearly over – thank God! – as we are surely required to say.

For the God and Father of our Lord Jesus Christ is not and never has been identified with any age, era, civilization or culture whatever. He identified himself with Jesus and identified himself through Jesus. But Jesus is 'the despised and rejected of men'. He 'came unto his own' and 'his own received him not' because 'his own' had *identified* their particular pattern of society and religion with God. And this despite the fact that they, the Jews, owed their very existence to the discovery that God was not identified with the civilization of the tribe of Judah or the Temple of the people of Judah. The glory of the Lord was departed from the Temple with the fall of Jerusalem but this did not mean that the glorious and living God was dead. He was rediscovered or rather he revealed himself again, by 'the waters of Babylon' and he was known to and through his suffering remnant. Again and again the people of God have had to go through the experience of thinking and feeling that their God was dead because they have insisted on identifying him with the means by which he once came to them and locating him in the institutions through which, at one particular stage in history and culture, they tried to respond to him. But he is the Lord, he does not change. He remains absolutely freely himself and he does not dwell in temples made with hands, nor does he have a favourite age or era. All times are equally his and he is as much to be discovered and responded to in an age that is avowedly godless as in an age that is avowedly godly. Neither godlessness, so-called, nor godliness, so-claimed, have the last word on God. God keeps that last word for himself, he has uttered it in Jesus and he will utter it when all things are summed up in Jesus. Meanwhile we are called to Christian faith in God, not to the defence of so-called Christian institutions or Christian formulae.

It is the nature, being and activity of God which makes the present debate about God and the present ferment of faith so truly radical. So-called radicals rarely get to the root of the matter, just as so-called conservatives rarely penetrate to the fundamentals which cannot be shaken. 'Radicals' attack, 'conservatives' defend, but God lives and challenges us through and beyond the self-centredness of attacking or the self-cowardice of defending. The question with which God is facing us, individually and collectively, is of the form: 'Do you believe in what men believe or do you believe in God?'; 'Do you believe in the church or do you believe in God?'; 'Do you believe in the capacity to give answers to questions or do you believe in God?'; 'Do you believe in belief in the creeds or do you believe in God?'. But how can we face this question posed by God himself as to whether we know him, whether we are committed to him? What can we say positively and constructively about Christian faith in God?

We can say this. God has always gathered a people for himself and so he will continue to do. People believe in God because people believe in God and God sees to it that a sufficiency of believing people are maintained for his purposes in the world and for the world. This is a basic picture of the Bible and a repeated message in the Bible. God is the Living and Holy One who gathers people for himself and who makes himself known to his people in and through their very vicissitudes. The knowledge of himself which God gave to his people was, when hammered out on the anvil of their history, so sure a knowledge of so reliable and active a God that his people were sure that he would act among them and for them in accordance with his abiding reality and his ever-lasting concern. They believed that he would send his Messiah to bring in his Kingdom, to establish the affairs of his people consistently with his own love and being. Christianity exists because a Jew called Jesus believed himself to be called to announce this Kingdom of God. He lived out his conviction to the very death, even the death of a cross and then, in the unexpected eyes and reluctant hearts of a handful of his followers, he was vindicated. To them, in them and for them he was raised from the dead. They knew that the God whom Jesus served and the God for whom Jesus died had raised him up. They knew, therefore, that it was in Jesus that they had encountered the very power of God, the very Kingdom of God. He was Jesus the Christ, and, as the very embodiment of God's power and reality, he was Jesus Christ their Lord. Henceforth he was the focus of God's people.

And so he proved to be. For the original handful of

disciples, turned apostles, were able to share their faith in
God and their experience of Jesus with an increasing number
of men and women of an increasing number of races, classes
and conditions. This, to them, was evidently the work of the
Spirit of God who was the Holy Spirit of Jesus. God who was
at work in Jesus, God who raised up Jesus, continued to be
God at work gathering in his people as God the Holy Spirit.
And this activity of God, Father, Son and Holy Spirit,
continues to this day bringing about Christian faith in God
and working through Christian faith in God.

We must realize that this is the living activity of a personal
God with, in and through, persons. There is no other basic
and guaranteed continuity of Christian faith in God, no other
source for it and no other foundation to it, than the living
faith maintained by the Spirit of God through a living people
in a living God. Thus, we, as individuals, as a congregation of
Christian people, and as members together of the Christian
Church, can neither enjoy faith in God nor be a means of the
kindling of faith in others unless we are ready to receive the
grace to live faith as an experiment and an experience.
Nothing can establish God. We can hope only to be established
by God in God.

We are not in a post-Christian era but we are in a post-
Christendom era. Civilization and culture do not take God or
Christianity for granted. This puts us back into the situation
of the people of God for most of their history, certainly into
the position of the New Testament church and of the church
of the first creative centuries. The world does not help us to
believe in God nor do we strengthen our faith through
conformity. Rather we have to find out whether God will
build up our faith within his people and often against the
stream of current fashion of what is taken for granted. This
does not, however, mean that we are to withdraw into the
church and seek somehow to cultivate our faith with our backs
to the world. Such church-centredness can only be the death
of faith. God is to be found in what he makes of the world for
his people and in what he makes of his people for the world.
It is abundantly clear from the Bible that his people always
lost their living faith in the living God when they supposed

that they themselves were the focus both of God's activity and of his reality.

I believe that the practical way to Christian faith in God in our present ferment of faith lies in this understanding that 'God is to be found in what he makes of the world for his people and in what he makes of his people for the world'. This means again, as I have already said, that we must 'live faith as an experiment and an experience'. Our possibility of faith in God has come to us through our association with the people who call themselves Christians, even if now we find that many manifestations of the church's life seem to count against faith in God. We must start, therefore, from what has been given to us and expose this through ourselves to the world and thus learn by experience what it is good for.

We have been given membership of the people of God through Baptism. Do we find that we experience a Christian community as an open and a sustaining group which on the one hand helps us to come to terms with ourselves and to know that there is a God who forgives and accepts, and on the other gives us strength to face the problems and perplexities of our lives and to know that God the Father Almighty is at work through his Holy Spirit to give purpose and pattern to creation and human living? If our baptism means nothing about belonging and being sustained then we must set about realizing our baptism openly and find others with us to move towards this sort of open and sustaining community. For clearly unless baptism is, so to speak, practised we shall find nothing in it to rely on, and it will become a meaningless and magical formula. God is not known through labels. He is known through obedient, risky and lively action.

Similarly we receive the reality of the presence of Christ in the celebration of the Holy Communion. What does the reality of our worship then have to say about the realizing of worthwhileness in all that we are involved with in our daily lives and responsibilities? How can we bring thankfulness from our weekdays to Sunday Eucharist, and what power of thankful receiving expectant openness does the gift of Christ to us enable us to have on each and every day? If we find no connection, can we face the nothingness at the Eucharist and

have the courage to face our lack of faith there, and see if the
sacrament is indeed a real gift through which God makes
himself real to us? How do we offer our weekly failures for
the forgiveness and re-creation of Jesus Christ who gave
himself and gives himself 'for us men and our salvation'?
We must risk finding that our Sunday worship means nothing
to our daily lives so that the Spirit of God is free to re-create
both our faith and our worship and so, also, our daily lives.

We have been given the Bible as the record of the creative
experience of the people of God. Are we prepared to admit
that we find it absolute nonsense and then wrestle with it
until we find that it makes sense of our nonsense and nonsense
of much of our sense? Are we ready to risk getting our views
of God and ourselves changed by putting the Bible furiously
to question because of our experience, and exposing our
questionings and our experiences to judgment and radical
re-evaluation? Such a readiness presupposes very long
perseverance, a never-ending experimentation and willingness
really to find out what way of life seems to be required if we
are to begin to understand the biblical experiences for
ourselves.

We are presented with the faith of the Christian people
symbolized in the creeds. Are we prepared to try and get at
what is behind them? To ask how descending into Hell can
be related to actual depths of human suffering and bewilderment and to probe into the relationship between the allegation
that Christ is seated at the right hand of God the Father
Almighty and the hope that we can discover a possibility of
love that can never be defeated, i.e. are we prepared to risk
the sort of experiment that would be required if we really
believed that love reigns?

If the Bible is anything to go by, such experimental
approaches to the reality and the realizing of faith will not
guarantee any one of us necessarily comforting and reassuring
experiences. We may be taken out of the half-light of a
pseudo-faith or semi-faith into the darkness of doubt which is
the ante-chamber to the reality of God. But if the experience
of the people of God is anything to go by, if the life of Jesus
Christ is anything to follow and to gain hope from, then we

may be sure that anyone who will throw in his or her lot with
the people of God and who will join with them in going out
into the world's uncertainties and into the depths of their
own perplexities will find, in God's time and not their own,
that they are not alone in this journeying. Rather they will
learn that they are on the way to a city whose builder and
founder is God and that on this way they are given enough
knowledge of God or, at least, sufficient hope that God will
be known, to continue hopefully. Together we shall find
growing in us a Christian faith in God which is not shaken by
ferment nor defeated by frustration but rather strengthened
and deepened because its source and its end lies in God alone.

PART TWO

Concerning Man
and Concerning Jesus

I | *Personality and Freedom*

Can you study personality in a scientific manner and a scientific way? Clearly this partly depends on what you mean by 'person' and what you mean by 'scientific'. But whatever it is decided to mean by those terms, there is a problem to which I wish to draw attention. To do so I cannot do better than begin my discussion with a quotation from Lady Wootton's *Social Science and Social Pathology*. I do so as she so well raises the problem and dilemma in question. In the course of her discussion of 'Mental Disorder and Criminal Responsibility', she writes (p. 252):

> In this and some others matters the only ultimate proof of the pudding must be in the eating; and that proof is essentially a statistical one. Subject only to the over-riding social and moral limitations mentioned below, the role of medical or psychiatric, as against educational, or what are now regarded as penal, methods in the treatment of backsliders will depend upon the actual success which each can show in dealing with different types of case. Dr Glueck's concept of the 'anti-social individual as a sick person' must stand or fall, not by the compelling logic of psychiatric theories, but by a simple demonstration of the degree to which doctors are more successful than other people in inducing favourable modifications of deplorable behaviour; and that is a matter that can only be demonstrated in statistical terms. No matter who has the first word, the last is always with the statistician. The task of the social sciences is to mobilize indifferently the results of *every* form of expertise and the evidence of *all* available methods of handling cases of anti-social behaviour; and it is not by deductive argument but only by willingness to submit to the test of experience and by a temper at once 'critical, distrustful of elaborate speculation, sceptical, candid, and tough' that psychiatry or any other science can hope to justify whatever claims it ventures to make.

The problem which is pin-pointed by the language of this paragraph, although it is not clear to me that Lady Wootton is aware of it, is that which is concealed or revealed by the phrase 'social sciences', and which would be posed even more sharply if we were allowed to call the social sciences 'human sciences', in the sense that they are the sciences which deal with human beings in the various aspects of their operations which express and exercise their humanness. The problem is this. To be essentially scientific is to be essentially concerned with that which is measurable. As Lady Wootton says, in the scientific field the ultimate proof 'is essentially a statistical one'. 'No matter who has the first word, the last is always with the statistician.' That this is the view taken by many psychologists and psychiatrists is made evident enough by the way in which they take great pains to lace their articles and books with stiff doses of diagrams, statistical tables and, above all, graphs. As Lady Wootton makes clear enough elsewhere (compare, e.g., p. 221), the object of this procedure is to remain clearly in the field of science by arriving at and operating with value-free definitions and judgments. The point I wish to make is that this is a logical, theoretical and practical impossibility. It may be therefore that the phrase 'social sciences' or 'human sciences' is a logical contradiction. (I myself think that it is more likely that we should make the decision to allow the use of the word 'science' in a rather broader sense than that which is tied to measurement and statistics. But this is a wider theoretical question than can be pursued here.) The point is this. Anything that can justifiably be given the description 'social', where the reference is to human society, automatically includes the notion of value and must operate at all times with the complication that the notion of value introduces. In the paragraph which I have quoted, Lady Wootton is unable to exclude the two adjectives 'favourable' and 'deplorable'. Although, no doubt, an attempt would be made to assert that these two adjectives are to be taken as strictly descriptive in the sense that their meaning can be defined by determining what the particular society involved in fact favours and deplores, we do well to remain sceptical about the possibility of a total value-free description being produced. Procedures for determining what groups of human beings in fact do, always require initial choices about what constitutes a significant grouping and about the significant features which are to be statistically organized. If the scientific conscience rebels against the arrogance and ignorance of these philosophical statements, then it is to be pointed out that we can never demonstrate that the value-free procedure is in fact a possibility. It is simply a presupposition and a faith that it is so. My presupposition, which I hold to be more in accordance with the evidence of the actual procedures involved, although it cannot be decisively established, is that belief in value-free procedures is mistaken. Value-free observations of human beings operating as human beings is not possible for a human being. Science does not provide an escape route from our humanity, as scientists must be human, for scientific activity is an activity of human beings.

This truism is not rhetoric, but logic. And obvious as it is, it is the sort of truism which has constantly to be reiterated in view of its practical importance and of the way in which it is constantly neglected. The particular area on which I wish to bring these considerations to bear is that of personality and freedom. And here let me stress that the arguments which I have just used and also those which I am going on to develop are not based on religion but on logic and practice. The basic considerations with regard to personality and freedom are philosophical and theoretical ones long before we get to religious considerations. The basic consideration is this. The real possibility of freedom is a necessary part of what it is to be human, not least of what it is to be a human being engaged in scientific activity. This is so, regardless of any facts of any sort which may be validly established about human beings by the scientific method. The basis for this statement is twofold, having one of its foundations firmly rooted in logic and the other equally firmly rooted in experience. The logical point is that the 'distinct perceptions' (as Hume called them) which are the subject matter and constitute the facts of science, presuppose a 'perceiver' (i.e. observer), who, as far as this particular set of observations goes, stands over against, or transcends (logically) the observed facts. Logically speaking, objects presuppose a subject who is opposed to them. And the fact that any given person who is a subject in respect of a given set of observations can himself, together with his observations, become an object for another observing subject, does not alter the logical point that there must always be a subject who is not determined by the observed facts, but free enough to observe them.

This logical point of the necessary independence of some observer passes over into the experimental point of what it is like to be an observer of a subject. Here one must insist on the uniqueness of self-awareness, and one must be clear that the self-awareness in question is not what I make of your self-awareness or what you make of anyone else's self-awareness, for that is a question of what an observer makes of that which is to him an *object* characterized by self-awareness, i.e. by the fact that he is aware of himself as a person. The unique self-awareness which is decisive for the argument which we are at present pursuing is the self-awareness which each man has of himself as he has it to himself. This true self-awareness (a subject's awareness of himself as a subject) is the 'experiential inside', so to speak, of the logical necessity of the transcendent observer. Anyone who sets out to give an exhaustive account of human behaviour and experience and who does so simply on the basis of his observations of other humans (who to him are objects) plus an attempt to treat himself purely as an object to himself, is leaving out of the account both the logical and experiential fact which makes his observations possible. He is failing to take into account the unique fact and experience of what it is to be a subject, i.e. a person. However mistaken may be the factual information about oneself which self-awareness may give, this does not alter the significance of the uniqueness of subjective self-awareness (of what it is like to me to be me), nor reduce its necessity for the possibility of there being any objective knowledge at all.

The above line of argument is one which cannot be refuted by facts of any kind, for it is about the process by which the observation of facts is made possible. I would maintain that to reduce human personality to the sum total of the facts which are actually or theoretically discoverable by scientific methods is in the first place always to make a decision which does not fall within the scope of the scientific method. So the weight of science cannot be put behind such a choice. And in the second place, it is a wrong decision because it precludes the possibility of that which is a presupposition of any knowledge or scientific activity at all. Therefore, however uncomfortable and complicating it may be for a proper scientific study of human beings, we have unavoidably built into our field of study what I would call the irreducibility of 'I'. Indeed I would be so bold as to insist that one should call it the *mystery* of the 'I'. We are back here to our initial problem, which I suggested was pin-pointed by the possible contradiction in the term 'social sciences'. Science implies in essence the clarity and definition achieved by measurements. The possibility of measurement implies the 'mystery' of the subject who measures. How, then, can the scientific study as objects of persons who for the possibility of science must exist uniquely as subjects, be carried on?

It may be thought that whatever the superficial plausibility of the above treated as a self-contained philosophical argument, it remains manifestly untrue in practice. It suffers, in fact, from being self-contained and philosophical and therefore cut off from the practical world. For the fact is that human beings in groups are susceptible to observations which can be reduced to statistics, and their behaviour can be the subject of statistically probable prediction. Moreover, there are manifest and notorious cases in which the individual person suffers from defects, whether physiological or psychological or a complex combination of both, which render any notion of personal freedom in these cases quite nugatory. The scientific observation of persons as objects in the most objective manner possible has already increased our capacity to deal with personality disorders in remarkable ways, and to introduce the notion of mystery is to threaten a return to the dark ages (scarcely yet fully passed), in which madness was attributed to evil spirits and in which flogging and hanging were thought to be righteously appropriate to a terrifyingly wide range of human deviant behaviour. It is certainly clear that to go back on the discoveries and procedures of psychology

Living with Questions

and psychiatry would be scientifically outrageous and morally disastrous. It is from this very fact that the urgent need arises of a confrontation and consultation between psychology and psychiatry, philosophy and religion. For I would maintain that it is as a matter of fact in theory and practice true, on the one hand, that there is the mystery of the 'I' which we could reasonably call the mystery of personality. But, on the other hand, it is equally true that human beings, whether as individuals or in groups, are affected by and even determined by, forces and factors which are open to discovery, measurement and manipulation by scientific methods. It would seem, therefore, that we have to consider how we may best pursue our knowledge of the structure and dynamics of personality, whether in the case of the individual or in the case of groups or even of 'humanity at large', with the proper awareness of the fact that the actual or theoretical sum total of this knowledge is not exhaustive of the total understanding of what it is to be a human being (the mystery of personality).

But even supposing it is granted that the concept of the mystery of personality is allowable, indeed required, by the logic and facts of the case, it is quite clear that this mystery is pretty strictly interconnected with the dynamic structure which is exhaustively observable by the methods of science. This is clearly and acutely brought out by what I would call *limiting cases*. These are cases in which, in my terms, the mystery of the personality or the 'I' does seem to have been reduced to the sum total of the structure. The sort of things I have in mind here are, for example, cases of acute physical lack which prevent the development of personality and cases of intense psychopathic determinism which lock personality in a seemingly incurable distortion. It seems to me that cases of this nature do count for the idea that the mystery of personality should ultimately be reduced to scientific observables and count against taking the decision that it is a mystery which is the defining thing about being human. But while the fact that some human beings seem to have to be regarded as objects alone, without the capacity to be free subjects, is certainly a difficulty for believers in any sort of good and omnipotent deity, I do not think that these limiting cases decisively alter the logical and practical position for which I have been arguing. The fact that the mystery of the 'I' is so interrelated with the structure and dynamics of physical and psychological relations that, in some cases, the former is reduced to the latter, does not alter the prior fact that even to know of and to be capable of describing these limiting cases requires observers within these limits who are free from the reduction which the limiting cases exemplify. Moreover, this problem is perhaps eased by the very fact that our increasing knowledge and understanding of the structural and dynamic features which produce these limiting cases is continually enhancing our capacity to push back these limits and to increase the number of cases in which human beings are given the opportunity to develop into free personalities. In all this very difficult field it is of the utmost importance to remember that knowledge of determinants facilitates freedom. Hence on all grounds we find reinforcements of the need for a full and open interplay between an awareness of the mystery of human personality and a scientific knowledge of the structure which is the basis of such personality. It is here, surely, that religion and the human sciences must enter, and must be able to enter, into dialogue if both are validly concerned with the humanity of man.

The following considerations, among others, would seem to support the view that the development of such a dialogue is urgently necessary. First, all who have any concern for the humanness of men must find one practical focus of that concern to be an urgent desire to do all that is possible in all possible cases to free as many human beings as possible for greater human freedom. Hence the possibilities already referred to which arise, in the advance of psychological and psychiatric understanding, for removing some of the defects and disorders which inhibit or limit the development of personality, are of the utmost practical interest to all who have a religious or ethical concern for their fellows. The increase and dissemination of such liberating knowledge cannot but increase the opportunities for a practical, responsible caring for one's fellows which is both the aim and the heart of love. Secondly, and this point develops out of the first, knowledge of this sort is a great and therefore potentially dangerous responsibility. Knowledge which gives the possibility of liberating or enhancing the development of personality in any individual or group at the same time creates the possibility, indeed involves the responsibility of shaping and directing the personality thus liberated, at any rate to some extent. Hence it is of supreme importance that the very difficult line be drawn between liberating a personality and manipulating it. This is a matter which demands the utmost human sensitivity, the most critical self-awareness and constant reassessment. No one must ever be allowed to settle down into the complacent belief that he is really quite certain precisely how any human being is to be directed in becoming himself. The practical procedures of psychiatry and psychotherapy need to have their explicit, and still more their implicit, assumptions constantly challenged by the posing of questions from the ethical and religious point of view.

But, and this leads on to a third point, such challenging must not be done in any offensive or superior way. It must take the form of questions sincerely and humbly posed as between human disciplines and activities which are all equally concerned with the furthering of humanness. And while ethics and religion have questions to put to psychology and psychiatry, they have also questions which they need to have answered by these disciplines. These questions extend further than those about the removing of limitations to personality development already referred to. Even if we insist, as I believe we must, on the impossibility of reducing the mystery of the 'I' to the observables of its dynamics and structure, it is surely also clear, if I may put it this way, that the mystery cannot be moved towards its true goal against the grain of its structure. The sort of thing I have in mind here is probably illustrated as well as anywhere in the field of punishment. Here it becomes increasingly clear that the motives of punishers and the effects of punishment are by no means as simple or as productive of desired and desirable effects as much ethical and religious practice or exhortation supposes. The understanding of the 'grain of the structure' of personality which psychological research can here supply is clearly vital in assisting religion and morality to move practically towards their self-confessed aims for men. But, and once again the pendulum swings in the opposite direction, we may, fourthly, point out that all programming of experimentation in the sciences of human behaviour almost certainly involves both prior and continuing evaluation, whether explicit or implicit. Nowhere will this be more true than in investigations concerned with concepts like 'guilt', 'blame', and 'ideals'. Hence, once again, it is not only proper, but necessary, that religion and ethics should have their say in a dialogue. Finally, just to touch on perhaps the biggest and the most controversial issue of all, it is generally agreed that the continuing happiness of a human being is related to his or her capacity for adjustment to reality. And what a problem is concealed by that last word! Here dialogue is more than ever necessary, for while I would not suppose that we dare leave the definition of reality to any scientist to be settled in terms of his science alone, I am quite clear that the religious man who does not care to correlate his approach to life with the realities discovered and organized by the scientist is only an escapist who is betraying his religious faith.

I would wish to close my paper with a few comments arising out of my last point, but now made from a specifically Christian point of view, whereas the argument hitherto has been of a more generally philosophical nature.

As I see it, developments in the social and biological sciences are requiring Christians to take absolutely seriously a fundamental aspect of the doctrine of man which is assumed by and required by a proper understanding of the biblical and Christian doctrine of creation, but which has rarely been taken sufficiently seriously in the actual practice of the Christian tradition. This is the fundamental axiom of the unity of man. The structure of the human being has physical, mental and social aspects. The studies of biology, psychology, and sociology overlap more and more and so both demonstrate and assert that these various aspects coalesce into such a unity that the drawing of distinctions with a view, for instance, of deciding what is the 'cause' of what, seems to

become increasingly arbitrary. This is so much the case that
there is always a plausible case for anyone to claim that the
whole structure and significance of personality must be
reduced to its physical, or at any rate determined, aspects.
There is a homogeneity and continuity between the 'highest'
and 'lowest' functionings of the human organism. Knowledge
of human 'plumbing' (e.g. of the functioning of the kidneys)
can be relevant to the liberation of the human spirit. And
yet, as I have argued, the logic of knowing, the experience
which I have of what it is to be 'I', and the impossibility of
value-free judgment about human activities requires that,
together with this concept of homogeneity, we hold the
concept of the mystery of the 'I'.

Christian anthropology, when it is true to its biblical basis
and refuses to be led astray by the strong tendencies to
dualism in the Graeco-Roman tradition, understands man as
a creature with a purely material beginning and basis who
has a spiritual purpose and destiny. This is symbolized by the
whole creation myth and, indeed, by the doctrine of creation
as a whole, which is simply and precisely the assertion that
the material universe is related to and capable of sustaining a
spiritual purpose. Hence, to refuse to take physical factors
seriously, or to resist the implications of valid scientific
knowledge is to be false to the biblical and Christian understanding of the world and man as created. Moreover, to resist
this valid and necessary approach to the created in its
material givenness is to put oneself in a false position with
regard to the development and fulfilment of the Creation's
spiritual potentialities (the possibilities of the mystery, the
development of life with God, the entering into life of God).
This false position arises both because to deny manifestly
given facts is to put oneself out of court as a source of relevant
attitudes towards the facts as a whole, and also because to
insist on remaining in ignorance of the basic grain of the
structure is to persist in remaining in a primitive position
with regard to developing the spiritual possibilities of that
structure.

While the doctrine of creation requires the Christian to take
absolutely seriously the physical basis of the structure of

human personality, other aspects of the Christian understanding of man fix attention upon the fact that human beings must be understood, as on the one hand of the utmost importance as *individuals*, and yet at the same time as essentially *social* beings. Every man in and as himself is the object of the love (and therefore of the judgment) of God. That is to say, he is of concern to the Ultimate Reality and Purpose of the whole of things, so that he has a definite and eternal status for himself, although he does not have this in himself but in his relation to God. But as this Ultimate Reality and Purpose is love (defined in terms of holiness and righteousness, and not of sentimentality!), the destined perfection of particular individuals can only be worked towards and ultimately achieved in terms of perfected social relationships, where the relationship with God is reflected and expressed in relationships with fellow human beings and vice versa. (The pre-eminent symbol for this notion in Christian thinking is the Body of Christ.) Hence, Christianity is bound by its own understanding to welcome, as validly based and as ultimately of the utmost practical and spiritual importance, empirical investigation into the physical-mental-social structure of human beings and human society. On the other hand, despite the hindrances which Christians in practice have not infrequently offered to the development of true humanness, Christianity must continue to resist all reductionism and to demand a continuing judgment of the presuppositions and sufficiency of the procedures and evaluations of the sciences concerned, in order that the way may be kept open for the fulfilment of the mystery of personality in the direction of the freedom of perfected relationships.

For Christianity believes that to be truly human is to be truly free, and that it is in this true freedom that true happiness lies. In the Christian understanding, which requires all the corrective aid which the human sciences can give for its valid practice, the way to this freedom and happiness is to be found through entering into the knowledge and experience that we are accepted by God as we are. Therefore we may have the strength to accept ourselves and our neighbours as we and they at present are on the basis of this acceptance by

God and with the consequent hope of growth into the
infinite possibilities of increasingly adequate relationships with
increasingly adequate persons. That this is the way forward to
freedom and happiness, however, both makes possible and
demands adjustment to current realities in oneself and in
one's personal and impersonal environment. Because of the
homogeneity of the structure of human personality, this
adjustment to current realities is the necessary means of being
open to and of developing into the infinite possibilities of the
reality of God which Christians believe transcends all lesser
realities and in which alone, so they hold, the mystery of 'I'
can ultimately and only be sustained and fulfilled. Hence, the
practice of the Christian understanding of and faith about
man requires, by its own nature and understanding of things,
to be brought down to earth and to be given the tools for
effective application in particular cases by all the tested
biological, psychological and sociological information that can
be scientifically made available. But for the sake of the
humanness of human beings, Christianity, despite its failures
in practice, must continue to insist that the human sciences
do not mar *their* practice by ignoring the fact which makes
them possible, that is, that the human beings which they
study as objects transcend them as personal subjects.

2 | *The Christian Idea of a Free Person*

In contributing to discussions between those based in the disciplines of psychiatry, psychology and the social sciences and those whose discipline is theology, my task would seem to be to speak from a definitely theological basis in the hope that we may be able to build a bridge between our different ways of approaching questions of personality and the like.

I do this because I take the view – which I know is not shared by all Christians or all theologians at the present time – that there is a real sense in which theology may be an independent source of data. That is to say that I am not prepared to surrender the concept of revelation. I am certain that at the present time what theologians most need to do is *listen*, but I remain convinced that in the long run Christians and Christian theologians have something distinctive of their own to say when they have, by listening to other disciplines, learned how to say it.

Hence I must try to make some contribution to our discussions from the Christian tradition about freedom and persons. The first thing that struck me when reflecting on this matter was that the Christian idea of freedom is intimately related to the idea of service. The following words of St Paul pinpoint the sort of thing I have in mind. 'You know well enough that if you put yourselves at the disposal of a master, to obey him, you are slaves of the master whom you obey; and this is true whether you serve sin, with death as its result; or obedience, with righteousness as its result' (Rom. 6.16ff.). The authentic Christian notion of freedom is not what I should call a primary notion. Freedom does not exist in its own right.

I may perhaps illustrate this by taking the notion of salvation. Let us assume that it is right and meaningful to talk of God acting to save men. Then the end of this saving activity of God is not that men should be free. Salvation does not consist in a man's being set free, although if and when he is saved he will be free. Indeed, I would argue that in the Christian understanding of freedom it is impossible to be free unless you *are* saved. But freedom and salvation are not equivalents. Freedom is a concomitant of the service of God. Which brings us straight to a point of central importance. The Christian idea of freedom is a *theological* notion. It is a theological notion because it has to be understood in relation to God. Indeed, freedom itself depends upon, or perhaps even consists in, relationship to God.

Freedom is not independence but dependence. For the moment I will say that it is proper dependence upon God. But I would also generalize the point from a theological to a philosophical one and say that freedom is not an absolute but a relational notion. Freedom is concerned with freedom from and freedom for, and the idea of a free person taken in isolation is an abstract notion which does not have and cannot have any content. When one is discussing questions like grace and freedom, or freedom and sin, this point about the relational and non-independent notion of freedom seems constantly to be forgotten.

I shall now proceed from this by picking up certain ideas out of the old but always continuing controversy between Pelagianism and Augustinianism. A few technical terms may perhaps be excused, as I think that they can be made clear to non-theologians and they have a certain precise meaning which will be useful for our purposes. Pelagianism (reputed to be the favourite heresy of the British) is the view that up to a very real point you can get on perfectly well without God. Grace, whatever it is, is only something which gives you help but it does not in any way penetrate into the centre of your being. Indeed, it must not, if you are going to be really free, for to be really free is to be totally dependent in some way upon yourself. It is necessary, therefore, to have only an external relationship with God.

It is useful in the sort of debate we are engaged in to consider Pelagianism because it is typical of a *theoretical* approach to the problem of freedom. In this it is typical of the way we are all liable to proceed. That is to say that (more often implicitly than explicitly) we approach situations with theoretical concepts in our minds and we allow the concepts to dominate our understanding of the facts. In connection with freedom, I see Pelagius as typical of the person who has views on what *must* be involved if a person is to be free, rather than on what *is* involved. (I myself believe that if Christianity were true to its own tradition it would always have a pragmatic approach to such questions.)

In the fourth century the important question was: What is the proper way of understanding man's relationship to God so that man is, on the one hand, responsible as he ought to be and, on the other, dependent as he ought to be? Pelagius, in trying to analyse a man and his actions, arrived at a threefold division. One had to consider the *esse*, the *velle* and the *posse*; the being, the willing, and the capacity to act. Man is an active and willing being. He wills to act. He (sometimes) carries his will into action. The *esse* is the fact that he has this capacity, the *velle* is the direction which he chooses to give it, and the *posse* is the capacity to bring this off. Pelagius in, as I think, his theoretical way allotted the *esse* to God. Man was dependent upon God for his existence as an active and willing being and God was the source of this. The *velle* and the *posse*, however, were allotted to man. Hence the thought that it had been made sure that man was free; the concept of the free person had been preserved. Man was given the chance of doing something that was God's part; he did it, that was his part, the part of freedom.

But underlying this analysis of freedom, as many others, there seems to be a 'model' of freedom which is somewhat as follows. To be free is assumed to be something like the state of a frictionless object poised on another frictionless object so that the first is 'free' to move in any direction it likes without any outside determination. So, in this case, the *velle* and the *posse*, the willing and the putting of the will into action, depend entirely and independently upon the man. But in the particular controversy that we are considering, a deeper insight, indeed a deeper psychological and philosophical understanding, emerged. It was Augustine who pointed out that this type of analysis is really quite hopeless. First, it is theologically hopeless. It is inconceivable to think of the biblical, Christian, personal type of God with whom the tradition deals and with whom Augustine believed himself to be actually dealing, as being excluded from anything. It is not possible that there should be anything which could be understood as so separated from him that it could be allotted to man in independent contradistinction to allotment to God. Therefore, from the theological point of view, God must be related to all three phases of man's existence and activity. And this has to be related to a more general and more obviously practical point. A man's willing and a man's capacity to carry out what he wills are neither of them simple and independent as a matter of fact. They are independent notions only as a matter of analysis. Men have their wills conditioned in various directions; they are conditioned to will in certain ways, and it is also patent that men are able to do certain things, both for internal and for external reasons. Hence the Pelagian analysis, which allots something to the given-ness, which is put on one side, and then something to the activity of man, which is then put over against this, so that the two may be separate in the interests of preserving freedom, is superficial in two vital respects. First, it is superficial with respect to dependence on God. For the understanding of the relationship to God which goes with the Bible and with the Christian tradition is not that of a remote relationship, nor is it that of a simple causal relationship. The picture is not that God must be 'over there' giving you the possibility for and ground of doing something or other. This is a too superficial understanding of dependence upon God.

But there is also a superficial understanding of the problem which we all know comes up in one way or another – the problem which, in theological language, is called the problem of 'sin'. It seems to be a fact that the human situation has a 'twist' in it (the technical term in the fourth century was *vitium* – flaw). Whether you consider human beings as individuals or consider the various human groupings which give shape to human life, it seems that neither the individual organisms nor the social organizations are at present so articulated that they 'work' smoothly. Rather, there is a real sense in which both the organisms and the organizations are 'at odds' with themselves. They need at least some measure of correction before they can work smoothly towards the expression or fulfilment of their own nature. This is not primarily a fact about any particular individual or any particular human organization or society. It is rather a *condition* common to and affecting all. This common condition is referred to in the Christian tradition as 'sin', and the fact that the way things are seems to be 'at odds with' or 'twisted away from' the way things ought to be (if the organisms and organizations are to run smoothly and with fulfilment), is symbolized by referring to the Fall. It is important to notice that the holding of a doctrine of the Fall (and its concomitant, the doctrine of Original Sin, i.e. that every man is in a sinful condition – see above) does not depend upon the possibility of giving a satisfactory account of the Fall in a historical or psychological or some sort of causal way. The main function of such a doctrine is to describe the facts about man's situation, which is: first, that he is dependent upon God; and secondly, that he is in a situation which is best described as fallen or sinful. Any attempt at explanation is strictly mythological, and a desire to do away with the mythology does not do away with the facts of the case. For instance, inability to make anything of the picture of the Garden of Eden does not alter the fact that man has to be understood in the context of dependence upon God and in a context which has now to be characterized as fallen.

Since man has to be understood in the light of these two aspects of his situation, freedom has to be so understood also. In relation to this question of freedom Augustine produced a famous distinction which can, I believe, be helpful and clarifying for us. It was the distinction between *libertas* and *liberum arbitrium*. *Libertas* is the perfect liberty of the children of God. It is the freedom which men are meant to have, the freedom which exists when men are truly free, the freedom which enables men to be truly themselves. *Liberum arbitrium* (to be translated 'free will') is what men do have. This is what men have at the moment, what one is dealing with when one is dealing with a person – a person who is thought of as in one sense free but in another sense determined. A man's free will depends upon what a man is, whereas *libertas*, the perfect liberty of the children of God, depends upon what men are meant to be. Therefore in the Christian tradition we have what may be called Freedom 1 and Freedom 2. Freedom 2 in fact exists, that is, free will. Freedom 1 is *libertas*, which is the aim or the goal.

It is necessary for anyone who is concerned with the development of persons and of personality to retain and act upon this twofold notion of freedom, the freedom we have and the freedom we aim at, whatever the precise framework into which the notion is fitted. It is here that one has some sort of basis for operational co-operation whether there is a common Christian or theological or religious view or not. The freedom men have, free will, is something which proceeds from what men are. When a man is willing he is willing what he is conditioned to will, but the fact that he is conditioned to will thus does not mean that he is not *willing* nor that it is not *he* who thus wills. His willing, for it to be his, must be conditioned by what he is. Men, in willing and doing, are being themselves, and this is to be acting freely.

But the Christian understanding (and I would suppose that Christianity is not alone in this) goes on to say that the trouble or problem (the problem with which both the pastor and the psychotherapist is dealing) lies precisely in what men are. And in considering the freedom of persons, the Christian tradition would maintain that the right understanding or diagnosis is that men are free to be themselves, but that, as they are, they are not free to be free. As free to be themselves they have *liberum arbitrium*, and within the terms of this type of existence of free will there can be the usual discussions about whether a man acted freely or not, about whether a man acts willingly or is forced into acting against his will. A man who has a gun stuck in his ribs is acting under external pressure and is not acting freely, while a man who has certain ideas and certain psychological and other internal conditionings and is acting in accordance with these is acting freely. His trouble lies in the fact that he is the sort of person who acts freely in this way.

Men are free (under broadly recognizable conditions) to be themselves, but they are not free to be free. Hence the *second* main point is that the notion of freedom is not held in the Christian tradition in opposition to some notion of determinism but along with it. Nor is it held that this holding together of the notion of freedom and the notion of determinism destroys the notion of responsibility. Free will, *liberum arbitrium*, is freedom as it is but not freedom as it might and should be.

Now, this insistence on holding together notions of free will, determinism and responsibility, together with a demand to talk about freedom on two levels is clearly something very problematical about which a great deal more ought to be said. Here, however, I will pursue my argument by means of dogmatic assertion.

Christians insist that all this must be held together if persons are to be properly treated as persons, because of two mysteries. The mysteries refer to matters of fact but are properly called 'mysteries' because they are not open to total explanation. They are the mystery of personality and the mystery of evil. Of the mystery of personality Christians would insist that because every man is, at least potentially, capable of relationship with God, any reductionist description of man which attempts to fit him without remainder into any theoretical frame, physiological, psychological, sociological or what you will, is bound, *as a matter of fact*, to fail to do justice to the totality of the facts about man. This Christian insistence on the mystery of personality involves the prediction that, in the long run, any theory which does reduce man within a particular framework will be shown to be false. It also involves the assertion that limiting cases of human beings, who can be shown to be conditioned beyond any hope of showing freedom or even personality, cannot be taken as definitive of, or decisive for, our understanding of personality or of the nature of man. Great care is needed in connection with these assertions as they can easily become part of an attitude of obscurantism to valid scientific findings, but I have no doubt that they are required by the Christian understanding of the total context in which man is, as a matter of fact, placed.

The mystery of evil is another assertion, on the basis of Christian belief and understanding, about something which as a matter of fact characterizes human existence but which cannot be satisfactorily factually explained. The immediately observable basis for the mystery of evil is the fact already referred to, that the human situation is characterized by a twist or a flaw. There is a contrast and a contradiction between what men are and what men ought to be. One of the aspects of this is that it is meaningful to say that men are free to be themselves but that as they are they are not free to be free. But this contradiction is a mystery, not just a flat descriptive fact about the human situation. That is to say that we are not to see this evil as decisive for our understanding of what it is to be a man. The human situation as we know it is distorted and has truly evil features, but this is not the deepest nor the determining truth about the situation. The things which militate against freedom and against personality must not be accepted or evaluated as indicating the general run or overall direction of the human situation, but rather as being contrary to the true possibilities and purposes of that situation.

The acceptance or assertion of these two interrelated mysteries of personality and evil as referring to factual, although not totally explicable, features of human life means that it is necessary to hold together notions that cannot at present be wholly reconciled in theory, and to make use of each one of them for practical evaluations of the present human situation, either in general or in dealing with particular men and women. In particular, we have to hold together these two notions of freedom – the freedom that there is which is limited and determined in ways which are constantly interfering with and even threatening to destroy personality, and the freedom which would be the fulfilment of the person-

ality. So we have to work with the practical concept of
freedom as a relational notion to be held with determinism of
a form which both does justice to the facts and yet does not
totally destroy the importance of the notion of responsibility.
And here we reach a point where I would suppose that those
with pastoral and those with psychotherapeutic concerns
would have a common aim. On this ambivalent and two-
valued understanding of freedom, which I am arguing is the
Christian one, we are concerned with both the existence of
freedom and responsibility and with the emergence, evocation
and, indeed, creation of freedom and responsibility. In
dealing with people who are both free and yet not free to be
free, we are working within a situation (of determined and
sometimes totally inhibited freedom) towards another situation (freedom as fulfilment in *libertas*), which both has
continuity with the present situation and yet represents a real
break out from it.

So the third point in the Christian understanding of freedom
is that *libertas* is a gift of God which God works to give men.
Without the right context and the right relationships men
cannot be truly free, cannot be free to be themselves as they
are meant to be. For the Christian, 'meant to be' has a
particular meaning. It does not just mean 'fulfilling the
internal possibilities of the organism which can be discovered
by a careful examination of the organism'. It does include
this meaning, but internal teleology is not enough. As a
Christian theologian, I have to insist that revelation is itself a
source of data about the context within which the possibilities
of the human organism are to be understood. And, of men,
'free as they are meant to be' means free as intended by God.
This freedom is a gift of God. In this there is freedom to
develop the internal possibilities until they are secured,
crowned and fulfilled by the possibility of God. Spiritual
health, in the Christian understanding, is when one ceases to
fall short of the glory of God. This is not a metaphorical
expression pure and simple, but it indicates that there are
literally infinite possibilities in human personality and that we
have not fulfilled the possibilities of human personality until

we have reached this infinite possibility which is God. Thus in the Christian understanding of freedom we are concerned with freedom from sin and freedom for God. And the Christian idea of a free person is necessarily related to that.

In practice, this insistence on the glory of God as the end and only fulfilment of the internal possibilities of men and women comes down to an insistence on the supreme importance of open-endedness; human beings must not be shut up within the framework of any theory or theories whatsoever. Here Christian practice has again and again failed, quite as much as any other theory of man has failed. So-called Christian dogmatic theories of man have often resulted in human personality being shut up rather than opened up. But it seems to me that in the authentic tradition of Christian spirituality, wherever and however it is expressed, there is always an insistence on the infinite open-endedness of the human personality, an insistence on breaking every mould and on not being content with any solution or resting place but on going on to yet further possibilities. And in this connection I am clear that there is much in the dialogue between Christianity and psychotherapy which is to be seen as an activity of the Spirit of God setting us free from those things in various types of Christian spirituality which have developed both on the basis of, and as contributions to, the repression and suppression of personality. But the liberation made possible here can develop properly only as it is related to freedom from sin for the limitless possibilities of God.

And here, I feel, we have to come back to the matter-of-factness which I believe Christians are obliged to assert about their faith. The Christian assertion (indeed, I would suppose that it is one way of putting the Christian gospel) is that this possibility is not 'pie-in-the-sky' or idealistic nonsense, but a real possibility held out by God. But I still think that there should here be common ground between people who believe in the Christian sort of God and people who do not on the grounds that whether this state exists or not, and whether it can ever be expected to exist or not, it is still plainly worth aiming at. And therefore, although from the Christian point of view I am not merely defining a direction by stating what

I believe to be an existent goal, from the point of view of the present discussion it might be possible to take this understanding of personality and freedom as simply defining a direction which everyone who is concerned for the development of truly human personality should seek to move in.

Finally, I would just add that this truly human freedom, this *libertas*, requires the appropriate context and coherence which both permits such freedom and determines such freedom. It is necessary for freedom to be both permitted by the context and determined by the context. And this, I fancy, is the theological and the psychological and the philosophical point behind the famous and much misused – 'Love God and then what you like, do'. The Christian tradition is quite clear that this permissive and determining context for freedom is the context of personal relationships. And the tradition is quite clear that there can be no perfection of relationships between persons without the gift of God. And it is also quite clear that the gift of God is precisely the perfection of relationships between persons through the perfection of relationships with himself.

The two symbols for this in Christian thinking, which have the utmost practical significance, are the symbols of the Trinity and of the Body of Christ. The Trinity is a symbol (distilled from history in a manner which we cannot now consider) that Ultimate Reality himself is rightly to be thought of as perfect unity and perfect relationships. The symbol of the Body of Christ stands for the fact that there is a way open for men to share in the life which constitutes the unity of the Trinity. Therefore, the statement that God is love is not merely the affirmation of an attitude, a sort of groan from the spirit putting an exclamation mark over the mystery and muddle of the world as it really is, but a cognitive description of that which actually exists. Ultimate reality is personal and is rightly understood as being concerned with the perfection of relationships between persons.

Therefore I would say that the Christian idea of freedom is the determinism of the love of God. Which would bring us, if we had time, to the whole matter of the Spirit. For the Spirit of God is love. 'The love of God is shed abroad in our hearts by the Holy Spirit which is given unto us.' And if one wishes to know whether the 'spirit' in which one is approaching some therapeutic task is indeed the Holy Spirit, the question to ask is how much of one's approach and one's activities are related to love as defined in terms of relationships between persons, the ultimate terms of relationships between persons being defined by the sort of love which is manifested in Jesus Christ. Here, too, I would think, in this matter of 'discerning the spirit', is an operational basis for working together between a devout Western atheist and a devout Christian. ('Devoutness' I take to be connected with an approach of openness and humility which comes from an awareness that one is up against something of great value and something which is more than one can fully comprehend.) That basis would lie in a common desire to discern precisely what, in the activity in which one was engaged, and in the spirit in which one was approaching it, there was which was truly concerned with the sort of love which builds personal relationships in the direction of the liberation of persons. The respective roles, say, of insulin and of absolution* in this would be something to be worked out in the doing.

---

* For a brief reflection on the sacraments in relation to personal living, see 'The Sacraments in the Church in Relation to Healing', pp. 190ff.

3 | *The Christian Counsellor*

First, what is the basis for Christian counselling? The basis is twofold: there is faith and there is 'know-how'. In practice these two are, of course, always mixed, but it is very important for practice to get the distinction clear.

Our faith, our commitment as Christians, is distinct from our scientific know-how, however closely the two need to be intertwined. Scientific know-how covers all that is to be learnt from the social sciences and the practice of the social services, together with all that is to be learnt in theory and practice from psychology and psychiatry. It is most important to be clear that faith as such has no control over, or privileged position with regard to, scientific know-how. The facts must never be distorted in the alleged interests of faith. Indeed, faith which attempts to ignore or distort facts is essentially unfaithful. For Christian faith is clear that this is God's world. The doctrine of creation is the assertion of this, and the doctrine of the Incarnation asserts that the world is so much God's concern that he is rightly known to have been personally and humanly present in it. The God in whom the Christian puts his faith is truly God over the world and at the same time truly God in the world. Therefore Christian faith demands a positive attitude to all valid science. Hence it must be the case that in the long run valid faith and valid know-how will illuminate one another.

Of course, we are clear also that there is 'sin', i.e. something wrong with the way we actually practise our faith and our science. Neither are as yet operated with full validity. And in any case we are only *en route* for the truth. Hence we always have to reckon with our two bases of activity. We have the commitment of faith and we have the responsibility of scientific knowledge. These two check one another; sometimes they obviously assist one another, sometimes they exist very much in tension, even temporarily in apparent contradiction.

A sphere of particular concern to us where this is very clear is that of guilt. Christians know that a man is, or can be, responsible before and to God and his fellows. But there are all sorts of questions concerning the 'mechanism' of guilt, false guilt, assessment of responsibility and so on. Here there are many valid scientific questions. Christians must not distort or fear the issue. We have to hold temporary tensions as part of our commitment of faith. Responsibility remains our presupposition and our aim. But where, for example, a set of valid psychological data and arguments for the moment leaves no scientific room for the concept and where, in particular circumstances, it has no therapeutic use, then we must have faith and not distort either the facts or the treatment. We have to face these tensions between faith and know-how faithfully and leave the eventual creativity to God. It is faithless to run to premature answers which abandon science or faith and thereby abandon both.

Granted the twofold basis, what is the aim of the Christian counsellor? This follows from his basis in the commitment of faith, which is faith in the God who is so concerned with humanity that he has chosen to be human. The aim of the Christian counsellor is to be used to help people to be themselves. This provides an ample basis for co-operation with all engaged in social and counselling work, whatever their 'faith'. Further, it is a completely sufficient basis. Our Christian faith sets us free from the need to make any other terms for co-operation. We know that God can look after his own interests. We, in following Jesus, are to obey him by sharing in his care for people, and this we are to do with anyone else who will care. We have no right nor need to insist that those with whom we work shall share our deeper insight into the whole context of the human situation.

Our common aim, therefore, is to help people to be themselves. We see this as a translation into practice of God's purpose of salvation, for salvation is to do with personal wholeness and personal fulfilment, the purpose and gift of

God for every man in fulfilled and fulfilling social relationships with all other men. This totality of salvation is the whole work of the kingdom of God and therefore the whole work of the church. Counselling is a particular work within this whole work, and it is limited by its specific nature. Counselling does not aim either at conversion or at recruitment. As Christians we are clear that for the fullness of sharing in the fullness of salvation men need both to be converted into Jesus Christ and to be recruited into membership of his body, but all this is the work of the Holy Spirit in the whole church and at large.

Counselling has the limited aim within the whole of setting people more free for this and of putting them in the way of this by helping them to be themselves at whatever stage they are at. We must not faithlessly try to do God's whole work for him at once, nor try to take short cuts which do violence to the personal integrity of those whom we have the chance to serve. The aim of the Christian counsellor, therefore, is to play his part in God's work of salvation by being concerned in a limited way in helping people to be themselves. And this limited work presupposes and needs the whole work of the whole church.

Finally, what is the method of the Christian counsellor? It is the practice of openness based on justification by faith. The Christian counsellor knows (although he still has to learn so much of what it means in practice) that his own possibility of being himself lies in his acceptance by God in Jesus Christ. Here it has been made quite clear that God identifies himself with us and accepts us as we are. This is the meaning and power of forgiveness. As we are accepted by God as we are, we are free to accept ourselves as we are and everyone else just as they are. This acceptance (God's acceptance of us and then God's gift to us of being able to accept) frees us for openness to the transforming power of God at work in us and in other people.

For example, we may go back to the question of our twofold basis. As we are grounded in our acceptance by God, we have no cause to see science as a threat to faith. Rather, we are free to be open to all that science has to teach us,

however much it may correct us. We do not need to be right
to be right with God. Being right with God on his initiative,
we are completely free to be put right. Similarly with regard
to our aim; we have no need to convert men or to recruit
them to our way of thinking in order to persuade ourselves
that we are on the right lines. God in his acceptance of us has
set us free from any need to know that we are on the right
lines. We are simply free to learn to love with all others who
wish to learn, and the ultimate issue is, as always, with God
who is love and who has already based us in his love. Hence
we come to the essence of the method of the Christian
counsellor. It is absolute openness to and acceptance of the
'client', of the neighbour in need. There must be no fear. (If I
accept this sort of 'sin', how shall I deal with my own secret
longings and fears? Have no fear, for God has already dealt
with your secrets, fully open to him!) And there must be no
judgment. (Forgive as you are forgiven, and leave judgment
of sin, yours and your neighbour's, to God who knows,
forgives and transforms.)

Of course, such absolute openness requires the practice of
the presence of God, the renewed and renewing gift of grace.
For absolute openness to and acceptance of another is a real
threat to oneself. But we are accepted, and we can therefore
have strength to accept. We ourselves hope to reach God's
standards, that is the reality of Jesus Christ, by the help of
the presence of God and not by any self-centred, moralistic
efforts. Therefore we have no calling to judge the client or to
threaten him or her with standards. We are to sympathize, to
suffer with, by being truly and humanly open to him as he is.
In this we hope so to be used that in and through our
acceptance our neighbour in need is helped to the courage of
self-acceptance and thus helped to freedom to change. For
we can never be free to change until we are free to face
ourselves.

This receiving of freedom to face oneself and to be changed
is a real experience of the grace of the God and Father of our
Lord Jesus Christ. And of this grace the Christian counsellor
is called to be a minister. Later it may be that there will be
recognition of the source of this grace, the dawning of

conscious conversion and the joining of the Christian community. But this lies elsewhere in the purpose of God and in the pattern of the Christian community.

The Christian counsellor is to help to self-acceptance by the completeness of his acceptance. This is the heart of his role. It is based on his faith (and he will be challenged to more training in and understanding of his faith!) and he will need all the expert advice and help he can get. He will have to know how to refer people to the expert help they individually need, whether it be legal, social, medical or psychological. But the heart of the matter is that he is set free to be himself because God in Jesus Christ has wholly accepted him. He is therefore both called and set free wholly to accept his neighbour in his distress and need. And this he may do to the glory of God, for the glory of God is his accepting and identifying love.

4 | *What is There to Know?*

In the first term of a new university it may not be inappropriate to discuss the question of knowledge. In any case, I wish to do so because I am clear that it is a question which is fundamental to the present debate about God, Christianity, and very much else, including, indeed, the purposes and pattern of a university.

The basic question is quite simply this: What do you know? You may believe so and so, you may feel such and such, you may even assert this and that and take up attitudes of one kind and another, but what do you *know*?

Behind this question is another one which is not always noticed, which is: What is it to know? Do you know when you have an existential intuition? Do you know when your carefully planned experiment comes off, and do you know when you are overcome with guilt or transfigured with joy? Just what is it to know?

Perhaps we might get further on this question by asking: What is there to know? The obvious answer to this for us today is data, that which is given to us to observe and to measure. In fact, what there is to know is the subject matter of science, all that which is amenable to scientific method. It is in the picture of the scientist scientifically finding out what there is to know that we have the current model for knowing, knowledge, and he who knows. It may well be that what we have here is a myth. Certainly, there are probably as many problems in the philosophy of science as in the philosophy of religion, but I want to concentrate on our approach on somewhere near the common sense level, at the level of what we normally and largely unconsciously find 'thinkable'.

Here the model for 'he who knows' is 'the scientist', seen as a detached, precise and clinically operating observer with a method and a body of information supporting him, which is likewise clinical, detached and precise. What he knows is data. When he has verified his data and the organization of these data, then he knows. In fact, knowing is what he does and what there is to know is what there is for him to observe, measure and articulate into law-like theories.

Important features of this way of knowing are precision, prediction and generalization, or perhaps better, universifiability. Precision is aimed at through techniques of measurement, use of mathematics, the employment of formulae and graphs. Prediction is a feature of the whole approach, because you verify that your knowledge is indeed knowledge by experimenting on the pattern that, if you observe so and so and do such and such, then you get the following predictable result. Universifiability is demonstrated by the fact that any sane person who is above a certain IQ and who has had the necessary training can be got into the same position of knowing *vis-à-vis* the same knowledge as those who instruct him. In all this we have here, *prima facie*, a pretty clear idea of knowing and knowledge and a manifest set of known data – and above all, this sort of knowing works.

But it is at this point of 'working' that uneasiness may arise. Certainly the knowledge of the physicist works. It produces more and more efficient fusion and fission processes, but what might be called a by-product of this is the H-bomb. Certainly the knowledge of the physiologist, psychologist and pharmacologist works. It produces more and more efficient techniques for curing mental disorders. It also gives better and better opportunities for efficient brainwashing. This sort of ambiguity may legitimately direct us to another possible answer to the question, What is there to know? This answer would be not primarily data, but persons. But here it is not nearly so easy to proceed with the preservation of clarity and with a steady expectation of ensuring nearly universal consent.

Precision, prediction and universifiability are by no means assured. For knowing persons raises questions of depth and value. One is moved into the field of intuitions, attitudes and commitments, judgments which seem to take one into a dangerously subjective realm, and to land one with questions which look very like those of aesthetics and matters of taste.

Therefore, with regard to the question of 'what is there to know?' we seem to have two possible answers. On the one hand data, and on the other hand persons. Data is the area of 'hard' knowledge where you know where you are, and persons is the area of 'soft' knowledge where it is very difficult to know where you are. But, is not the point of knowing precisely that you do know where you are? Further, if the questions of value and the like which seem to arise in connection with knowing persons are as important as they *feel*, then is it not all the more necessary – indeed all the more to be expected – that one should really know where one is or can be in these matters? Now, the man who knows where he is is the data-knower, not the person-knower. We are therefore obliged to wonder whether the person-knower is really knowing at all. Is not real knowledge of persons that type of knowledge which is reducible to hard data, to statistics and rule-like predictions, to sociological graphs and to rules for treatment for varying types of carefully classified cases? Clearly there is a very strong case for assuming such a conclusion. Personal *attitudes* will remain, but knowledge is to do with data and persons as objects of knowledge are reducible to data.

In addition to the general pressure to come to this conclusion provided by our whole implicit attitude to knowledge which I have symbolized in the mythical figure of 'the scientist', there are two considerations which encourage this conclusion, i.e. that what there is to know about persons is reducible to data-knowledge and, indeed, is not real knowledge until it is so reduced.

The first is that truly scientific developments over the whole range from organic chemistry, through biochemistry and the biological sciences, to psychology and the social sciences, have immensely enhanced our knowledge of the processes involved in being a human being. They have vastly increased our capacity for individual and social human 'engineering' – using this term in a sense which is at least morally neutral, but which tends to be morally approving.

There seems to be a strong practical case for saying that if we really know, or perhaps, rather, when we really know, we shall be able to see *how* knowing persons is reducible to knowing data.

Secondly, in the absence of strong evidence to the contrary, the natural thing to believe about human beings would seem to be that they do, as a matter of sheer fact, emerge out of the material which is the material of data-knowledge and that they dissolve back into it. As a matter of fact persons are reducible to data: 'Dust thou art and unto dust thou shalt return.'

Hence there is great pressure to conclude that *in reality* person-knowledge, if it is to be real knowledge, must be reduced to data-knowledge, that data-knowledge is the only real knowledge and that indeed all that there is to know is, in the end, mere data. The implications of such a conclusion, whether it is come to explicitly or whether it is rather more implicitly underlying one's whole approach to knowledge and indeed to life in general, are pretty far-reaching. In effect, knowledge must be thought of as a temporary (although valid) arrangement of partial (though real) data, which arrangement is the temporary possession of a purely temporary existent or class of existents. That is to say, that we exist, if I may be allowed to put it so, in a situation of absolute relativeness.

I believe that although this picture I have drawn is very roughly and crudely drawn, none the less it does in rough outline represent the underlying situation as it strikes most of us most of the time. Our implicit understanding of knowledge and reality, of what it is to know and of what there is to know, is back, for all its necessary modernity, to that of Heraclitus: *panta rei*, everything flows; we have absolute relativeness.

A variety of consequences, some of them logical, some of them practical, follow from this. Among them I may mention the following.

First, as far as reality goes, neither persons nor knowledge matters. The 'stuff' of the universe, the data of knowledge, what really is 'there' to be the object of 'real' knowledge – is quite indifferent to knowing persons and to what they do or do not know. As objects of knowledge persons are reducible to data, and, as a matter of fact, knowing persons are ultimately reduced to data. When that has fully happened there is no knowing persons and therefore no data. In this sense reality is absolutely indifferent to persons and knowledge.

But, of course, knowing persons do not share this indifference! So certain practical reactions follow, of which three strike me as particularly current and important.

First, there is the response of *commitment* – we must individually make some limited area of reality or sector of experience significant by our commitment to it. The commitment proceeds from us and any value there is in it lies in the commitment as such. Hence the vogue for words like commitment, relevance and freedom, used absolutely.

Secondly, there is a response which is particularly prevalent in academic circles, though not confined to them. You sell yourself to one approach – naturally that discipline or science in which you yourself are, in however minor a way, a luminary, and you stick to this approach as providing *the* unifying force and the explanatory key.

It used to be physics, now it is much more likely to be the biological sciences, psychology or sociology.

This is really only a form of the general reductionism we have been discussing, but one can keep oneself sufficiently busy in a sufficiently significant way not to be troubled by this.

A third possible and common reaction is to be concerned not with any particular commitment nor with any particular pattern of co-ordinating and making sense of human life, but rather with immediate reactions to and experiences in the moment. *This* is typified in much current literature and drama and expressed in a great deal of current discussion of morals. The utmost possible significance or satisfaction or forgetfulness or what you will is to be obtained by seeking unrestrained self-expression in whatever circumstances happen to be obtaining or in whatever opportunities happen to be offered.

The effect of these and kindred common trends is to produce much fragmentation of knowledge, many tendencies to intellectual imperialism and a great deal of sheer moral anarchy.

With regard to fragmentation of knowledge, we can see it is reflected in answering the question, 'What is a university?', and by the doubts which this raises in our minds as to whether there can be such a thing nowadays, in the sense of something that is corporately concerned as a whole with knowledge as a whole. With regard to intellectual imperialism, I should perhaps not make specific charges without careful documentation, but I would suggest that we should easily find examples in the works of some sociologists, in such a field as that of criminology, and in the works of some psychologists, especially perhaps those concerned with the behaviourist approach. As to what I mean by moral anarchy, this is sufficiently indicated by the easily recognizable fact that the one rule which is universally applauded in the sphere of human activity is that every man and every woman should do that which is right in his or her own eyes.

I am arguing, or perhaps rather suggesting that it could be argued, that all this and much more like it follows from the assumed position with regard to knowledge. If one is looking for a knowledgeable approach to things, where can one start from? What assumed or authoritative basis is there for making sense of life and experience or for living one's life realistically? You simply have to start from wherever you happen to be.

If you have landed in an interesting discipline of experimentation and practice, medical, biological or sociological, then the thing to do is to stay busily in the middle of this. It is necessary to stay in the middle to avoid being confronted with questions which are too difficult, i.e. which cannot be answered in terms of your own discipline. But you can give yourself a methodological reason for what might be called this intellectual cowardice by saying that questions which cannot be answered within your own disciplines are not real questions.

Or, if you have more courage (belligerence?), you can

proceed from your discipline to claim that this discipline *is* the arbiter of what is knowledge, of what is real, of what is truly human.

Or if you have no taste for the routine of intellectual disciplines and no stomach for intellectual empire building, then you must clearly start always from your immediate reactions. There *is* no such thing as a *knowledgeable* approach – there is just *my* approach. And who can suggest a better one? Clearly there are *others*; but on what grounds are they *better*, at any rate, for me?

Now this is where, as I understand it, Jesus Christ comes in. A Christian is a man who is convinced that there is an answer to the question about the possibility of a knowledgeable approach to reality – and that this answer is both a given answer and a potentially universifiable one.

Where can you start from? From Jesus Christ – or rather from Jesus of Nazareth who was recognized to be the Christ. We have here a matter of fact starting-point, the datum of a particular person who establishes himself as the basis for a particular understanding of the reality of the world, of the reality of human life in the world and of the possibilities involved in human life by virtue of that reality.

The manner in which Jesus of Nazareth establishes himself as the starting point for knowing and evaluating the reality of the world may be briefly indicated as follows:

1. We have a given historical reality, the Jewish people, with their tradition of an experienced living God known to them through the ups and downs (mostly downs) of their intensely varied history.

So confident were the Jews that the living God whom they had experienced was really God and really living, that there had grown up among them a Messianic hope. The forms of this hope varied and it was naturally expressed in imagery drawn from their history and given shape by their particular experiences. A clear example of this is the form of the Messianic expectation which took its shape from King David. He had indeed been the Lord's anointed in that he was a king, and particularly favoured – particularly associated with the establishment of Israel. Now the Jews were sure that these experiences of God in the past could be vindicated in the future.

God was the Lord, living, powerful *and* consistent in his purposes and attitudes of holiness, righteousness and love. Therefore, they expected him to send another decisive anointed king, a son of David, one analogous to David in God's purposes for his people, but greater than David in that he would bring about the decisive settlement of the affairs of the world in accordance with the reality, the character and purpose of the Lord God.

Confidence in God, assurance of his reality, was thus expressed in this and other forms of Messianic expectation. With regard to the establishment of Jesus of Nazareth as the decisive starting point for understanding the reality of the world this tradition, assurance and hope of the Jews forms the *context of recognition*.

2. In this tradition there appears the historical individual Jesus of Nazareth, about whom one thing is as clear as any historical fact can be, i.e. it is not provable beyond all shadow of doubt, but it is 'morally certain'. Jesus of Nazareth believed that he had a mission connected with the kingdom of God. That is to say, he had a calling from God which placed him somehow very close to the centre of the purpose of God relied upon by the Jews in their Messianic expectations. Real experience of the real God had shown that he was indeed 'there' and had purposes of holiness, righteousness and love. As he really was God and was a God of this nature, he was bound sooner or later to establish his kingdom, i.e. show that he was God, by aligning everything in accordance with his character, his goodness. Jesus of Nazareth was convinced that he was called to play a part in God's establishing of his kingdom.

'The kingdom of heaven is at hand.' In obedience to this calling, he taught, collected disciples, and followed a policy which brought him, not without shrinking, but eventually by deliberate choice, to the death of the cross.

Jesus of Nazareth was undoubtedly a man for God, a man with a mission concerning the Kingdom of God, and in pursuit of this mission he died.

3. His disciples had accepted the fact that Jesus had this mission in connection with the kingdom of God; they had placed him in that context of recognition which at least associated him in a central and decisive way with the fulfilment of the Messianic hope of the Jews. But they were brought to a full stop by his death.

The reason that any claims are made about the significance of Jesus of Nazareth for an evaluation of reality, is that this full stop was removed. For some reason the disciples became unshakably convinced that death had not put a stop to Jesus and his mission. They were convinced that, as a plain matter of fact, as matter of fact as the fact of Jesus' calling and Jesus' death, Jesus was once again alive. The incidents and experiences which partly produced and partly reflected this conviction are to some extent mirrored in what we call the narratives of the Resurrection. The *central* conviction was – and is – that Jesus' calling and Jesus' mission for which he had died were vindicated. Jesus had died in obedience to God, and God had shown that this was obedience by 'raising him up' – establishing him as not dead, not brought to a full stop, but alive and fulfilling his mission.

This matter of the resurrection and its credibility must be returned to. But first let me complete the historical sketch of the way in which Jesus of Nazareth was established as the criterion of knowledge and reality.

Jesus had identified himself with the general context of the messianic expectation of the Jews and followed a calling connected with the coming of the kingdom of God. In following this calling he had been crucified. His disciples were convinced that God had raised him up.

Therefore, 4. Jesus of Nazareth was to be recognized as the Christ. Jesus' mission concerning the kingdom of God had been vindicated by God's raising him up.

Hence, the way Jesus had carried out his mission, with its pattern of teaching and service leading through his death to resurrection, was to be received as the pattern by which God established his kingdom.

Once Jesus has been recognized as God's Christ, the particular details of his approach to life and his encounter with death have now to be understood as the essential clues to the way in which God arrives at his purpose – indeed as the essential clues to the shape of that purpose.

To recognize Jesus as the Christ requires the *context of recognition* of Judaism and the Old Testament tradition of faith in God. But once Jesus is recognized as the Christ, he himself becomes the *context of definition*. This is expressed by the well-known and extremely primitive Christian confession, 'Jesus Christ is Lord'. That is to say that the dominating and decisive factor concerning the understanding of God and the world is Jesus Christ. This is where we return to the question of the credibility of the resurrection.

It is not a question which can be settled by the immediate application of criteria relating to what we or anyone else habitually find thinkable. For the whole point about the proclaiming of the Resurrection of Christ is that it is a claim to *define what is thinkable*.

We have, as a matter of history, the tradition of the Jews with their faith in a living God distilled from their corporate experience and producing their Messianic hopes. We have also as a matter of history Jesus of Nazareth, who believed himself to be called to serve the kingdom of this same God in whom the Jews believed and whom they thought they knew. And we have as a matter of history, Jesus of Nazareth crucified in the course of this mission and his disciples convinced that the God whom Jesus served and for whom Jesus had died had raised him up.

We are therefore faced with deciding whether what *we* think to be reality swamps Jesus Christ or whether Jesus Christ defines reality. It is the old question of whether or not Jesus Christ is Lord, and it is a perfectly proper question. It is not a mythological or superstitious or religious one. It is simply a question about reality, directly related to the questions 'What do you know?' and 'What is there to know?' For if Jesus Christ is Lord, then – starting from him – we may be clear that God is, that he is properly thought of as the Father with purposes consistent with his holiness, righteousness and love, and that God the Father can be relied upon as being involved in this world with a view to bringing his purposes out of it.

This being so, we return to our discussion of questions of knowledge in a very different frame of mind. It becomes clear that we have to tackle the whole matter of the relation between data-knowledge and person-knowledge with the conviction that persons are not, in the end, to be reduced to data.

Rather, data exist to serve and to develop persons. With *that* assurance we must then be extremely careful to see that every possible piece of data-knowledge is treated with the respect it deserves and made scientifically available for the service of personal purposes.

We must be clear that commitment is indeed demanded if we are to experience worthwhileness and serve worthwhileness, but it is not undefined commitment or mere commitment. It is commitment to all that promotes personal purposes and the development of persons as defined by the holiness, righteousness and love of God. As to attempts to articulate particular disciplines into arbiters of what reality is and what is truly human by way either of limitation or of possibility – we must be clear that no system and no theory can be of more than limited use. For the context of the possibilities of men is the infinite and transcendent reality of God, and anything which shuts man into any theory or framework whatever is an enemy of his eventual humanness. It is, incidentally, important to notice that this applies to theology too. The only theology which does justice to the reality defined by Jesus Christ is a broken theology in which all theories are systematically and constantly being broken up so that they may be open to further possibilities.

And finally, in relation to self-expression, in relation to the question of everyone doing what is right in his or her own eyes, in relation to the question of the freedom to be oneself, it becomes clear in the light of Jesus Christ as the definition of reality that all self-expression is deceitful and destructive unless and until it is aligned on the expression of oneself in love. And love is to be defined not by the impulses of the moment or the instinctive reactions of an animal make-up but as love which harnesses these impulses and directs these instincts in the direction of that total self-giving for the sake of the personalities of others which was demonstrated by and vindicated in Jesus Christ.

I fear I have attempted the impossible and my over-reaching has brought its own destruction. But perhaps I could sum up the thesis I have attempted to set out like this:

The answer we give to the question whether Jesus Christ is Lord makes literally all the difference in the world and to the world.

Neither Christians nor non-Christians have begun to assess Jesus of Nazareth until they have begun to face up to this.

5 | *The Christian and Other Faiths*

On the question of how a Christian stands with regard to other faiths, I find that I have to begin at the beginning, and ask myself how indeed one does approach this question, which has obvious theoretical implications and increasingly practical ones. We are forced to begin at the beginning because one of the really splendid things about the present situation is that we cannot escape realizing that we are in one world. Consequently it cannot be the case that one can have one's understanding of the world, one's understanding of one's self, one's understanding of one's commitment dictated by something which is of purely local interest. Even if our faith in Jesus Christ has been a purely local matter, conditioned, say, by our cultural life in a part of Western 'Christendom', it cannot now remain so. We are faced with a question very similar to that which arose for the first Christians. In a Judaic culture, localized for them in Palestine, they discovered that Jesus was the Christ. But was it the case that Jesus was of significance for the whole Hellenistic world? Was he truly Jesus Christ the Lord in that wider world? So now we are faced with the question whether Jesus Christ the Lord is indeed in any real sense the Lord of the whole earth. And this is being forced upon us in a way which really, in one sense, threatens us, so that we are therefore forced to real exploration.

How, then, does one start on this exploration? First of all, we must be quite clear that traditionally Christians are entirely exclusive and absolute about Jesus Christ. This is well symbolized in that symbol of the Christian faith, that sort of distilled summary of Christian experience, the creed, where Jesus is referred to as being 'of one substance with the Father', one of those apparent pieces of mumbo-jumbo which either points to a mystery, or to nothing. And if one investigates what it points to, one is faced with the fact that this is a claim that in Christian faith and understanding, in the understanding of the world provoked by Jesus, in the understanding of man focused on Jesus, Jesus is known to be of the very stuff of God. What we are up against in Jesus is God. Jesus is God's decisive act, his decisive act to bring in his kingdom. That is to say, that Jesus is what God does to establish everything in the world in accordance with his own reality. God is the living and the active God, he is the God who cares. This he has made clear to his people and through his people, and because he cares, he will act consistently with his caring. And he does act, such is the Christian understanding, he sends his Christ, his Christ is Jesus. So Jesus turns out to be God's decisive act.

Or another way of putting it is: Jesus is what it is all about. We may symbolize this by speaking of him as the word of the creator; that is to say, he is the embodiment of the pattern and of the purpose of the universe, and, therefore, he is what it will all come to. We may symbolize *that* by saying that he will come again, to judge both the quick and the dead. What did it all start from? That pattern in God's mind which is seen to be embodied in Jesus. What will it come to? That pattern which is seen to be embodied in Jesus. Jesus is the stuff of God, a God who is love. He embodies what God had in mind at the beginning, he is God's word, he is the shape of things which will dominate in the end. Jesus is Lord. That which is embodied in him is that which will overrule all things in the end. And therefore in Jesus Christ we have what we may say is God in person. God in person showing us what man is, showing us what man will be, showing us what man can be, and further showing us that the ultimate reality of the universe, that which is at work in, through and beyond the stuff of the universe, is at work to bring man to this fulfilment, to this shape, to these opportunities, to the enjoyment of the possibilities which are embodied here. And therefore for Christians, here in Jesus Christ, as far as our understanding of ourselves goes, is the clue to reality. This is what I have a chance of becoming, this is what we all have a chance of becoming, and what is more, this is related to the very stuff of the universe. Here is the transcendent in the midst.

Further, Christians hold, this is not a theory. There are all sorts of theories which can be based on Christianity, there are all sorts of deductions which can supposedly be drawn from it, but the centre of the matter is a happening, is a man, is a piece of history. And, consequently, Christianity is not a view of life, it is not a theory about the universe, it is a basis on which one will have to work out all sorts of views on life. It is a point of vantage from which one will have to wrestle with all sorts of theories about the universe. Basically it is a reaction to the happening who was Jesus, and it is believed to be continued, because it is a reaction to the reality who is Jesus. It is a reaction to this happening, who is Jesus, and all that led up to him, and all that follows from him. The scope of this is believed to be total, because all that led up to him goes back to the creative purpose of God and all that follows from him goes on to the fulfilment and very end of all things. The first point, then, is that Christians are committed to absolutely exclusive claims about Jesus Christ. Reality demands this. This is how things are, and therefore this is what always must be taken into account.

One proceeds from the first point to the second. Which is this. It follows, therefore, that anything in other faiths which contradicts Jesus Christ, anything in other faiths which goes against the reality of Jesus Christ, in the Christian view is wrong. And it is wrong, not as a matter of intellect but as a matter of reality and practice, so that it must be combatted. It must be stood up against for the sake of reality, for the sake of the truth of things, for the sake of the development of man. Now to state it this way is such a scandal, such an occasion of stumbling, that it is necessary to pay very careful attention to the true implications and the true applications of this. My second point is that anything in other faiths which contradicts or goes against Jesus, on the Christian view, is wrong and must be opposed. I do not agree for one minute that everybody is going the same way, or believes the same thing – I believe that is wholly contrary to the situation and the logic of the various faiths. This may mean that Christianity is false. But one must at least be quite clear about the situation. And in order simply to make the point I shall have to give a series of examples of the sort of things which might be involved. Pressure of time forces me to put these examples extremely crudely, and therefore, very probably, offensively, but I see no way of avoiding this.

For example, then, it seems to me that the Christian is clear that the Jews are wrong. They have failed to identify the essential clue to the way their God and ours worked for men and among men. And one of the results of this is Zionism, Zionism with its consequent misery which arises from the assertion of the wrong sort of power, in the wrong sort of situation. Zionism, which has even become a religious failure, because nowadays, in Israel, many Israelis are prepared to assert that they are Israelis and not Jews. This point must be picked up later, because it must be noted that one of the causes of Zionism is clearly Christian persecution. But our concern at the moment is that it seems quite clear that the Christian must understand the Jew as having made a fatally wrong mistake here.

Similarly, if Islam is wedded to a rigoristic view of law, if Islam is wedded to a performance of religious duties, which is based on this understanding of the law, if Islam is wedded to the view that understanding of God is wholly transcendent, so that one is ruled by a predetermined fate, if all this is true, then Islam is wrong. The reality of God is not so.

Men are not to be fulfilled in the way in which the religious duties of Islam point. There is too much rigidity here to cope with the demands and opportunities of science and to respond to the true situation of man in the world under God.

Again, if the teaching of the Buddha is basically atheistic, that is to say, makes it clear that there is no God of concern, if, the teaching of the Buddha interprets man as needing to escape from rather than to fulfil his personality, if the teaching of the Buddha holds the world to be a fantasy and

an illusion rather than the very material of human life and
development, then the Buddha is wrong. This is a false
reaction, which goes against the grain of reality, which
wrongly faces the possibilities of science, and the challenges
and, admittedly, the threats to man. Again, if Hinduism
dissolves the significance of individuality, through a reincar-
national circle, if Hinduism finds room to worship both the
evil and the good aspects of what is manifested to us, then
this is presenting a gross distortion of the truth, a distortion
from which humanity in Christ's name needs to be rescued. I
must stress that I am simply using these things as examples of
the sort of thing that seems to me would follow from point
one, if my brief examples from other faiths did not turn out,
on closer investigation, to be simply misrepresentation.

I believe that there is bound to be the possibility, and
indeed at times the necessity, of a sharp clash between the
following of Jesus Christ and all these religions and faiths,
and others, which I have not time to mention (and I
particularly leave aside what might be called faiths, Marxism,
for example, and secular Humanism because I think we do
not want to concentrate on the faiths of the West). As was
pointed out at the beginning of this second point, where
anything contradicts and goes against Jesus Christ, it must be
opposed as wrong.

To proceed, therefore, to the third point. Here we come up
against a strong caveat, a very big '*but*'! My subject is
Christianity and other faiths, and so far I have not spoken
about Christianity at all. I have spoken about Jesus Christ. It
is very important to be clear that Jesus Christ is not to be
equated with Christianity, that is to say, with the particular
cultural and institutional embodiments which have so far
historically arisen as attempts to respond to him. This is quite
vital. Jesus Christ is not to be equated with Christianity,
where 'Christianity' means the particular cultural and
institutional embodiment which has so far historically arisen
as a consequence of attempts to respond to him. There is a
good deal of Jesus Christ in these things, but they are not
equivalent to him. The whole of him is certainly not in them,
and quite a lot of them do not coincide with him at all. This

may perhaps be made clear by discussing the distinction between Jesus Christ and Christianity as affecting the relationship between Christianity and other faiths.

First, nothing I have said so far denies the necessity of dialogue with other faiths. In my view, quite the contrary. For what, *in fact*, contradicts the reality of Jesus Christ? On the Christian belief, Jesus Christ is the embodiment in history of the ultimate reality God, who is before all things, and who brings all things, and all men, to fulfilment. Jesus Christ is the man in the middle who is related to the beginning and the end of things. It is impossible, therefore, on the Christian understanding of Jesus Christ, for any present understanding to have the monopoly of the reality of Jesus Christ, or indeed for it to embrace the totality of the reality of Jesus Christ. No matter how carefully any present understanding is built on past understandings, there must be more to discover, to embrace the totality of that reality. It therefore seems quite clear that we need the help of all men to learn about and to expose the reality of Jesus Christ. And men who have tried to respond to reality, men who have tried to explore the human condition, along the ways it may be of Islam, of the Buddha, or of many others, such men, we may suppose (and it seems to me that there is much evidence to force us to that supposition if we were reluctant about it), have achieved experiences and insights into the possibilities of the world which are clues to the true reality of God. Loyalty to Jesus Christ requires us to be exposed to these insights; requires us to enter into fearless and faithful dialogue, so that we can together learn more of what is truly involved in seeking to become really human, more of what is truly involved in the human condition and the possibilities of the human condition in the world, in the world in which Christ lived, died and rose again. I believe that Jesus Christ does, at some essential points, if I may put it shortly, put all religions in the wrong. But Christians must be clear about two things here. First, that he puts much in Christianity in the wrong. And secondly, that he does not therefore condemn all other religions. Although he puts much in the wrong he is to be related to, and he is to be understood, through many

insights of many men in many other religions, which sometimes reflect his reality better than so-called Christian understandings. And therefore the absolute claim of Jesus Christ
does not forbid, but rather requires dialogue with other faiths.
That is the first point. And it moves on to a second point.

It is not really Christianity and other faiths with which we
ought to be concerned. Rather, our concern is men and
women exploring and responding to reality as Christians,
Buddhists, Jews, Muslims, Hindus. For surely Jesus Christ
makes it clear that not doctrine but human beings are basic
to the religious quest, are basic to human living. And,
consequently, these absolute claims of Jesus Christ are to be
received primarily and centrally and decisively in terms of
obedience, in terms of response to the possibilities revealed, in
terms of practice in our relations to our fellows and to the
world at large, in terms of commitment to explore further
and more deeply the sort of things that we are put on to. And
the questions which therefore have to be faced are of the type
'How are we to love our neighbours?', 'Who am I?', 'Who
are you?', 'What are the possibilities involved in our existence
and in the context in which we operate?', 'What resources are
available for being human in the world as we now have to
face it?'. And, 'How can we go more deeply into what is
involved in what we allege to be our faith?, How can we
respond so as to get a better understanding both in heart and
in mind to those things which our faith, which our religious
understanding begin to give us glimpses of?'. Dialogue
between religions which is consistent with the reality of Jesus
Christ must take on this form of concern for practical truth,
for commitment to response, for going deeper into the reality
which we believe we have so far seen. That makes it clear
that there must be no question in any dialogue between
faiths of any kind of intellectual or cultural imperialism. It is
a conversation between human beings about human living.

This brings me to the third point, which is really my
summing-up point in the question of the nature of the
dialogue of faiths. We must learn (and it is going to take
some learning, to get clarity into our system and systems) that
what has been called Christendom is not Jesus Christ. The

ways of thinking of the West must not be identified with
Christianity, still less with Jesus Christ. One of the ways in
which it will appear whether or not Jesus is Lord, in the
broader sense which our present situation now demands, is
whether the faith of Jesus Christ and the life in Jesus Christ
remains clearly a living option when it is quite clear that the
West no longer dominates. If Jesus is the Christ, if Jesus
Christ is Lord in the way in which I believe he has been
proclaimed to be at the heart of Christianity, then there must
be a disentanglement of Christianity from the cultural taken-
for-granteds, if I may so put it, of the West. For the sake of
Jesus Christ and in the name of Jesus Christ, cultural
equivalence between a form of Christianity and Western
society has finally to be broken down. One of the splendid
things is that Western atheism is finally assisting in this. But it
is surprising how far Western atheists are often Christianly
cultural imperialists at heart. They may be atheists, but they
are still Christian ones, in the sense in which I am using the
adjective here, related to cultural realities and embodiments
which at some stage in the history of things were a proper
response to, and a means of, passing on the Christian Gospel,
but have now become fossilized misidentifications. And that is
why, basically and fundamentally, dialogue with other faiths,
which are many of them rooted in other cultures, is quite
essential. For if Jesus Christ is what I believe him to be, then
he will challenge all. He will challenge all Western
particularism and imperialism which has got bound up with a
thing called Christian society. He will challenge all oriental
pessimism, which goes deep into the culture which is bound
up with Hinduism and Buddhism. He will challenge all
Jewish particularism and so on, just as he will bring out the
insights in Buddhism, Hinduism, Judaism and Christianity
which we all need to be human. Certainly in many ways
Christianity, as a religion, is in the same position as other
religions. It has much to be set free from, it has many
authentic insights, it has much to repent for.

   Here I must return to my perhaps brutal remarks about the
Jews earlier, because it is surely clear that whatever sin has
been committed in connection with the state of Israel is really

the sin of the world. That is to say, that any misunderstanding of national power or of national possibilities which has misled the Jews in connection with the founding and developing of Israel, is the sin of Christendom. For why must they turn to having a national home of their own? Because they have never been safe anywhere else? But that is not their sin. Speaking as a Christian, it is our sin. Therefore it is quite clear that in the dialogue with other faiths there must be no self-righteousness. One of the things that becomes more and more striking is the way in which the Bible so often turns out to be true. On reflection it is so justly clear that 'all our righteousnesses are as filthy rags' (Isa. 64.6), and they do not clothe us for the future. So there must be no self-righteousness; rather there must be solidarity in penitence, in search for forgiveness and for grace, solidarity in mutual service for reconciliation. For loyalty to the reality of Jesus Christ, which is also loyalty to the reality of humanity, requires not imperialism, but service. The very shape of Jesus Christ, his living and his dying, his cross and his rising again, surely makes this clear, though it is the sort of clarity to which we do not readily respond. Jesus Christ, therefore, is not to be equated with Christianity. This is the third point, and there is just a brief postscript.

The above is the merest outline of a possible approach to the question of Christianity and other faiths. In closing, I wish to draw attention to the perspective within which all our thinking about Christianity and other faiths should be done. The authentic Christian viewpoint is, surely, given by the phrase in Ephesians about it being the good pleasure of God to 'sum up all things in Jesus Christ' (Eph. 1.10). Christians are called to see, and to help others to see, that Jesus Christ is the shape of the future – God's future and man's future. And this future has to be entered into. It has to be entered into by Christians and by Christianity as well as by other faiths and non-faiths.

This future, because it is the future of the God of the whole earth who is also the father of Jesus Christ, must hold the fullness of the primal vision of Africa, the fullness of the wisdom of China, the fullness of the riches of oriental men

who have lived through cultures so different, and in many
ways so much older, and so much richer than our own. It
will embrace also the fullness of the purified riches of Western
Christendom and of the churches of the East. We are offered
a vision. The vision is that of the one true man in Christ
Jesus who would have in him as a community some of the
things that one is enabled to glimpse through one's African
friends, some of the depth that one is offered through one's
Indian friends, some of the struggles of the Chinese, some of
the simplicity of the Aboriginals, some of the multiplicity of
resources of the Europeans, something of the Amer-indians,
and much more. We need one another in our human and in
our religious explorations, and in our living. We need one
another, just as we cannot be fulfilled without one another.
Loyalty to the absolute and exclusive claims of Jesus Christ, a
loyalty which is shaped by the reality of Jesus Christ, requires
absolute openness to all the faiths of men, and complete
readiness to serve in a common exploration and in a common
living.

6 | *What is There to Hope For?*

I find it odd. I become more and more sure that the people
who said that Jesus was risen from the dead are quite right.
Risen he was and risen he is. There is a fact here which is a
fact of the world and a fact for the world. My intelligence
and my imagination seem to be more and more ready to
accept the Resurrection as a fact of the past. But, and this is
what I find odd, disturbing and provocative, I do not seem
to be able to get to grips in the same way with what
presumably follows, that is with the Resurrection as a fact of
the future.

I know, of course, that people who are not Christians are
quite clear that the Resurrection of Jesus is in no sense a fact.
I know, too, that Christian belief is alleged to be on the
wane. I am further aware that very many people who declare
themselves to be Christians, and whom I, for what it's worth,
would certainly recognize as such, hold that the Resurrection
is not a fact but a symbol. All this, and all the argumentation
that lies behind it, is very weighty. I can quite see why Paul
should have been laughed at when, on Mars Hill at Athens,
he got to his talk about Jesus and the Resurrection. But –
although this still rather surprises me – I think that Paul was
right and that those who take a contrary view are wrong.
Jesus was dead and God raised him up.

At Easter I am not really concerned to argue for my faith
in Jesus and the Resurrection but to try to face what at
present I see involved in that faith – in particular this matter
of the fact of the Resurrection, past and future, but I still find
here an argument with myself. I consider my study of the
Gospel narratives of the so-called resurrection appearances. I
compare this with the shape of the preaching presented in the

Acts of the Apostles and with the relevant references in the
Epistles. Scholars, of whom I suppose I might count myself
one, argue back and forth about how to evaluate these
writings. At times one wonders how so few New Testament
words can sustain so extensive a volume of scholarly sentences.
But through it all I find a simple conclusion emerging. We
can be pretty clear about what the first disciples believed had
happened.

Some of them were familiar with the shape of Jesus in his
living, that is to say that they knew him as a person. Some
of them were well aware of the shape of Jesus' dying. He had
become involved with the Jewish and Roman authorities and
was killed. Some of them were equally aware of a new living
of Jesus, a living as real and actual as the living of Jesus from
Nazareth to the cross and a living as much present, and as
much to be reckoned with, as the dying, becoming a corpse
and being buried. Further, Jesus had directed his living, the
Jewish and Roman authorities had directed his dying and
God had directed his new living. This was so concrete and
fact-like that it was perfectly appropriate to include in the
story of the incidents which led to the discovery of this new
living of Jesus, the incident of the empty tomb. I cannot, for
my part, decide whether the actual discovery of the empty
tomb was one of the preludes to discovering Jesus to be alive
or whether the story came to be told as a symbol of the
discovery that Jesus was alive. But either way, the shape of
the discovery and of the belief seems to be clear and one and
the same. The burying was real and the being alive again was
real and that in the same categories of reality. The fact of
Jesus' death had been taken up into, and overcome by, the
fact of Jesus' resurrection.

Jesus had lived, men had killed him and God had raised
him up. This is what had happened. And from now on the
responses of our living and the expectations of our living are
to be made and developed in the perspective of these happenings. I can see no escape from the awkward shape of this
belief of the first Christians, of this belief which constituted
the first Christians. I get no escape from the awkwardness by
transposing the statement 'God raised up Jesus' into the

statement 'there arose a belief that Jesus was as good as alive'. If this means that the disciples spontaneously persuaded themselves to carry on in this manner, then we are dealing with a delusion of considerable historical and, it may be, pathological interest but of no ultimate religious and human significance. Further, we are doing quite impermissible violence to the logic and spirit of the New Testament simply considered as a literary work. No literary or historical critic of any integrity would permit such a violation of any other document. A piece of writing must be allowed the authenticity of its own approach and its own errors, whatever conclusions this may force us to about its value. As I say, I am unable to escape the conclusion that the shape of what the first Christians believed to have happened is clear enough.

If, on the other hand, by 'there arose a belief that Jesus was as good as alive' we mean that God enabled some men to perceive the lasting significance of the shape of Jesus' personality, then we are back with talk and belief about God acting. To cause a belief, and *a fortiori* to cause a true belief, is just as much a happening as, say, raising up Jesus.

So, try as I will, I have not been able to avoid the conclusion that I am presented with the Resurrection of Jesus as a fact of the past. Indeed, I now find that, far from wishing to avoid this conclusion, it is resuming its place as part of the basic stuff of my Christian faith. Paul wrote that if Christ be not risen then Christian preaching is vain and so is Christian faith. Right now it is not conceivable to me that the faith which I share with my fellow-Christians is vain. I find it too much of a gift, too much of a resource, too much of a personal presence and provocation. Of course, I am intellectually aware that all faith may be folly but my only concern now is to try to be clearer about the shape of Christian folly, the implications of Easter foolishness.

God raised up Jesus, dead and buried when Pontius Pilate was procurator of Judaea, and established him in his person, in his achievements, in his continuing significance. Since this has been done, what will be done? Paul, with whom I have been daring to agree – with some surprise – has a short and strong word for anyone who asks 'How are the dead raised up? And with what body do they come?' (I Cor. 15.35). It is *aphrōn* – mindless, ignorant, 'Thou fool!', as the Authorized Version has it. But I shall persevere with the questions and accept the epithet. For I seem quite often to find myself caught up in a sort of expectant puzzlement between being more and more sure that I have been given something to believe and less and less sure that I know what it means.

God did raise up Jesus. What then will he do through and in the spirit of Jesus? What am I to expect, what am I to look out for now and to look forward to in the future? Death and resurrection, I suppose, dying and rising, confronting being brought to an end and discovering offers of a new beginning. But this will have to have specific meaning through and in relation to specific happenings if the Resurrection is a fact of the future as it is a fact of the past.

The Resurrection means that God acted to establish Jesus in his person, in his achievements and in his continuing effect. Hence, it must be possible in fact to discover the shape of Jesus Christ in and through the events, circumstances and persons with whom I get involved, and it must be possible to see any set of persons, events and circumstances in the perspective of this shape of Jesus Christ. Further, must I not expect ultimately to see the shape of Jesus Christ established beyond and over all events, circumstances and persons?

I think that this must mean inextinguishable hope *in* the world and a final hope *beyond* the world.

For by 'the shape of Jesus Christ' I mean the person that he was, the expectations which he aroused and the promises which were thereby held out. The Resurrection as a fact of the past is God's re-establishing of *this* person, that is of Jesus Christ, in his own personal pattern and presence, through and beyond death. The particularity of the Resurrection seems to be an essential part of its meaning and its universal significance. It was Jesus who was known to be living again, not the spirit of Christ, nor the essence of love nor the embodiment of humanity. The Resurrection is a preservation of identity and a declaration of identity. In raising up Jesus, God makes it plain that his resources are at work for, and are at the disposal of, the establishment, development and liberation of human identity. This identity, moreover, is your identity and my identity. We are meant to have our own proper names and it is those names, not our surnames or class names or categorizing labels, which are our real names and which denote the real in us which is offered the possibility of establishment and fulfilment.

Here something in me joins fiercely with much from outside me to say 'nonsense' – look at the world, look at the news, look at your neighbour, look at yourself. But this seems to be precisely the point of the Resurrection of Jesus Christ. His identity is established and declared through and then beyond everything that counted against it. It was a rising again from the dead. Hence all human endings and all inhuman absurdities are put in question. The last word is claimed by God as the establisher of identity.

Not that this identity must be confused with mere individuality. For the shape of Jesus Christ is not merely the person that he was but also the expectations which he aroused and the promises thereby held out. These expectations and promises are all to do with the fulfilment of the life of the people of God, they have a communal dimension and they are concerned with relationships. The love which he embodied and the love which he encouraged saw every man in need as my neighbour, prayed that we might receive the same forgiveness from God as we extend to those who trespass against our identity, and had a vision of a body in which unity overcame all differences of class, status, sex, nationality or religion. Hence the establishment of identity, which is declared in and promised by the Resurrection, is also the establishment of community. The Resurrection of Jesus Christ promises that I shall be me, but only and excellently in oneness with all men.

Perhaps, then, it is not so very odd that while I find my intelligence and my imagination increasingly accepting the Resurrection as a fact of the past I do not find a corresponding increase in my understanding of the Resurrection as a fact of the future. What will my identity be when it is fully established in openness to all men in God and to God in all men? How will the dead be raised up and with what body will they come? The only answer can be that they will be raised up by the God who raised up Jesus and that they will come with the body and in the body of Jesus Christ. This will be the establishment and the declaration of an identity and a community in a way that is now unidentifiable.

But although we cannot visualize how we shall enjoy our identity in this community, the establishment of this community is assured. The definiteness of death no more puts a limit upon the possibilities of our human identity than it did upon the identity of Jesus Christ. Our hope, therefore, goes beyond the world into the future which is the future of the God who raised up Jesus. But this hope stems from the Resurrection as a fact of the past and of the future. Such a fact must also, in bridging past and future, have its existence in the present. If there is anything in these wonderings and wanderings of mine, then the reality of the Resurrection should be looked out for and expected wherever we are offered possibilities of, or faced with problems about, identity and community. This is where we shall find possibilities of dying and rising, of being brought to an end and of discovering offers of new beginnings which are reflections and realizations of the power of the Resurrection.

Every threat, as I receive it, to my being me can be received as an opportunity to discover some new way and some renewing way of living. Dying itself is the opportunity to discover that life can be received only as a gift, in total and unmitigated dependence on others and on the source of life beyond all others. Every opportunity to be me can be received as a step towards a greater openness of community and a greater opportunity of sharing in the one bundle of life into which we are all called for the fulfilment of all. Similarly, every threat to community, at whatever level we are involved in it, can be received as a challenge to live into the Resurrection, to be part of a bringing of death to that which impedes community, to suffer with and for the bringing to life of that which develops community. Every development of community is itself a sign of the Resurrection to be received with thankfulness and hope and to be used for still wider building and sharing.

But there will come a time when we find our identity finally threatened by the inevitable fact of death. Our hopes of building community will seem decisively checked by the ineluctable facts of human nature and the tangles of politics, indifference and greed. It is then our faith in the Resurrection will be finally put to the test. If God has raised up Jesus, then we shall find that it is the threats and the checks which are temporary and the identity and the community which are final and everlasting.

PART THREE

Concerning being a Christian

I | *How much Doctrine do We Need?*

Questions – that is what we are faced with at every turn. Everything is under question. The word 'God', it seems, is either a meaningless noise or else describes simply one's attitude to the world. Morality, whether it be new, old, or indifferent, is constantly under fire. Society is rapidly changing – yet in what direction and what, if anything, can or should be done about that direction is not at all clear. The church, the university, the educational system and well-nigh everything else is being questioned and questioning itself. Nothing is to be taken for granted. So much is this so that many people come by sheer exhaustion and bewilderment to the conclusion that there can never be any agreed or any reasonably assured answer to any question of any importance. Hence the only thing to do is to give up asking questions and make whatever you can of whatever section of comparatively ordered life that comes your way.

But there is one simple question which underlies and is relevant to all the questions and all this questioning. It is put to us in every question we now face and it is posed to us in the hour of our death. It is, 'Is man alone?'.

Has man any resources beyond his own for dealing with his life and his living? What is the sum total of the environment in which he lives? What is the last descriptive word about this universe? Are the possibilities and powers available to man, or acting upon man, exhausted by the sum total of the particles or of the quanta of energy which in a real, measurable and definable sense constitute the universe? Is there anything else, or is man, as far as his destiny and his possibilities go, on his own?

To this simple and perfectly understandable question Christians have always had an assured, confident and simple answer – *no*, man is not alone for there is also God. Indeed, first of all there is God, and he is for man. This is the Christian Gospel, which is decisively good news. You are not alone. Over against you and yet wholly with you there is God – and he is for you. He takes your part. And the Christian Gospel goes on to address itself to men in the very midst of their questionings, relativities, uncertainties. Therefore, says the Christian Gospel, since there is God and since he takes man's part, two things follow.

First, the maturity of man, the fulfilment of man is built into the purpose of the universe. Questions – yes: putting to the most radical and disintegrating tests, bewilderment, despair in the face of meaningless evil. Hope, yes, hope destroyed, hope deferred. What can it all come to? How can we speak of 'all' at all? All these questions do rightly arise – radically arise – existentially arise. But since there is God and since he is for man, the making and fulfilment of man is built into the purpose of the universe.

Therefore all complacency is challenged. There is no excuse for accepting situations contrary to humanness. You may never say, 'This is the best we can do . . .'. Nor can anyone, in the end, get away with the cynical repudiation of humanness and humanity. Moreover, the challenge is not only to all complacency which accepts the situation, but also to all despair and indifference which is overwhelmed by the situation. So all despair and indifference is challenged. It is not true that there is no hope, that nothing can be done. Everything that makes for the true maturity and fulfilment of man can be done and will be done, and there is strength available and avenues open to start doing it. Man is not alone; therefore no man dare be complacent, no man need despair, no man may excuse himself with the escapism of indifference.

But the Gospel has a greater challenge and a greater promise even than this. Since man is not alone but there is God and he takes man's part, this maturity of man which is built into the purpose of the universe is an infinite possibility, the possibility of infiniteness. God is, and he is for man: therefore, there is offered to man the possibility of fulfilling all the matured possibilities of this universe in the infinite possibility of the life of God.

In practice, this means that the maturity which is offered to man is always open. There are always further possibilities to be grown into, further possibilities of love, of truth, and of beauty. This is why this maturity is life indeed – true life – everlasting life – the life of infinite possibilities – not an achievement which reaches a static stage of fulfilment and then withers and dies. Since God is and God is for man, there is no end to man's maturity – only more growth into the infinite possibilities of the divine life.

So, to the simple question, 'Is man alone?', the Christian Gospel returns the simple answer *no*. There is God and he is for man. Therefore the maturity of man is both a real possibility and an infinite possibility.

But how do we know? How do we know that this is Gospel? That this is Gospel truth?

Our knowledge is the result of a three-stranded cord woven by the Spirit of God which binds the knowledge and assurance of the Gospel to our hearts and minds. We know because we are told. We know because God finds us. We know because we find God.

We know because we are told. This is the whole *tradition* of the biblical and Christian faith. People believe in God because people believe in God. The Holy Spirit keeps alive a believing community who can meaningfully speak of their belief to others. There has been built up through long and varied experience of living, suffering and praying a way of talking about God which is to be found in the Bible and crystallized into the creeds, doctrines and prayers of the Christian church. This tradition is meaningfully handed on and speaks to us. So we are told about God and his ways and purposes. The Gospel is spoken to us.

But this is not enough. We know also because God finds us. That is to say in some, often more or less hidden, obscure and only occasionally remembered way, we have experienced a

presence, a power, a personality who is with us and for us
and if only that experience could be rekindled we know we
should be sure that God is and he is for us. Maybe we cannot
now pray. But we have truly prayed. Maybe now the inward
but assured presence, like the still small voice of which the
Elijah narrative speaks, is not very evident to us. But he has
been evident. Therefore we know that God has found us and
that he will find us again, and therefore we may know that
the traditional Gospel of which we are told is about a present
and living God. As the Holy Spirit has touched our hearts,
we rightly believe others when they speak in the name of
that Spirit.

But tradition and the experience of God finding us are
bound together into living truth by the fact that not only does
God find us but we also find God. We are called to live our
lives on the policy which the tradition suggests to us and in
the light of such vision as God has given to us. And as we
seek to follow this Christian policy to be obedient to the Holy
Spirit, in company with other Christians brought together by
the Holy Spirit, we sufficiently find that life is enhanced in
this living, experience is deepened and the tradition is
illuminated. And we also find that tradition illuminates our
experience and experience calls us to new policies of Christian
living. So this threefold cord – the tradition; our experience;
the policy of common living – assures us that the Gospel is
indeed true. Man is not alone. God is and he takes our part.

Since we have this assurance, we come finally and briefly
to the needs of the church today. We come to this on the basis
of the Gospel and of our assurance concerning the Gospel
given to us by the Holy Spirit. The church does not need a
Gospel which is 'relevant'. The church is created by the
Gospel and continues to exist because the God of the Gospel
keeps her in existence. What the church needs is to be
faithful to the Gospel, to the God of the Gospel. Christians
are not called to be relevant. If you allow 'relevance' to
determine you, you are being conformed to the world and
man is heading once again for being alone. Christians are
called to be faithful. What the church needs is faith and
obedience to that which constitutes her. Out of this God will

give saving relevance to, and encounter with, the world. But this faith and obedience certainly do demand involvement with the world.

Let me try to illustrate what I mean by referring to the need for dynamic doctrine. Out of the biblical and Christian experience of God, there have been crystallized in the tradition certain central doctrines. Concerning God – the Trinity; concerning God and his relation to the world – the Incarnation; concerning God taking man's part – the Atonement; concerning man – sin and grace; concerning the universe – the doctrine of creation. Now we are told that such doctrines as these are almost, if not entirely, mythological, pictures without any logical reference to reality. Therefore they are unthinkable and irrelevant.

That they have become unthinkable to many people and fossilized into irrelevance for most cannot be denied, or they would not be so lightly written off. But as they are truly part of the tradition which tells us of God and of his Gospel, to write them off is to run the gravest danger of stopping the Gospel being any sort of news, good, bad or indifferent, and of losing our grasp on the very existence of God. What we have to do is to work from the faith which the Gospel gives us – that God is, that he is for man and that consequently his purpose of maturity for man is woven into the universe. On this basis we take the doctrines which the tradition which hands us the Gospel has handed to us and we submit them to the questions which man's speaking of the universe has raised for them, and we submit the current dogmas of man's speaking of the universe to the questioning of the doctrines.

As examples of areas in which this might happen I would mention the following. The doctrine of the Trinity assures us that the Ultimate Reality of the universe (God) is truly personal, for he is rightly to be thought of (although not sufficiently to be thought of) as a really personal unity of an absolute oneness fulfilled in perfect relations and a perfect relationship which *is* oneness. We now have much evidence from psychological and sociological work and elsewhere that personality cannot be reduced either to an individual focus or to a set of social relationships, but must be understood in terms of both. There is clearly much room for dialogue here.

As psychology, psychiatry and the study of man's social relationships give us more and more insight into the mechanism of blame and of guilt and of the part which self-acceptance and acceptance of others must play in developing mature and healthy persons, so we are provided with much that questions and much that illuminates the doctrines of the atonement and the role and purpose of the church as a community based on reconciliation which comes from the acceptance by God of men as they are. Also, the doctrines of the church and the atonement have much to say on these vital questions of human relationships and realities.

Since the doctrine of creation assures us that the world is related to the purpose and pattern of God, we cannot but welcome everything that a valid science validly discerns about that universe. We have to seek to bear witness to scientists that the universe as a whole demands a more worshipful consideration than they sometimes give it. But they have to remind us and, indeed, to inform us for the first time, of much about the universe in many particulars.

So we are called to a faithful and fearless dialogue. Christians must not suffer faithlessly from an inferiority complex and let all the disciplines of science and the social sciences call the tune so much that all the given doctrines are dissolved away – and the Gospel with them. But even more importantly, Christians are forbidden by the heart of their faith, their Lord, the Suffering Servant, to indulge in superiority complexes and think they may dictate to modern investigators what they shall think or what they shall discover. In quietness and confidence we are, in matters of doctrine and of understanding, to open ourselves wholeheartedly to all the questions which modern thought and science put to us or to our doctrines. Where the doctrines truly are part of what God has given us as part of his giving of the Gospel they can only be re-established, re-invigorated and re-illuminated by this openness. And as they are so renewed to us and through us, so these great doctrines will shine afresh with a saving relevance to man in his aloneness. They will once again become the means under God of making it clear to the church and to the world that God is, that he is for man and that man is called to a maturity of infinite possibility in the very life of God himself.

2 | *The Nature of Theology and Theological Education*

In view of what may be called the 'vast fluidity of the theological field' at the moment, it is perhaps desirable that I should outline in a somewhat rash way what my own position, as I understand it at the moment, is. My position is that theology is an entirely valid and, at its heart, distinctive area of study and of human enquiry. By saying 'at its heart distinctive', I mean 'has its own distinctive proper subject or object not in its entirety shared by any other area of study'. The difficulty, of course, is that the proper object of theology must be the proper subject of theology, to wit God, and this creates a quite exceptional number of difficulties. I am sure myself that the word 'God' is the proper name for the Existent and the Existence who wholly transcends all that is normally designated the universe and that in discussing theology I am discussing a proper area of study whose subject is God. I reject as theologically, philosophically and psychologically unsatisfactory all immanentism that cannot be distinguished from pantheism and all process philosophy that is not clear that the source and goal of the process is greater than the process itself. In other words, I believe that the word 'transcendent' in relation to God must have a continuing and unique use. I am further clear that the word 'God' in the use which I have here very crudely indicated and the phrase 'the God and Father of Jesus' designate one and the same Existence. I am not concerned to give any reasons for these positions, but only to indicate what some may call the basis, and others may call the prejudices, from which I approach the subject. Theology is ultimately a properly independent subject because it has ultimately a properly independent object.

But the proper procedure of theological education, as I understand it, needs to be guided by two factors. First, what I may be allowed to call my basis, which I have so crudely and roughly indicated, is extrinsically debatable. I need only touch on some of these areas of debate. We are all familiar with them. There are immense difficulties in the notion of transcendence, and it is a very proper question as to whether the notion of transcendence can be given a continuing and satisfactory content. There is also the question of the relation of this notion of transcendence to the worshipful. The very existence, indeed, of anything which can properly be called worshipful is quite rightly, in many ways, called in question. I myself believe that the atheistic existentialist has a very powerful case, a case which those people who welcome the arrival of atheism in Christianity would do well to examine. For, as Nietzsche knew, the death of God is a much greater tragedy than many of our latter-day atheists have yet discovered. But it may very well be the case that God is dead. There are immense difficulties in continuing the notion of God, in continuing even the notion of the fact that the universe as a whole may be considered as a whole. I see very strong grounds, often, against any sort of rational or idealistic assumption that 'the whole' makes sense. Some things may make some sense some of the time but that there is overall sense to be made seems to me very often to be highly debatable. Further, we know that there are very strong religious traditions other than the tradition of theism, and these are religious traditions that deal with the worshipful and with such matters as values. And then, again, there is the particular point which I put in the form that the word 'God' designates the same existence as the phrase, 'the God and Father of Jesus'. Here we come to the question of what I might be allowed to call the 'hypostatic centrality of Jesus', namely that the person who was designated Jesus is at the very centre of our understanding of God, man and the universe. We know, of course, that this is extrinsically debatable and that there are good grounds for wondering whether it is either nonsense or overweening arrogance. Therefore, the basis for theology, for Christian theology, for the sort of theology which I think it proper for us to be concerned with here, is extrinsically debatable. It is under challenge and it is challengeable. This does not mean that it is not true, but the question is at issue and properly at issue.

But not only is it the case that my basis is extrinsically debatable. I think it very important to observe that my basis is, if I may so put it, intrinsically explosive. Transcendence is transcendence, that is to say, it must pass beyond any account that one can give of it, any understanding one may have of it, and one is always committed as much to the *via negativa* as to positive utterance, and it is true that anything which is said about God, if it is truly said about God, must be untrue. Further, theism of the sort with which I believe we have to do in the biblical tradition and in its culmination in Jesus Christ and in its understanding in the Christian tradition – theism of this sort, transcendent as it is, precisely demands immanence and process. The God with whom I believe we have to do is a God who is very present in, and very concerned with, the whole process of the universe. It therefore follows that we are bound to be committed to a constant reconsideration of the meaning of our theological terms as the processes of the universe continue.

And there is a third reason why this basis is intrinsically explosive. That is, that the central figure in our understanding of this humanly speaking, Jesus the Christ, has the form of the servant, and if we consider the form that he took, the life which he lived, we are bound to be confronted with the fact that the dimensions of love are constantly to be extended, that the dimensions of love are explored by the total self-giving of those who love, and therefore that every horizon which we believe defines what we understand about love, which is at the heart of our understanding of God through Jesus, must be an horizon which must always be extended. And, therefore, not only is it the case that the basis of this theology is extrinsically debatable, challengeable by much in the universe and in our own lives and in our own experience, but it is also the case that any true understanding of a theology which is

about such a God as I believe it to be about, is always
bound by its own understanding of this God, its own commitment to the involvement of this God in the world and its
own following of the crucified Jesus, to be constantly blown
apart, to be constantly obliged to rethink and go further.
Therefore, although theology is a proper subject, it cannot be
an isolated subject. It cannot be a subject on its own, and at
any given time and situation the very internal logic, if I may
so put it, of this theology may require it to find its form, the
form in which it expresses itself, the form, therefore, in which
it is to be studied and taught, from other subjects. God is, as
far as we can see, very much committed to and involved in
all those things which are the proper areas of study of the
other subjects.

Therefore, I would seem to be obliged to reformulate my
original way of putting what I have to discuss, namely
theological education. It is true we have to consider education
in theology and ministerial education, but both of these
things have to be considered in the light of the fact that the
ultimate scope of theology, properly so called, must be
universal and that therefore the particular theology which we
can pursue is a proper subject only if it is properly related to
other subjects. What sort of thing, then, would this or does
this imply in practice?

First, by way of preface or introduction, it implies, I am
clear, that in our theological education and in our concern
for theological education we must always start from the
particular place where we happen to be. One of the present
tendencies which I find particularly tiresome is that persons
suppose that because everything is in a state of flux one has to
arrive at some firm ground before one can start going anywhere. Whereas, in fact, the essential theological principle of
involvement requires that we should always have the confidence of knowing that we can start right from where we are.
Not only can we not help starting from where we are, but
above all we must not be afraid of it. The God and Father of
Jesus and what we know about him both licenses and
requires us to start from involvement right where we are, and
to start hopefully and seriously from where we are. The God

and Father of our Lord Jesus Christ licenses this hopeful
starting, because the whole of the biblical revelation makes
clear to us that in some real sense it is precisely out of
historical particularity and situations, as men encounter
them, that God makes himself known and works out his
purpose. The God and Father of our Lord Jesus Christ
requires us to start hopefully with this involvement, because
the incarnation of Jesus makes it clear that God furthers his
purpose by clothing himself, if I may so put it, in ordinary
reality, in ordinary history, not in some specially significant
history.

Here I might break off to observe that it seems to me that
Bultmann's insistence on decisively separating historic
Historie as 'one damned thing after another' from *Geschichte*,
'something which has meaning', is a fundamental gnostic
error, and a destruction of the Gospel. It is precisely because
God is involved in one damned thing after another that we
have the Gospel. Therefore, we must be quite clear – and
particularly clear at a time like this when everybody, even
Oxford, is inventing new syllabuses – that this does not mean
that we wait until we have the perfect syllabus before we do
theology: we do theology by starting from even the impossible
syllabus that we have now, and there must be no looking for
theoretical starting places.

The fact that I have thought it necessary to draw attention
to some intrinsic definitions about theology does not mean
that I suggest for one moment that we have to do anything
like start all over again. There must be no looking for
theoretical starting places; rather, an attempt to be obedient
right where we are, on the basis which we have, moving our
obedience in a certain direction, the direction which is defined
by facing the demands of the situation. The very questioning
of syllabuses can be faithfully and not neurotically undertaken
by seeking to look for the demands of God in Jesus Christ.
And this must be done on the basis of where we are. Therefore, the theology which we are concerned to educate people
in and the theological education which we are concerned to
give must be strictly *emergent* theology. We must not get
ourselves in any way into that very common and insidious

and sapping error of adopting what I call an 'If only . . .'
approach; if only we were able to have brighter pupils, if
only we were able to have better teachers, if only we were
able to understand better what the role of the clergy was, if
only we knew better what we are up to, then. . . . We do not
answer any of those questions until we actually do something
about it. Thus we need an emergent theology. We proceed
from the confidence that it is related to the ultimate given of
God's revelation of himself which climaxes in and through
Jesus Christ, and yet which has to be opened to the future
fulfilment of God's purposes for the universe.

Then, when we come to consider this emergent theology,
we are confronted with the fact that the basis of our theology
is extrinsically debatable, and that requires that our emergent
theology should be *open* theology; a theology which takes care
that it makes use of the given of all that has been passed on
in the Bible, and in addition is open to all the questions put
to it by the world. Doctrine cannot be taught without openness to philosophy, the Bible cannot be taught without openness to history, the doctrine of the church cannot be taught
without openness to sociology, and much else in each case of
course – these are examples only. The doctrines of man and
of the Atonement cannot be taught without openness to
psychology. And openness must be *openness*, so that there may
be a real encounter between the data of the tradition, the
data which lie behind and give birth to the record of the
Bible, the worship and understanding of the church and our
present faith, and the data of the current world, the questions
which are validly proposed by any valid discipline, as it is at
present validly practised. Of course, taking current disciplines
seriously does not necessarily mean taking them at their own
evaluation. Each new advance in a particular field of human
study tends to suffer for a while from *hybris*, a thing which
theology permanently suffers from. So we can throw no
stones. None the less, I think truth requires that one should
be aware that there is no necessary need to take any particular
development at the face value of the discoverers or developers.
But they had better be given a hearing because they are
likely to know better than us what they are up to. Therefore,

there must be real openness. And I am much inclined to the
view that in theological education the precise syllabus hardly
matters. It must clearly fall within a certain area, but as long
as the syllabus gives time for openness and the method of
openness is applied – then, I suspect, theology will be done.
What we have to be careful about is that there is no escape
into mere theology, theology on its own, which is no theology
at all because it is not about God, but is the biblical version
of either classical or oriental studies or archaeology. There is
a detached study about what some men thought in some way,
at some time, about some being who might be called God.
This may well be a perfectly proper study, but on its own it
is not theology. Theology is about the actual relationship of
God to actualities and the study of archaeology, history or
other men's concepts is simply a means to that end,
theologically speaking.

Further, not only do we require an emergent theology and
an open theology, we have to take into account the fact that
our basis is not only extrinsically debatable but also intrinsically explosive, as I have sought to indicate, and therefore
our emergent theology, which must be open theology, must
be *broken* theology. Perhaps this hardly needs illustrating in
view of what I said earlier. But in view of the Godness of
God, we have to be clear that in our doctrine we are
concerned as much with an apophatic way, a way of denial, a
way of having to warn ourselves that we must go beyond, as
with a cataphatic way, a way of statement and affirmation.
And in this connection we have to be quite clear that it is
impossible to do theology apart from a spiritual discipline
which is related to worship and prayer. If you want the cash
value, if I may be allowed to use that term, of the word
'God', you can get nowhere near it without worship and
prayer, and I cannot see how any theology can be done
except by men who worship and pray. But even that means,
or that means more than ever, that we are confronted with
necessary brokenness. In this area of theology shading into
worship and prayer, I think we are confronted with the same
sort of problem as the scientist or any seeker after the truth
has, when he comes into the area where he knows he is

encountering his responsibility for truth, to the facts which
build up into the truth. There is a commitment here without
which there can be no real theology, and this demands
brokenness, and because theology demands brokenness, there
is no real tension between commitment to theology and open
theology. That is the way forward, I am sure, in the matter
of theology in a secular university or indeed in a secular
world. If we are true to our theology, we must be so open
that we cannot be accused of wrongly distorting the secular
possibilities. That, any rate, is the goal; that, at any rate, is
the ideal. In practice it is much more difficult. Since also, as
I have said, we must be concerned with immanence and with
process, it will always be the case that in our theology we
shall never know in theory, only in practice, where to draw
the line. Where *do* you draw the line? The answer is, 'you
don't know until you try', and it is no excuse for holding back
from such an inquiry that once you start you don't know
where you're going to stop, because if there is a God and if
he has made himself known in Jesus Christ and if the Holy
Spirit is still the personal presence of such a God, then we
shall not all go over the precipice. And if there is not a God
then we should be thankful that we do go over the precipice.
But we cannot suppose that in advance we may draw a line
on mythology, on restatement of doctrine, on reconsideration
of morals, though we must be clear that since there is a God
we shall find a line to draw.

Thirdly, on this matter of broken theology: since we are
concerned with him who is in the form of the servant, we
must be quite clear that our theological method involves
quite as much listening as speaking. Theology cannot and
must not claim an empire. She is not the queen of the sciences
but the servant of all, at the service of other subjects in which
we have to enable the terms of our service to emerge. For
example, it is quite hopeless to suppose that we may dictate
to psychology, psychiatry and so on the way in which we
shall discuss human nature. On the other hand, when
theology has listened to what these disciplines have to say,
then she will be ready to make her contribution by maintaining that human nature cannot be discussed without the

insights that lie behind, and are sometimes expressed in, such things as the doctrine of the Atonement and the doctrine of Original Sin.

So theology is a proper subject, but to proceed properly it must be emergent, open and broken. What, then, of the actual practice of theology at the present time? There are signs of a concern to rebuild syllabuses and to construct departments which will be much more immediately related to the practical situation as we now have it, rather than to the situation as we have inherited it. Thankfully, there is a good deal of looking for openness, a good deal of concern that the boundaries between theology and other subjects should be fully explored, and, as far as possible, integrated and opened up to one another. But I am not at all sure that many of us are really very ready for what I would call positive brokenness, that is to say a real readiness to reconsider our whole position which does not stem from a weak belief that the positions have been dissolved into other positions, but from positive belief that a very costly openness is required if we are to enter fully into our heritage. There is, I think, in many areas still a fear of commitment, still a tendency to retreat into scholarship in the name of keeping up standards, when it is not at all clear that this is really the issue. However, it ought to be noted here that there is a failure of nerve in very many subjects at the moment, and a refusal to venture outside any very small area of specializing in which certainty can reasonably be obtained. Here there is a great opportunity for theology to be bold. For theology, because she believes in God, must believe that there is still the possibility of building towards a synthesis, of getting something unified out of human studies. Theology, therefore, might very well play an important part in recovering the nerve of the studies in universities where people have withdrawn more and more into their own compartments. There are signs elsewhere that others are becoming aware that this compartmentalization must stop. The way in which theology responds to this opportunity constitutes a challenge, and could become a judgment.

If one turns to theological colleges, it is possible to see a considerable desire to emerge into openness and a readiness to take up subjects which clearly both bite into Christian tradition and bite into our present problems. Many of the demands and unrest and debates about what goes on in theological colleges arise out of the desire to be more open and to have the whole of our training much more directly related to the problems which God is pressing upon the church. It is also clear that there are very interesting experiments going on between particular theological colleges and groups of theological colleges and practical studies in such areas as mental hospitals, relations with social services and so on.

But while there are many hopeful signs of experimentation, there are a number of grounds for concern.

The first is that it still seems to be the case that over a large area of theological college thinking, 'theology' is itself a dirty word. I imagine that the blame for this must fall on persons like myself who are supposed to be academic theologians. We have not yet recovered our nerve about the proper role of theology within all our other concerns, so as to be aware that all our concerns have to be theologically aligned and orientated if they are to be true and proper concerns for the Christian church and the Christian ministry. And then there is, I suspect, no desire to emerge very far; there is too much readiness to fall back on the saying, 'Prepare me for the job', – the picture of the job being some image in people's heads rather than the rather alarming prospect that there is actually on the ground. It is not at all plain that people are really sufficiently confident in their faith to prepare for the openness, let alone for the brokenness, which real theology and valid ministerial training today requires. Further, it is to be questioned how colleges can face the rigours of responding to the situation at the present when their staffs are so clericalized. I am bound to say that I myself find much more interesting theology going on, though it is not always recognizable immediately, when I am mixed up with certain types of debate among psychologists, psychiatrists, economists, than when I am mixed up in most of the debates with my theological colleagues. Surely, until the laity are playing a full part in demanding theology and requiring theology and contributing to theology, we shall not get the open and broken theology which we require.

One fact remains. The practice of theology and the practices of theological education require a great deal of change. It often seems that the Church of England, along with many other churches, is in favour of change as long as it makes no difference. For making differences involves risking what you have. But failure to risk what one has for the sake of development shows lack of faith in the viability and validity of what we have. We have to recover our theological nerve sufficiently to put our theology really at risk. Until we risk theology as emergent, open and broken, theology will be neither educationally exciting nor excitingly educational.

3 | Ethics, Authority and the Christian Tradition

If we are to live with questions, we have to work out methods for facing the questions. What follows is a barely edited version of an introduction to part of a syllabus for the teaching of Christian ethics in the theological colleges of the Church of England. It is included here because it is a working attempt to reflect on the ways in which some Christians should be helped to prepare themselves to face, and help others to face, questions of behaviour and morals.

We have to consider what approach should be adopted in preparing candidates for the ordained ministry of the church for their role in relation to Christian behaviour. What resources have they to draw on and, therefore, with what material ought they to be put in touch? What is the type of authoritativeness which this material has and, consequently, with what type of authority should the ordained minister hope to fulfil his part in this particular sphere? The assumption of the approach outlined is that traditional formulae in the ethical sphere and traditional appeals to traditional authorities no longer carry weight or are relevant simply by virtue of their traditional form. Therefore, it is neither realistic nor relevant to attempt to teach Christians ethics on the basis of some traditional scheme, however classical or biblical it may be. This is to say nothing about the reality or relevance of the authority underlying the traditional approaches. Nor is it to be taken as denying the importance of the insights involved in the traditional formulations. In fact, the need is to evolve methods of teaching and thinking which will enable Christians with teaching and pastoral

responsibilities to see through the traditional forms to the
abiding authority and continuing insights which are their
raison d'être. Hence the method which the following discussion
seeks to outline is as follows:

Basic imperative: Attend to what is given.

(*a*) It is assumed that God has given a revelation of himself
to and through his chosen people, the record of which is to be
found in *the Bible*.

(*b*) It is also assumed that God has not left his people
without the guidance of the Holy Spirit in facing up to the
problems of Christian obedience and Christian witness during
the course of their history and that the record of this is to be
perceived in *the history and tradition of the church*.

(*c*) It is also assumed that the questions which are posed to
the church by the world through developments in thought,
science, technology, psychology, sociology, comparative
religion and so on are not meaningless or purely accidental.
It is assumed that, despite the complications and confusions
of sin, the world is God's world and that God remains at
work in it. It is therefore assumed that his present word can
be heard by attentive listening to current questions in their
contemporary form. Hence included in the given there is *the
challenge of the situation*.

Therefore the basic imperative – attend to what is given –
is held to involve:

attend to *the Bible*
attend to *the history and tradition of the church*
attend to *the challenge of the situation*.

Next it is assumed that there is a sense in which the whole
life of a theological college is conducted explicitly or
implicitly in the context of *the challenge of the situation*, and that
the focus of formal instruction is *the Bible* and *tradition*. These
have to be studied in such a way that the material contained
in them is readily available for the encounter with *the challenge
of the situation*.

It is suggested that in the sphere of ethics this involves a
procedure such as the following:

Study *the morals* actually commended and practised in the

Bible and in the Christian tradition.

Consider *the ethics* which are implied by or were stated to lie behind this morality.

Analyse *the theology* presupposed by or held to be determinant of this ethical understanding.

Morals is taken as meaning the actual conduct commended and practised as a matter of fact. Morals has to do with the decisions taken and the advice given in matters of conduct, individual and corporate.

Ethics is taken as referring to reflection and analysis on the matter of morals. It is concerned with generalization on the one hand and justification on the other. What *classes* of action are taken to be right? What *type* of advice *ought* to be given? Why?

Theology is taken to refer to the systematic understanding of the Gospel and of the Christian revelation in general which has to be brought to bear on the '*Why?*' questions in ethics and the practice of decision-taking and putting into action in morals.

The above three formulations are simply put out as rough and ready definitions for the purpose of clarification in formulating a method. They are not systematic statements of what the words do, in practice, mean or ought to mean. Such a threefold division is clearly artificial in practice. Also, the application of it to any particular area of morals or ethical inquiry will be found to require a blurring of the distinctions. But some such analytical tool as this is required if the bridge is to be found from what was done, required, judged under those circumstances to what is to be done, required, judged under these circumstances. Not many people are very good at sustained efforts at analysis. So handling three elements related to two different sets of circumstances ('now' and 'then') may seem to guarantee bewilderment. But a clear understanding of the method should prevent this, for the questions which need to be raised are always related to practice.

The starting point is an 'area of moral botherment' – where people clearly go wrong, are said by some to go wrong, or wonder what is right or wrong. Such an area is sufficiently identifiable in practice. Then it is necessary to identify a similar-looking area in the Bible and in the tradition. One is then already passing from 'morals' to 'ethics', because questions of classification are involved. One has to show why it is correct to look for ethical help in *this* area of modern moral botherment in *that* area of biblical or later tradition. While one is doing that it will be found that the theological questions are already arising. For an important reason for holding that *that* area of ethical teaching is relevant to *this* area of moral concern is that it can be shown that both here and there the same questions are being faced about obedience to God in Christ through the Spirit. The essence of the method is that it is an attempt to find a practical way of bringing together what is given in the Bible and the Christian tradition with what is given in the challenge of the situation so that God may be heard and obeyed. A way back to a fresh start when the inquiry has run into bewilderment is therefore always to re-ask the question, 'But what is to be done?'. If it is borne in mind that the rest of this discussion of 'Ethics and the Christian Tradition' is meant to contribute material for such a method of working, it may be possible to find something helpful in it.

First, however, it is necessary to face the problem of authority. This is a problem of which every reflective Christian cannot but be aware. It is clear that in the foreseeable future Christians will have to live with this problem and with the fact that there is disagreement among themselves about the precise nature of the authority which is proper to Christianity. What is true of Christians at large is true of the Church of England within her own life. Anyone who has to write about teaching Christian ethics finds himself right in the middle of the question of authority. Clearly there must be a specific place in any syllabus or outline for considering the question.

(i) Authority cannot be confined to a particular topic. It is involved and implied at every turn. If the method of study is in any way related to considering moral behaviour with a view to ethical analysis and theological insight, then the practical understanding of authority is constantly involved.

What *weight* is given or to be given to traditional ethical formulations? What is the *source* of our systematic theological understanding and how *given* are its forms – or even its content? It will be necessary, therefore, to include in the process of teaching over the whole range of Christian Ethics a clarification of the position with regard to authority. What standpoint on authority is implied by, read out of or read into the material immediately under discussion? It is not necessary constantly to be seeking to justify the position habitually taken up on the matter. That would be to show lack of faith and would tend to lead to paralysis of action. But it is necessary to be *aware* of the position taken up and to be aware that, at any rate to those who do not take that position, it is not its own justification.

(ii) If follows from what has just been said that it is impossible to write a document such as this present one without taking and implying a position on authority. For the sake of clarity, the present writer's position is here stated, although in a somewhat crude, over-simplified and therefore possibly shocking form:

(*a*) In practice there is no available, applicable and absolutely infallible authority in Christianity. (This point *must* be read with the point to be mentioned last.)

(*b*) It is not legitimate to suppose that there comes a point at which it is possible to obtain absolute clarity and complete assurance by hearing a voice which says either (i) 'The church has spoken' – whether that voice is the voice of Rome or any other which claims to be a defining voice, or (ii) 'It is in the Bible' – however that voice may claim to speak the true, simple and fundamental meaning of the allegedly relevant and decisive biblical texts.

(*c*) Despite the prophetic achievement and theological insight of Karl Barth, the proper biblical and Christian understanding of man does not require us to demote reason to the role of a slave of revelation.

(*d*) It is therefore necessary and Christian (and not merely Anglican and old-fashioned) to rely on the inter-action of the trio of Scripture, Tradition and Reason under the guidance of the Holy Spirit in the fellowship of the *corpus mixtum* of believers.

(*e*) God will see to it that his servants are given sufficient authoritativeness to bear witness to the emptying and the exaltation of his Servant, sufficient forgiveness to restore them to effective service despite repeated failures, and sufficient grace to enable them to make a creative use in his name of their share in the bewilderments of the world.

One's position on the points outlined above is directly relevant to the way in which it is thought possible for the study of moral data to lead via ethical reflection to theological insight. Conversely, that position determines or at least reflects on the manner in which theological understanding is held to influence that ethical reflection which provides a critique of moral decisions. How *does* revelation relate to conduct? What *is* the defining effect of the Christian Gospel on the imperatives of daily life? If we were certain of the answer to these questions we should already be enjoying the Beatific Vision. As it is we tackle the questions obliquely from a number of differing positions. Training in Christian ethics is thus very largely to do with training in self-awareness. We must become aware of precisely what it is we are doing or trying to do and of why we think we ought to try to do it. Trained self-awareness leads to sensitivity of application and openness to correction.

But enough has probably been said to show why all these pages on the Christian tradition are concerned more with method than with content and with merely pointing to areas in which the content is to be found. It will also be clear why, in the discussion which follows, there is space spent on natural law and ordinary human fairness and a dismissal of total depravity. They follow from the writer's theological understanding. Those who hold that it is a misunderstanding will know how to decontaminate the material to put it to a safe use. *None the less* the material and the method remain available for and suitable to those who stand in any tradition. Teaching must clearly be done from a position. But the position must include the knowledge that the position is

challenged and challengeable (*cf.* 'what is given – the
challenge of the situation').

There is a further preliminary questioning. Why 'Christian'
ethics only? The challenge of the situation includes the
challenge of non-Christian ethical traditions including
Humanism (so-called), Marxism and the religions and
philosophies of the East. Further, the theology referred to
above implies that such traditions are sources of real insights.
It has, however, not seemed practicable in any way to
prescribe them for study. Any teacher who can include in his
material apposite references to and comparisons with these
other (very living) traditions is clearly to be encouraged to do
so. Indeed, teaching by contrast is highly fruitful and
stimulating, both paedagogically and theologically. The
matter is mentioned here simply as a reminder that it is not
and cannot be forgotten. It is to be hoped that it is hardly
necessary to add that inaccurate comparisons and the setting
up of Aunt Sallies is worse than useless – theologically and
ethically.

The assumptions and method of the approach having been
referred to, what follows is an attempt to argue further the
state of the question with regard to Christian ethics.

The concern of Christian ethics

Christian ethics is concerned with the connections between
the character of God and the doings of men. God is God. He
is therefore the ultimate reality of the universe. This being so,
he is the ultimate concern of every being self-conscious enough
to be aware of him and capable of responding to him. Hence
he must be decisively relevant to every act of every man. The
ethics, therefore, of believers in God must be basically concerned with the perception and application of this relevance.
Christians are believers in God who are convinced that the
recognition of Jesus of Nazareth as the Messiah expected by
the Jews was correct and that consequently Jesus Christ is
Lord. This means that it is Jesus who is the crux and the
focus, both as to definition and as to fulfilment, of the
purpose of God, the Lord of all, for his universe. Christian
ethics, therefore, will be concerned with bringing to bear on

the conduct of men the understanding of and response to God which Jesus Christ fulfils, requires and makes possible.

Christian ethical formulations

In the course of history, various formulations and formulae of Christian ethics have been produced. They have been held to be statements that in some way or other are derived from this Christian understanding of the character of God which reaches its full development in the things connected with Jesus. They are attempts distilled from the experience of the church to give more or less authoritative interpretations of how this understanding should influence the patterns and particularities of human life in the world. But the underlying reality of these ethical generalizations is not now readily perceived by very many Christians, let alone non-believers. Their precise contemporary relevance and application is also a source of much perplexity.

The Gospel and law

Clearly the status and role of laws, lawlike statements and the concept of law, as such, is a subject which is an important part of any study of Christian ethics. This subject has specific mention in the syllabus which follows, and it must also clearly be borne in mind whatever specific topic is being considered. But the syllabus does not provide extensive references to current debates about 'situation ethics' and the like. It is assumed that awareness of the questions raised, for example, in Chapter Six of *Honest to God*, will be part of that 'challenge of the situation' to which the introduction refers and that every teacher (and every student) will conduct his work on Christian ethics in this awareness. The way in to effective participation in such debates is to study the Christian tradition, from which material must be drawn one way or another to contribute to the settlement of such debates. (In practice, it is more a question of making possible effective living and the effective giving of guidance in the midst of such unsettled debates!)

Some sort of generalizing must be possible and necessary in the field of ethics, as in any other sphere of human experi-

ence. Unless generalization is possible, valid experience
cannot be passed on. The question is one about the role, as
much as about the possibility, of ethical formulation. And this
question can hardly be tackled with any degree of competence
by those who have no knowledge whatever of what formulations have been made, what they have been thought to do
and to what extent they can be held to have been successful
and unsuccessful. There is little reason to suppose that we are
wiser than our fathers, however certain it is that we live under
conditions and with presuppositions different from theirs.

What is the connection between God and goodness?

So the suggested method is to attend to what is given. The
sources upon which actual Christian ethical thinking has to
be based must be investigated. Some examples of the actual
development of such thinking need to be tested. Thus we may
hope to obtain material for such thinking today. In approaching this study, it is necessary to notice that ethical insights
seem sometimes to be derived from an understanding of the
character of God, while sometimes it seems that an understanding of the character of God is derived from ethical
insights. Take, for instance, the question, 'Which does God
prefer, mercy or sacrifices?' It is clear that the God and
Father of our Lord Jesus Christ *must* prefer mercy to sacrifices
(argument from the character of God to behaviour – God
requires goodness). But it is equally clear, at least after a
certain stage in ethical development, that if one reflects on
the ethical worth of merciful behaviour and of a sacrificial
routine, then God, if he *is* God, *must* be the sort of Being who
is more concerned with mercy than sacrifices (argument from
ethical insight to the character of God – goodness must belong
to God). Attempts to portray God as requiring what sensitive
consciences know to be barbarous and immoral, some would
say, have played and do play their part in keeping people
from belief in God.

The presuppositions of a critical study of Christian ethics

But to put the matter in this way is already to have taken
up a position on the question of the relation of revelation to

conduct. It is to assume that human reason in the form of developing human sensitivity does have its part to play in relation to biblical and church tradition. This is in accordance with the theological position briefly outlined in discussing the problem of authority. Whether that position is more or less accepted, or totally rejected, it is still necessary to be aware of the questions and of the form of one's answer to it. It might be expressed by asking how far ethics is to be thought of as a self-determining (autonomous) discipline in which basic questions of definition cannot be settled by an authoritarian appeal to revealed concepts *as revealed* and independently of their ethical value. Those who hold that (alleged) revelation cannot be judged by human ethical insights but must always *determine* human ethical insights must be clear what they are doing, why they are doing it and whether they can succeed in doing it consistently (e.g. is there never any question of evaluating different parts of the Bible differently for purposes of ethical instruction, or, in practice, does not every tradition exercise ethical insights on the Bible as well as receive them from the Bible?). This question must be consciously faced and an answer to it knowingly formulated, or there can be no hope of a coherent approach to Christian ethics, nor can there be any hope of an authoritative commendation of Christian ethical insights to a secular world. Is it ethically sufficient (i.e. is it moral?) to commend anything whatever on the sole grounds that God requires it – apart from a consideration of whether it is, in some sense, in its own right moral or not?

Ethics, the way things are and natural law

Such questions are not merely theoretical, but are particularly forced upon us when the challenge of the situation includes the fact that the authority of Christian revelation is not taken for granted. We have to be clear ourselves about what is involved in Christian morality. We have also the task of upholding it and commending it at large. For it is arguable that our concern as Christians is not ultimately with Christian morality but with universal morality (or, alternatively, that morality which is truly Christian – which is not necessarily the same thing as what any particular body of Christians alleges to be Christian morality – is universal morality). For Christian ethics, as we have seen, is concerned with the relevance of the character and being of God to the lives of men, and God is the ultimate concern of *all* men. Hence, the relationship of that which God wills and that which men (of various races, cultures, classes, etc.) hold to be good is of peculiar importance.

In this connection, consideration might perhaps usefully be given to a whole set of possibilities which either have been associated with or might be associated with the notion of 'natural law'. As part of this process of taking human ethical insights seriously (whatever caution our understanding of sin may require), attention should also be given to the ideas which men have of what is 'just', 'decent', 'fair'. Certainly such ideas are not sufficient for the Christian understanding of man. And there is the further question posed by the failure of men to live up to even the ideas which they have. None the less, in such ideas there may be found points of contact between believers and unbelievers. Moreover, it is necessary to investigate very carefully and sympathetically areas of alleged Christian doctrine and Christian ethics which seem to be totally contradictory of notions of fairness or decency. It is not always the common ideas of decency and justice which are found to be condemned by such an investigation.

Christians are clear that there is one universal constant in every situation who is relevant to every existent and every moment of existence, namely God. Whether one is suspicious of or sympathetic to many of the categories of traditional doctrinal and moral theology, the concept of what is 'natural' to man must be both meaningful and relevant, whether 'natural' means *what is inherent in* or *what is required by* the situation of being a man. Further, in any understanding of anthropology which is Christian, God must be relevant to what is natural to man and God must also be in some way or other and up to some point perceptible in what is natural to men. (The doctrine of total depravity being, as has been explained, rejected.) To put it another way, God must be absolutely relevant to what man *ought* to be (*pres*criptive sense of 'natural'), and must be to some extent perceptible in what men *are* (*des*criptive sense of 'natural').

The human animal, man, is distinguished from other animals precisely by the fact that there is a query about how the word 'natural' should apply to him. Purely animal conduct on the part of man is rightly called 'bestial' and condemned thereby. No other animals can have their behaviour described as 'bestial', for it is natural for them to behave like beasts. But what is natural for men is the subject of endless debate. Hence the need to consider the distinction between a descriptive use of 'natural' (the only use proper to all other animals – relating to habitat, physiology, etc.) and a prescriptive use which implies that men can somehow 'fall below' what they are capable of doing and being. The Christian doctrines of Creation and the Fall imply some link and some discontinuity between these two meanings. The assumption made here is that there is no total discontinuity in anyone who remains a man.

So it is contended that against the complete relativism of some anthropology, sociology and moral philosophy, a Christian must hold that it is possible to perceive certain general ethical insights which are common to all men, however much the mode of their expression is conditioned by all the relevant and relative factors in each society. Moreover, the more anthropology, sociology, psychology and other disciplined scientific inquiries enable us to understand the factors which both shape and distort men and societies, the more it should become possible to perceive the basic lineaments and requirements of being human which are natural and essential to men. Hence anyone concerned to understand, develop and make use of Christian ethics has the keenest possible interest in all that can be discovered about the facts of 'human nature', *viz.* information, scientifically determined, about what 'men are really like', about the way they actually behave and are influenced to behave. Somewhere in what men actually do conceive to be their ultimate concerns must be some inklings of what truly is their ultimate concern. And what truly is men's ultimate concern depends on what is ultimately really the case. To use 'old-fashioned' (but possibly simpler) terms, *being* is prior to *value*. If it is the case that God is the context and end of all men, then values, valuations and choices which ignore this fact or interpret it wrongly must be distorted and cause distortions. On the other hand, some trends in values, valuations and choices will reflect this ultimate factual situation even if it is not recognized for what it is.

Thus the notion of natural law is relevant to Christian ethics in at least three ways. First, there is the concern for what *are* the perceived laws of human behaviour (i.e. what general statements can be based on observation and investigation?). Secondly, there is the concern for what are the *requirements* of human behaviour if men are to respond to and be made fit for God. And thirdly, there is the concern to lead men to see the relevance and force of the requirements of Christian living by showing their continuity with (and *then* their fulfilment and re-direction of) that which men already tend to recognize as requirements. And, conversely, there is the need to check any *a priori* statements about what is universally required of all men against the facts of human nature and behaviour as they are descriptively known to us. There is, of course, the question of the role of sin in distorting and of grace in perfecting situations. But any moral theology or Christian ethics must pay attention to the *facts of the case*, both at the level of the autonomy of the physical, biological, psychological and social sciences and at the level of the understanding of man and God given through Jesus by the Spirit. Otherwise there is grave danger of producing only so much irrelevant pontification. Hence, the importance of the idea of natural law, despite the difficulties, ambiguities and abuses of the term.

Relating the unchanging character and purpose of God to problems of morals

While studying the material for and the tradition of Christian ethics, one must always be trying to see the reference to the universal constant of relationship to God. How is it reflected in the specific requirements recorded in the Bible and in the various incidents in the biblical records?

What is the insight behind codifications, laws and the Christian tradition at large? The task of perceiving this universal imperative (stemming from the unchanging nature of God) 'embodied' in the particular imperatives and judgments which men have believed themselves to be receiving or rejecting is no easy one. Social and other conditions change, and scientific knowledge which was not previously available becomes more and more extensive. The men whose experiences are recorded as normative for Christian thinking (i.e. the men of the Bible) and those whose opinions are held in some way to be traditionally authoritative knew of none of these things. Hence the need to get through the time-conditioned form to the abiding content becomes more and more urgent. This can be done by developing a sensitivity to and perceptiveness of the crux of obedience to God which lies at the heart of a commended action or pattern of actions. And even when and if this vital and unchangeable *'inwardness'* is perceived, there is still the problem of the necessary insight to see how this is to be 're-embodied' in the changed circumstances and changed understandings of today. Hence it must be clearly understood that the study of Christian ethics cannot be a detached academic study of the history of ideas. It is in fact a spiritual discipline which must be closely allied to the practice of Christian discipleship. The basic and committed motive of the study must be to search the records of what men have held to be required of them by the God who is ultimately known as the Father of our Lord Jesus Christ in order that we may understand what he requires of us now.

Ethics and practice

As we have seen, the Christian belief and contention is that the facts of the case always include the fact that God is the proper context and end of all human activity. Therefore, there must always be in fact a connection between the being and nature of God and right and proper conduct. But the question is how to perceive this connection, how to relate knowledge of God to human conduct in general and my, your or their behaviour in particular. In this connection, it has been argued that full consideration must be given to the way in which knowledge of God and understanding of his demands often comes from facing the ethical demands of current situations and considering current ethical insights. Approaching current situations with ready-made 'insights' which are, in fact, not 'tailor-made' (nor God-given!) for those situations may be more irresponsible than moral. In fact the method of obtaining the sensitivity and insight referred to in the previous paragraphs is very probably to allow our present ethical questionings and difficulties to force us back into an investigation of the biblical record and the Christian tradition to see what in them speaks to our condition.

In the course of the study of 'Ethics and the Christian Tradition', the question must be faced about the ideal and practicable model of the Christian (individually or collectively) tackling problems of behaviour. Is it correct to visualize him or her or the church, as having a ready-made set of ethical insights codified into injunctions obtained directly from 'revelation' which are then applied to situations? How are these situations recognized as requiring this particular application of this particular set of injunctions? It is not clear that the answer to this problem is flatly negative on 'revealed rules' and on some system of casuistry which endeavours to pass on experience of the insights required for their application. But it is clearly necessary to have a working model of some method of approach to the whole problem which 'engages' both with the Christian tradition and with the present human situation and does not simply aim formulae alleged to enshrine God's will at a situation from without. Above all, there must be openness to the Spirit.

It is not easy to perceive or to determine the work of the Holy Spirit in evoking in Christians individually or corporately this ethical sensitivity to the demands of God and to the appropriate and relevant responses to him to which reference has had to be made. But it is clear that it is only faith in the present working of the Spirit which makes the study of Christian ethics and the living of the Christian life a practicable proposition at all. Formalism and over-traditionalism may seek faithlessly to confine the Spirit to formulae and methods of approach which he has used (and may still use) as part of a wider whole. But those who are resigned to complete relativity and the incapacity to give or receive any corporate guidance would seem to be at least equally faithless. Training in Christian ethics must be designed to enable men to form, under God, a working hypothesis on these matters from which they can start to play their part in assisting in the ministry of the church to the world.

Clearly all our study must be made with some understanding of these questions raised by our present situation. This study, it has been argued, must aim at directing attention to (*a*) the material available and (*b*) the methods suitable for formulating a coherent ethical *policy*. We are concerned with the development of a conscious and disciplined way of living which seeks to bring to bear the Christian understanding of God on the life of men in the world. There must be no anxiety in this study nor in the uncertainties which surround many of its details. We are not concerned what to do or what to counsel others to do in order that we may be acceptable to God. Rather, on the basis of God's saving work in Jesus, we are seeking to be responsive and obedient to the task which in the Spirit we are given to do. We are not looking for the key to Christian behaviour. Having that key (Jesus Christ himself in the Spirit), we are looking to discern what avenues of conduct and what patterns of behaviour are therefore open to us.

4 | *To Whom do We Pray?*

The situation with regard to prayer, the spiritual life, knowledge of God, is both far worse than people in the church think and far better. There is no danger of God being dead; the situation is far better than a lot of people seem to think in that respect – or have the courage at any rate to live up to in that respect. But it is far worse than, for instance, the gentlemen who sit on the Anglican Liturgical Commission think.

Most of the church's investigations into the liturgy and the like today are in the form still of escapist activities of persons who will not face up either to God or the world. The main reason people think God is dead is the poverty of the spirituality of the church at large, for spirituality is central to the whole business of belief in God. Therefore, the question to start from is, 'To whom do we pray?'; and the answer is, 'To the God and Father of Jesus Christ'. That is, the God of Abraham, the God of Isaac, the God of Jacob and, as Pascal would say, not the God of the philosophers.

This is the starting-point, because if you start from the God of the philosophers or the fact that the philosophers have now decided there is no God, you are back into the realm of mythology, for all metaphysics are mythology. They represent the tales that men have told about the world on the basis of what they have thought the world to be – or what they might think the world to be. Thus scientific metaphysics are also mythology. But Abraham is probably not mythology; Isaac and Jacob might be; Jesus Christ certainly is not. The more I study these matters, the more it is clear to me that the question of starting-point, the question of that which is given, is fundamental, and I remain unrepentantly certain that the only religion which is finally based on anything other than mythology is Christianity. Science in its proper sphere has got something to go on; Christianity has got something ultimately given to go on; everything else is mythology in the end.

So we begin with the God and Father of Jesus Christ; and this is the God of Abraham, Isaac and Jacob. There are really only two possible foci for the spiritual life: one is God himself and the other is me now in the presence of God.

There is no answer to the question, 'To what do we pray?'. This is always the mistake of any sort of substitute-talk like 'ground of being' and so on; you cannot pray to a 'what'. In an address which Paul Tillich gave in the synagogue in New York on the death of Buber, he said that one of the things that Buber taught him was that the term 'God' is a primary term and there is no substitute for it.

I stand by what I understand to be the Augustinian and Anselmian, and I would indeed say Barthian, tradition of spirituality. Unless there is a discovering in encounter of God, then I see no possibility of putting meaning into the symbols of the church, because the symbols of the church are ultimately concerned with response to God, who can be described and defined in no other terms than that he is God. Therefore, unless there is direct encounter with the Reality who is God, there is no evidence for this Reality. And that is why prayer, in its fullest sense of the term, which in the end has got to become living, is at the heart of the matter. Tinkering with symbols is neither here nor there. When you see the problem properly, however, you may well have to do a lot of things with symbols, because any symbols which get in the way of this directness or do not facilitate our opening up to God are a menace.

So we pray to the God and Father of our Lord Jesus Christ, the God who is discovered in encounter, who is vindicated in Jesus, and whose discovery is renewed in experience. To put it bluntly: people believe in God because people believe in God, and if God does not keep people believing in himself, that will be the end of the matter.

This is why I find the focus of prayer – or I should say the
foci of prayer, which are in the end the same thing as the foci
of life – in the two areas which I would for convenience call
worship and grace. Worship stands for the response to the
supremely valuable, ultimately transcendent personalness,
who is God. Worship directs us to the reality and worthwhileness of God as God. If you say, 'We can only worship
now through working', and so on, you have at once made sure
that you will not have a proper use for the word 'God'. I am
not saying for a minute that the worship of God does not
demand work – that is another matter; but one focus of
prayer is worship, which in this context stands for the fact
that God is God. There is this indefinable 'other' who is God,
who is best described as the Father – the God and Father of
Jesus Christ – and to whom we are making response; and
the end of the response is God, just as the beginning is, I am
increasingly convinced, philosophically and practically, that
either this is true or everything is nonsense. In the end
language will not hold together, science will not hold together,
certainly psychology will not hold together, community will
not hold together, people will not hold together, humanity
will not hold together if everything has to be described in
terms of something else which requires something else to
describe it in terms of.

It occurred to me the other day as I was gazing in a tube
train at that poster which says 'There is no substitute for
wool', that if you go carefully into the development of
intellectual thought in the nineteenth century, if you go to
meetings of psychiatrists, psychologists and sociologists, if you
listen carefully to individual secular people who cannot in
truth accept a process that simply goes on and on and on,
then the other slogan to put beside it is 'There is no substitute
for God'. Indeed, to know what truly prayer might mean in a
secular age, we should read Sartre and see if we can do
better than he. For if we can do better than he, then,
providing the human situation is being faced as clearly as he
faces it, we have already got on to praying. Of course, many
people look as though they are doing better than he because
they have not analysed it as he has. Sartre is the man who

knows what it is to be a human being in a secular age in the
sense of 'there is no God'. Many of the Americans who speak
of the 'death of God' do not seem to know what this is at all.
They seem to be people who go around treating the death of
God as if it were a farce or perhaps a comedy. Nietzsche
knew it was a tragedy and went mad, and now Sartre knows
it is a tragedy but has not gone mad.

The other focus of prayer is grace: the awareness, or the
occasional possibility of awareness, or living in the hope that
there might be this awareness, of the presence of an otherness
which gives resources beyond one's own. This is the experience of worthwhileness actually here and now. It is an
experience of the immanence of the transcendent. Our
spirituality must be concerned with evoking and developing
and following up this awareness, this awareness of an otherness which is closer than ourselves. Indeed, the ultimate basis
for prayer must be Trinitarian. That is to say, we are
concerned with the God who is wholly God and therefore
wholly other, who is wholly incarnate in Jesus Christ without
in any way diminishing or detracting from his utter otherness,
and who is also present in personalities and through
personalities as the Holy Spirit. And it is this being taken up
by God for God which saves the whole of life from absurdity.

Prayer, then, is to the God and Father of our Lord Jesus
Christ, who is discovered in encounter, vindicated in Jesus,
and renewed in experience; and this experience has two loci,
worship and grace, in which God the Holy Spirit is imman-
ently at work. Once we have understood this, we may turn to
the question of what prayer means in a secular age. We then
get on to all the difficulties that arise over what is the really
distinctive thing about our secular age, which is its flatness.
We have produced a manner of thinking, which affects many
more people than reflect upon it, which is very largely 'flat'.
It has no room for the notion of transcendence in any way,
and has fallen into the habit of believing that the only way
language works satisfactorily is when it is literal. The model
of meaningful language is the instructions which you can
understand on the back of a television set or the instructions

which you could understand if you had the proper instruction in television mechanism and so on. This is where the whole Christian situation is so much up against it that it has caused people to panic and think that the thing to do is to throw over transcendence instead of to renew spirituality, so that Christians can live so authentically that people will want to learn the language.

It is true that the *Zeitgeist* is against even our authentic symbolism working. For example, people are overwhelmed by arguments like those based on size. Are you going to say that there is a possibility of personal response when the universe is so macroscopically and microscopically vast? But this sort of argument is simply a logical muddle which gains added force from our own psychology. Who has discovered that the universe is so macroscopically vast and so microscopically vast? Man. And there is no logical reason for deciding that what reason has told us obliterates our reason. I know that logical reasons often carry little psychological weight, but they are important with regard to truth, even if less so with regard to persuading people of truth. At any rate, we can be clear that arguments from size ought really to carry no weight. But one of the reasons why they have such an impact on the whole area of prayer is precisely because our spirituality has been so poor and people have largely lost the living awareness of absoluteness, infiniteness, the otherness of God. The spiritual poverty of the church makes it look as if God was the being who existed to keep in order a measurable universe, and now that we know that the universe is immeasurable, we know also that we have no one keeping it in order. Logically this is all wrong, but that does not mean that it is not a problem. It is a matter of authenticity, in the spiritual life as elsewhere. People learn or know that other people can learn about nuclear physics. They realize that beyond a certain stage even most educated people cannot go because only a few people can cope with certain types of mathematics, but they will still believe that those people are on to something because the whole operation is one of authenticity. Similarly, people will learn how to pray – or be prepared to learn how to pray – if it looks as though people who are praying are doing something authentic.

I have already referred to how, in the history of thought and in the present situation with regard to science and psychology, there is the possibility of awareness of mystery when I coined the phrase 'There is no substitute for God'. People in the church at large ought to be clear that there are no decisive reasons for holding that you cannot believe in God and that if we analyse, say, the biological sciences or the philosophical scene or the problems that doctors, social workers, psychiatrists and so on are up against in the community, there is quite as much evidence that no framework will satisfactorily include, explain and satisfy the human as there is evidence that any framework will. Indeed, this is to put the case at its least favourable. I stress this in relation to praying because it seems to me we have to have the nerve to pray, and one of the things which is related to praying in a secular age is the recovery of nerve. It is a pathetic fact, although I think there are understandable psychological reasons for this, but a large number of people are put off doing things or trying things by the sort of general feeling that they would be absurd or nonsensical. We may compare, for example, the frequent current use of the adjective 'thinkable'. I think that the only thing to do when we are told that nowadays we cannot think so and so is to get up and say, 'Oh, can't I? I can'; and if somebody says, 'How can a rational man be a Christian?', the answer is, 'I am a rational man and I am a Christian, therefore a rational man can be a Christian.' I may be no more rational than most and I'm a bad Christian, but there it is.

So there is no substitute for God. But it might be, of course, that although there is no substitute for God there is no God. My present argument is not an argument for the existence of God. I am only pointing out that the existence of God is as much a possibility as atheism. It is here that we see the central importance of praying. The really clinching business about the existence of God is the spiritual life, and you will not find the decisive evidence anywhere else.

Now the problems that arise over the possibility of believing in God in so vast a universe and of 'How can we talk about personal purpose responding to personal purpose in so vast a field?' are, I believe, to be tackled with the help of the unique Christian discovery of the relation between transcendence and immanence, or, if you like, between detachment and involvement, which I was referring to when I touched on the doctrine of the Trinity. If we study how it arose, we see that this doctrine reflects the Christian understanding of what seems to have been the last thing that men wanted to think. Therefore we may be clear that it has been experimentally discovered and is open to experimental vindication. In fact, the doctrine of the Trinity is an experimental doctrine which is related precisely to the question of transcendence and immanence. What those who have popularized the 'death of God' say is absolutely true – God, in his Godness, is to be encountered in the here and now, and God is as fully God hwen he is in the here and now as when he is God in his 'thereness'. The point about most ecclesiastical spirituality, most ecclesiastical use of the Bible, most ecclesiastical activity is that it is neither here nor there. That is, it does not key in with the actual concerns of living men, so it is not here, which is where God is; and it is not there, as it does not really have spiritual depth. To be out of touch with the 'here' is fatal for godly living. The spirituality of Christianity is precisely concerned with the 'here' which has the 'there' in it, and the 'there' which draws us out of the 'here', but not with a 'neither here nor there' in the 'betwixt and be-tween'.

But it might be said, 'Well, in that case, how do you pray?'. The first point to be considered is that contained in the oft-repeated and much-abused slogan of Dom Chapman, 'Pray as you can and don't pray as you can't'. This is not to be interpreted in such a way as to lead to the expectation of 'cheap grace', as seems to happen with many who use the last few pages of Bonhoeffer and do not seem to know about his life. We need to be liberated from the inhibiting burdens of past patterns of prayer still imposed upon us as if they were *the* ways to pray, so that we feel guilty when they do not help us. But prayer remains an activity which requires attention, effort and organization, however much this must be combined with tentativeness and sensibility. We can get a great deal of help from psychological insights into the way in which personalness is liberated. One of the things to be investigated carefully is what can we now learn from psychology about such things as regularity, patterns of praying and so on, in order that people may be liberated and not fettered in realizing the awareness of God in the midst. Everyone who lays down, or who is concerned with helping in, a pattern of prayer knows it is not the pattern that matters; it is whether the pattern will help us get on to something. But even I, in only twelve years of being a priest, have come up against people to whom I have had to say, 'Stop listening to your spiritual director, because until you stop, and stop trying harder and stop trying to fulfil his pattern, there will be no liberation towards the true end – God in you.' We must be set free, and set others free for, flexibility and openness.

One of the things we have to do is to get people to recognize what in their lives is really either praying or very nearly praying anyway. A phrase which helps me in this area is that of 'focused awareness'. 'Focused awareness': helping people to have time or to think it worthwhile to be quiet, to attend to whatever there is to attend to, in the belief that in the end this may lead them to discover that there is one sense in which they have been praying on and off all their lives. The whole question of attention, contemplation, focused awareness is very relevant to spirituality today. Of course, one knows from the history of Christian and general spirituality that this can go either way. Contemplation and awareness are not necessarily personal. We have nature mysticism, oriental mysticism and so on. But this is where the Christian tradition and the authentic living Christian fellowship comes in. I have actually seen, although admittedly on rare occasions, a man who has been set free to attend to what he was nearly attending to anyway, so that he has thereby become aware of what is really the dimension of God and then been able to recognize that this is really also what Christians are trying to be concerned with. But, of course, if there is no focused awareness or its equivalent in the particular Christian com-

munity he happens to be connected with or ever sees, there
never will be a tie-up.

Another aspect of all this is what I would call 'corporate
attention' in the sense of dedication to a common worthwhile
end. This seems to be a way in which many people –
especially young people – have a chance of getting on to the
dimension of God. They are concerned with 'What shall we
do about Vietnam?', 'What shall we do about mental health?',
and so on. And the coming together to work together is
another form of concentration, a form of concentration which
is much more corporate, which is much more a matter of the
will and the emotions and the desire to work something out.
This ties in with the fact that in many ways prayer should be
understood as a form of action rather than as a form of
thought.

The sketchy suggestions touched on here are related to the
earlier part of what has been said by the fact that the initial
assumption was that either God is there and is concerned to
make himself known or there is nothing one can do about it.
The question is, how to develop an awareness of the fact that
God is there. My first way was the individual matter of
focused attention, and the second one was the more active,
corporate attention to a worthwhile end. But we must be
aware that there is no reason why at any given time a
particular person should know that what he is engaged on is
the beginning of a response to a transcendent personality or
personalness. We have to be ready to allow this sort of thing
to go on for a long time in certain cases, and not try at once
to drag it into the church, where it will be killed off. There
will be many 'fringe activities' (on the fringe of the church,
that is) which are true spirituality and which will mean in the
end that those involved will be led into the fullness of their
ultimate meaning through the authenticity of the Christian
fellowship and the interpretation of the Christian tradition;
but at any given stage this will not necessarily be the case.
We must reckon with those people who use all their energy
in CND, social work and the like. This is the way their whole
energies go, and they have no time for the church. But the
energy they are developing is spiritual energy. And we have

to be sensitive to the ways in which this sort of energy leads on to the dimensions which raise questions of grace and worship and the whole matter of transcendence, mystery and the dimension of God.

Then, more within the Christian tradition, we need to have much more training at all levels than we have tended to do in what might be called, for the sake of brevity, 'openness to inspiration'. People must be trained to know that prayer is a form of action rather than a form of thought in the sense that it requires effort. Further, we ought now to be beyond the stage of saying, 'Well, the Bible is thoroughly undermined and archaic'. We ought to have understood that the Bible has no use so long as it is just treated as 'the Holy Bible'. We have to go beyond that and teach people to concentrate on it, not listen to it as if it was a 'holy book', but just listen to it. Similarly, we need to tell people just to look at and reflect on the record of Jesus. It is of interest that among some agnostic students of ancient history there is a revival of interest in the whole history of Christianity as part of culture. And after a detailed study of the New Testament they may say, 'Well, the Book of Acts is an extremely good piece of evidence about what the world was like in those days'; and then they go on and say, 'If you actually read the Gospels, Jesus makes quite an impression'. They feel free to say that so long as they do not have to fear that Christians are going to 'get at them' about it. We are, I believe, nearly at the stage when it will be possible to let the Bible speak for itself again because it no longer looks as if we are trying to bludgeon men over the head with it. If a man can attend to the Gospels in an unprejudiced manner, not supposing them to be holy books to be treated with caution and care, then it may well strike him how extraordinary Jesus truly is. But there must be unprejudiced openness to what is really there.

So openness to inspiration by concentration on what actually is in the Bible and to the patterns of Jesus is another way of rediscovering the possibility of transcendence wherein may be found the response to personalness. Finally, this may lead eventually to the position – and this seems to me to come last – where once again we may actually be able to

enter into intercessory and petitionary prayer, because as
we are alerted to this personal response to personalness we
may gradually be aware once again of what simple people
have always known, which is that you cannot really put
anything past God, that the transcendence-immanence
situation is such that even a miracle is not beyond the
bounds of possibility. It is very right and important to put it
this way round, because it is belief in and experience of the
possibility of a personal presence which is essential before
anything which 'miracle' in the biblical sense stands for can
be in any way thinkable today. Hence 'praying for', in any
powerfully individual sense of interceding and petitioning,
seems in the present climate of opinion the last thing that
people can be expected to do. But 'last' here should be used
in the teleological sense. I suspect that if one goes far enough
along this way of the knowledge of the response to personal
presence and purpose it will be possible to intercede without
any sense of embarrassment, which I, as still a 'secular' man,
continue to feel acutely.

5 | *The Sacraments in the Church in Relation to Healing*

Our concern is with that joyful response to the given-ness of Jesus Christ in his church which liberates the power of the Gospel and enables true health. Jesus Christ himself is *the* sacrament because in his incarnation he embodied the union of God and his creation which fulfils the possibilities of the world in the personal fullness of God. Our entering into the fullness of this possibility, discovering even that it is a possibility and what the possibility means is a process. The sacraments of Baptism and Eucharist focus the universal given-ness of Jesus Christ in the action of the church located in the particularity of the local church and congregation. So the universal reality of Jesus Christ is related to us within the particular, local and limited processes of which we are a part.

I suggest that this means that we have to understand Baptism into Jesus Christ in relation to health along the following lines. If we are baptized we are made part of the community of Jesus Christ and of the pattern of the life of Jesus. This is a life of being plunged into living through dying so that we may experience creative living. In practice, this is not to be understood romantically, but realistically. It means that there is strength available (the strength of Jesus Christ) to face hopefully and openly all the demands our living makes upon us. Situations in our lives are constantly, in small ways and great, making demands upon us to be altered. As we are baptized into Jesus Christ, we have the strength, if we wish, to face these demands and be altered into deeper and truer selves instead of being obliged to defend ourselves against life and to become more and more closed and defence-less. This strength is available to the individual through the community and to the community through the individual. Baptism in Christ means that all plunging into life can be hopeful, and what we learn in the little crises of our lives can be built up into the strength to see and know that our greater crises of suffering and doubt and our ultimate crisis of death are all likewise part of the pattern of the life of Jesus and therefore part of created living into the true, full and eternal life in which Jesus Christ unites God and man.

The Eucharist, the Lord's Supper, the Holy Communion stands in a similar way for the given-ness of Jesus Christ in relation to the processes of our lives. The sacrament under-stood as Eucharist is given to make real the fact that all life may be thankfully received and responded to as an oppor-tunity to receive, whether through brokenness or through a new wholeness, the pattern and process of living into divine fullness. Understood as the Lord's Supper, the sacrament is given to make real the fact that all men have a hopeful history within the history of the people of God. Fragmentation and hopelessness is not the dominating fact of our lives. God makes a pattern for his people, and each and every man can receive the reality of this pattern and be given direction, life and hope. Understood as Communion, the sacrament is given to make real the fellowship and family of God to which all men are called to belong and so be at home and be sustained in their journeying through the process of life to the realized fellowship of love which is the kingdom of God. The sacrament of the altar is given to make real the good news that any and every life in any situation can be thankfully received, hopefully directed, sustained through fellowship and developed through sacrifice.

Because we are given the Eucharist, we are to be enabled to receive the demands of life, of our neighbour, of the world as opportunities to receive more of the life of Christ. To give ourselves to our neighbour and to the world is to receive Christ in and through our neighbour and the world. It is by giving out life that we receive back life. Sacrifice is not the mutilation of life in ourselves, but the finding of life in our

neighbour. Such creative giving and receiving is the fruit
and the proclamation of that victory of Christ of which the
Eucharist is the given symbol with creative power.

But this given reality of the sacrament will not be realized
by us, we shall not show the fruits of sacramental living if we
withdraw to the sacrament of the altar and Lord's table as if
it was a private medical or even magical thing given to
privileged Christians to enable them to be sustained against
the world and away from its pressures and threats. For
example, to have ecclesiastically authorized ministers slipping
into hospitals to dole out the sacraments to the privileged few
who are marked out for this privileged and 'spiritual'
medication is not to respond to and speak of the universal
Gospel of God, but is to perpetuate churchly selfishness and
defensiveness. In such peddling of 'the medicine of
immortality', the church too often makes it look as if it has
no water of life even for its members, still less for all men. We
all have to learn – every congregation of Christians and every
ordained minister of the church – that eucharistic and
sacramental living in the world is not achieved by the
performing of the rite of the eucharistic sacrament as such
and in isolation. In too many congregations the celebration
of the sacrament is a mere rite. This rite has to have its
reality kindled in the lives of the members of the congregation, laity and minister alike, by a eucharistic and sacrificial
readiness for living in community. There will be no reality
experienced in and through the sacrament in the midst of the
congregation gathered if there is no sacramental living in the
midst of the world by the congregation dispersed. The
Eucharist offers strength for thankful living to those who
bring to it the desire and attempt to practise a thankful
receiving of the demands of their neighbours and their world.
The Holy Communion offers the strength of sustaining
fellowship to those who are open to the demands of being a
sustaining neighbour, member of a family, part of a profes-
sional, industrial or educational team. The Lord's Supper
offers the strength of direction and purpose to those who are
concerned to give purposeful hope to those by their side who
live in apathy, indifference or despair. If there is no reality of

encounter with the life of Christ in the world, then there will
be no reality of encounter with the life of Christ in the
sacrament. It is the demands of sacramental living, of drawing health from sickness, living from dying, believing from
doubting, response to the love of God from the indifference
and cruelty of men, which will send members of the Christian
congregation thankfully and hopefully to the Eucharist.
There they may receive the power to offer what they have so
far discovered of sacramentality, of the reality of God in the
realities of the world. And as they receive this power to offer,
so they will receive the power to be directed and the power
to be renewed for further and deeper creative living – but
living not at the Eucharist but in the world. The ineffective-
ness, either by way of power of creative living or of
faith-kindling proclamation of the Gospel, of the formal
presence of the sacraments in so many situations of sickness
and of healing, shows us that we are being called to receive
a renewal and a reform of our understanding and practice of
the sacraments by a faithful facing up to the opportunities
and possibilities of sacramental living in the world and for
the world.

In this connection, I would also suggest a wider consideration of the celebratory aspects of man's life in various
cultures. The actual liturgical 'doing' of the sacraments needs
to be given a celebratory aspect which is clearly so in terms
of the way of life as lived in the society, institution or
neighbourhood where the sacrament is being performed. And,
conversely, we need to be able to see and heighten the
sacramental aspects of the human celebrations of the rhythms
of personal and natural life. The Gospel declares that Jesus
Christ is life that men may have abundant life. Every
affirmation of life and of its abundance, birthday, anniversary,
turn of the year, gathering of the harvest and so on, needs to
be considered for what help and clue it can give us to living
life in a celebratory way which is thankful and truly life-
affirming. Thus celebration, sacramentality and sacrament
may become a chain through which a cleansing, uniting and
fulfilling power of the life of Jesus Christ may be received,
realized and expressed.

6 | *Worship and Doctrine*

I wish to investigate the meaning of the often quoted statement, '*Lex orandi, lex credendi*', that the law of our praying is the law of our believing. This presumably means that worship is relevant to doctrine. I would suggest, however, that it must also mean that doctrine is relevant to worship, and that we have two points here and not one: what you do affects your understanding of what you know, and what you know affects your understanding of what you do. It is worth dwelling upon this point, although it is so obvious, because, with regard to the whole notion of belief in God, we are in some ways in something of a crisis, which could be called a crisis of epistemology, a crisis about our knowing. In this situation, it is important to see that what you know is relevant to what you do, and what you do is relevant to what you know, and that what you know and what you do are not one and the same thing. As yet. I take it that one of *the* points about the Beatific Vision, as it is one of the points about the Being of God himself, is that with it there is a perfect coincidence between – not a coincidence between, but an actual equivalence of – knowing and doing. But here knowing and doing are different things; and when I am talking about knowing, I am talking about knowing in the doctrinal sense: knowing looked at primarily from the end of intellectual formulations, rather than existential impact, if I may put it in such a way.

That this is not merely an academic point, but a perfectly practical point can, I think, be illustrated like this: there are a good many people who say that they believe in the creeds, but it seems that very many people who say this do not really mean it in any sense which involves much of an existential impact. 'I believe in the creed' seems to mean in practice: 'I am worried when people tinker with clauses of the creed. It upsets me. I do not like people to suggest that there are difficulties about the Virgin Birth. I do not like people to suggest that the notion of Ascension is a difficult notion, and so on.' But in practice their belief in the creed makes absolutely no difference. That is to say, they do not seem to have any real understanding which informs the whole of their life and their activity and their commitment to their fellowmen. Nor do they appear to see what it means to say that in Jesus Christ there is a fresh start, such a fresh start that something like the Virgin Birth is appropriate to the beginning of it. They do not seem to understand anything about the nature of the Ascension in the sense of the life of man being taken up into the life of God, and there being a transfusion between the two.

It therefore emerges that in practice, for a very great number of persons, doctrinal formulations are really fragile shells, or magic symbols. They are something to do with an entity that is very difficult to get at, called 'my faith'. 'My faith' is enclosed in a fragile shell of doctrinal formulations to which no content can be given; but taking one piece out can cause a great deal of worry. Or it is a magic symbol – 'This is untamperable with: that's how I know that God exists.' Thus knowing can very easily become, and it seems to me, pastorally speaking, that it has become in very many cases to very many people, what I might call flatly propositional. It is just a question of sentences which people are prepared to recite. And there is no connection between this type of knowing when it has become this absurdly flat propositional sort, and acting.

On the other hand, there are plenty of people who want to concentrate very much on things like sincerity, warmth, depth of feeling, who would say, 'The great thing about the Christian is that I am committed,' full stop; 'The great thing about worship is that it comforts me,' full stop; 'The great thing about ethics is that I feel it right to do so and so.' Now it is perfectly true, as no less a person than Pascal has taught us, that the heart has its reasons; but it is also perfectly true that the heart is deceitful and desperately wicked – at least there are reasons for believing this. And it is therefore clear enough that doing, acting, committing oneself, can become concentratedly self-centred. We are confronted at the present time with a large quantity of so-called philosophical and theological understanding which turns the sentence 'This has meaning' into something like 'This sends me', or words to that effect. And to ask the question 'Where to?' is improper.

It is therefore obvious enough that doing and knowing are not necessarily related at the present, and that there are people who put far too much weight on knowing, in the sense of being committed to propositional statements, and there are people who put far too much weight on doing, in the sense of existential impact pure and simple. But I think it is further necessary to declare, and that was the point of my reference earlier on to the Beatific Vision, that here and now there will never be a perfect coincidence between knowing and doing. This is part of the dichotomy of our fallen state, it is part of the fact that it does not yet appear what we shall be. There will always be a tension between knowing and doing, there will always be the danger of over-emphasis in one direction or the other. And it is therefore very necessary, and particularly necessary in view of what may be called the crisis of belief, today, that one should investigate this notion of what is meant by, what is involved in, *lex orandi, lex credendi*. It seems that it must work both ways: that worship affects doctrine, that doctrine affects worship. And there are two particular ways in which the interaction between worship and doctrine is of particular importance at present.

There is, first, a very direct connection between the poverty of much worship, in both its practice and its shape, and the danger of losing grasp of the objectivity, of the otherness, of God. Misunderstanding of the inwardness and the nature and purpose of worship deprives us of the awareness that God is both transcendent and yet, although other than us, none the less real to us. For we must realize that worship is primarily *attending to God as God*. As a matter of fact it is only possible to do this in Christ, through the Spirit, but that is a doctrinal point which I shall come to in a minute. Worship is attending to God as God, and the church at worship is the church concentrating upon the purpose of her existence: that is to say, God. And when the church is concentrating upon the purpose of her existence, the church is in fact concentrating upon the purpose of all men, that is to say, God. For to attend to God, to be focused upon God, to give that attention to God which is worthy of God, which is only possible in Christ through the Spirit, is life. To attend to God is life in at least two senses: first, it is the source of life, for unless one is in relationship to God there can be no real life, no everlasting life; there can in fact be no life, there can only be existing until you die. To attend to God is life both in this sense of giving life, and also in the sense of making life worth living: there is no point in life ultimately, there is no fulfilment in being a human being, except and unless there is fulfilment in all the riches of God, in the perfection of God: so to attend to God is to be concerned with the purpose of life both in the sense of being concerned in the possibility of life, and in the sense of being concerned in the fulfilment of life.

It needs to be made as plain as possible to people who are struggling to believe, to people who would believe but think it is not possible, that it is attending to God with which the church is concerned, and that worship is the very heart and centre of this attending to God. To join in worship is to join in the church's attending to God, in the continuing tradition of what the church has learned through all the ages of how to attend to God. The liturgy brings to bear, crystallizes, focuses upon our daily concerns the whole living understanding which the church has had, and which the church has inherited from Israel, of encounter with the living God. Worship is thus the focus of the prayers of the faithful, both in the sense of distilling and carrying on the essence of the prayers of the faithful all through the age, and in the sense of drawing together the prayers of the faithful as they are praying at this very time.

In this way, to attend to worship cannot fail to root those who take part in it in the objectivity of God. It is clear in the worship of the church, when it is a true expression of the continuing life of the faithful people of God, that here we are attending to God: not that we are contemplating, full stop, whether it be contemplating our navel, or just contemplating, but that here we are in the presence, that here we are being confronted with a Presence. It is above all in worship that it is made clear beyond a peradventure, as a matter of fact, in the reality of our own lives, and yet a reality which takes us beyond our own lives, that we are indeed responding to God, that grace is not a question of 'You are accepted', but that it is a question of 'You are accepted *by God*'.

Unless this objective worship is at the very centre of the church's life, and conducted in a manner which takes the whole notion of objectivity into full account, it is no wonder that people lose their grasp of the fact that grace is being accepted by *God*, that worship is facing up to *God*, that the response of the Christian is response to *God*. And therefore there is an urgent necessity, in view of the need of making the knowledge of God something real to our contemporaries, to wrestle precisely with the question of the *lex orandi, lex credendi*, of the connection between the objectivity of worship and the assurance of faith that God *is*, and that it is not a question of a theistic attitude, but a question of a response to the living God, the Father of our Lord Jesus Christ. Thus the practice of worship is essentially connected with the continuing grasp on the objectivity of God, and this is a vital matter with regard to belief in the world today.

But it is necessary to see that, when one talks about the objectivity of God, one is talking about the otherness of God, and not about the object-likeness of God. It does not mean that God is an object like ourselves. That would be worship, but it would be idolatrous worship, worship concerned with an object. And this is the point at which it is necessary to change direction and to speak about doctrine in its effect upon worship, instead of worship in its effect upon doctrine. The shape of worship and the understanding of worship must be Trinitarian. All of us who have any concern with, or responsibility for liturgical reform, or make any contribution to it, must be clear that we are concerned in the shape of our worship with the worship of God the Father. This point is necessary both doctrinally and practically. Indeed, there is a complete connection between the two.

Worship of God the Father is what the whole Christian tradition both represents and requires. The whole biblical picture and presentation is consummated in response to and worship of the Father, and it is this presentation of God as God and Father which is sealed by Jesus Christ and presented to us through Jesus Christ. It is, moreover, this worship of the God who is above us, beyond us, transcends us, which is absolutely necessary to the fulfilment of man in his humanness. It is not possible to have the fulfilment of the humanness of man except in relation to God: the living God of the Bible, the God of the tradition of the church, the God who is the true and living God. For man to be fulfilled, he must be taken out of himself into God. It is no good allowing him to drop back into his ultimate concern, to drop back into his depth; he has to be taken out of the depth into the height of God. It is perfectly true that there are plenty of uses for depth imagery, and that they are very important, but I think the point is made clear to us by trinitarian doctrine, by the worship of the church – and I suspect the psychologists will get on to it in due course – that it is only as man is taken out of himself and beyond himself, that he is able to be fulfilled as himself in God. To put it another way would be to say that there is no point in salvation *from*, unless there is salvation *for*, and that the worship which is of God the Father, of the transcendent God, the overall and beyond, is the essential point of being saved because it is what we are saved *for*.

We worship God the Father, who is the Source of Godhead and the Fount of all things, and we worship through the Son. The proper place for our understanding of Jesus Christ is in relation to the Father and in relation to us. There must be no Jesus-cult: we worship through the Son, Jesus Christ, the Word of God, who is also the last Adam, Jesus Christ the Mediator between God and man because he is both the very expression (of one substance with the Father) of who and what God is, and also the embodiment of perfect manhood; Jesus Christ who shows us that God is for us, and therefore we dare to worship God, therefore we have a standing-ground in which to worship God; Jesus Christ who is the first

True Man, and the source of all real humanity. It is in Jesus
Christ that the gap – the gap that so worries people who want
to fall back purely into subjectivity – the gap between God
and Man, God who is truly other, and yet God who is
infinitely concerned with us, is finally and decisively closed.
It is Jesus Christ who is the At-one-ness, who is the union
between God and man, and the source therefore of the
possibility of our daring to stand before God, and daring to
hope to receive the life of God in the mode proper to a
creature. And in the present controversies and discussions it
seems very clear that we need this balance between otherness
and transcendence, and immanence and presence. We need
also the union between these two things, the union and
communion between God and man, which is established in
reality in Jesus Christ, and made possible through Jesus
Christ. And therefore we worship God the Father, but we
worship through the Son.

And then we worship in the Spirit. God himself is present
in his own self both in us and among us, and above all when
the church is at worship. That is how the worship is made
real, that is how there is the possibility of knowing God and
responding to God, that is how it is possible that Jesus Christ
himself should be present among us. He is not present among
us by an exercise of the historical imagination, by an attitude
of mind towards Jesus Christ which puts him in the position
of authentic existence; he is present among us because God
himself the Holy Spirit dwells both among us and in us,
realizing in us the very same reality of presence as is the
reality of the presence of God and man in Jesus Christ, as is
the reality of the presence of the Father in heaven: it is all
one reality, Father, Son and Holy Spirit. We worship God
the Father, we worship through the Son, and we worship in
the Spirit, and that is the way in which what you might call
our doctrinal understanding and the existential impact in
fact come together, by one and the same *physis* and *energeia*,
by one and the same activity of God in accordance with his
essential nature. We are not struggling, we are responding:
indeed God is responding in us, and it is on grounds such as
this that it seems quite clear that the only practicable shape

of worship, the only shape of worship which really makes
sense, the only shape of worship which enables worship to be
worship, is the pattern of 'Glory be to the Father in the Son
through the Holy Spirit,' in the Son because we are
Christians, through the Spirit which is the spirit of fellowship.

I have one more point: worship is *the* activity of the church
because doctrinally we know that the whole concern of the
church, which is the concern of man, is God. But as things
are, worship is a separate activity of the church: the church
has to have occasions of worship, foci of worship. This is
necessary because of sin. We are not yet in the presence of
God as we will be, and therefore it is not the case that the
whole of our lives are automatically worship; and it is
necessary also that the church should come apart to worship,
simply because of the distinction which exists between
Christians and the world: there are those who respond to
God, and there are those who do not as yet consciously
respond to God. And therefore there must be this separation
and this separateness of the church in worship. But – and this
is my last doctrinal point – such worship must not be an
isolated activity. Worship is *the* activity of the church, worship
has to be a separate activity of the church, but it must not be
an isolated activity of the church. If the doctrine of God
requires worship to be *the* activity, and the doctrine of sin
requires worship to be a separate activity, the doctrine of the
Incarnation requires that worship should not be an isolated
activity. The form of Christ is the form of the church; the
body of Christ exists for God and for the world, and the
church does not exist for herself. Detachment, separateness, is
for the sake of involvement, and I would suggest that the
grave danger in the practice of worship in the Catholic
tradition is really monophysitism. I know it is clean contrary
to the intention, but in practice I believe it to be true.

Let me give two examples as to why I think this is so.
Attending to God in practice very often would seem to have
been worked out in a way which has forgotten that he is the
God who became man. This can be seen in discussions about
liturgical reform where, for instance, it is said that worship is
the church's activity: what people must do is learn the forms

which have been hallowed by tradition. We must not water down anything, we must not pander to *hoi polloi*: we must not be concerned with people who cannot understand: they must be instructed: we have failed to instruct them through the ages, but they must be instructed. We must under no circumstances reform in such a way as to leave anything out: we must do archaeological research: we must go into the whole tradition of things, and make sure that everything is included. There is a great *hybris* here which is particularly given to the priest and those people who think they understand, and in thinking they understand show that they do not. We forget that the God who is attended to in worship is the God who for the purposes of salvation became man. And the notion of there being some virtue in the liturgy being incomprehensible is to my mind perilously near to a blasphemy.

Finally, a point about worship as the *opus Dei*. Here I would suggest that we consider whether worship really is the *opus Dei*, the work of God, any more than mission to man and service of man, in the involved sense of those terms. We know that one element of meaning in the doctrine of the church as the body of Christ is to show that some concentrate on this function of the church and some on that: the theory is all right, but what about the practice? Without a continual concern for involvement, not merely in God (as it seems to us) but in the concerns and affairs of men, of mission to men and service to men, there is very grave danger that the *opus Dei* becomes heretical, monophysite. And so it could cease to be *opus Dei*? To suggest such a thing would be over-Protestant? But the question which Protestants in fact put to this whole tradition is that a concentration upon attending to God, if you forget the total involvement of God in the world as it is seen in Jesus Christ, and the necessary response to that, in mission to men and service for men, can be in real danger of betraying the God who is revealed in Jesus Christ. I believe that the whole Catholic tradition is much under judgment here, of course, for being false to itself; not for being untrue in itself, but for being untrue to itself. A much deeper penitence and repentance will be required of the Catholic tradition before we shall find the one fullness which is in the will of God. If in a gathering like this we have been priding ourselves at all on preserving objectivity, let us wonder how far in preserving this we have in fact been obedient to the God who is involved, to the incarnate God; for we have to remember that the *doxa*, that the glory of God, the Shekinah which is the Presence of God, according to St John, is seen on the cross, in the suffering man who is wholly identified with the world.

We must attend to God in worship: that is the only way of objectivity, of reality, of truth, and this worship must be trinitarian, 'Glory to the Father, through the Son, in the Spirit'. But we need to remember that on earth the glory is manifested in Jesus Christ, and that worship is under the judgment of involvement, and that there is the necessity of making sense of worship to all the faithful, and there is the necessity of seeing that worship is united in the one hypostatic reality of the body of Jesus Christ with mission and service to all.

POSTSCRIPT

The Authority of Faith

In this Christian living with questions, is it possible, despite the fluidity and provisionality of the situation, to state where one *stands*? What account can be given of the basis, rather than the procedure, of the Christian position? The thesis I would put forward is that it is faith which is the only ultimate basis *from the human end* of the Christian Gospel and of the authority which church and Bible carry. For the knowledge of the truth of the Christian affirmations about God, the world and self is likewise arrived at by and ultimately rests upon faith. This does not mean that faith is to be opposed to either reason or knowledge, nor does it mean that the authority that is to be encountered in connection with the declaring of the Christian Gospel is either unreasoning or unreasonable. Still less does it mean that such authority is absent or is a mere matter of a subjective attitude of those who happen to be believers. But what needs to be exposed and spelled out is the true nature of the situation with regard to the basis of Christian truth and Christian authority. Until this is radically faced-up to, the Christian church will continue to fail to live and to witness with the authority and power to be expected and required of a body sent out and sustained by God.

Faith, then, is, from the human end, the ultimate basis and, ultimately, there is no basis for faith – from the human end. Before we attempt to clarify the concept of faith it is necessary to be clear about 'ultimately' and 'from the human end'.

'Ultimately' is not intended to be taken in, say, a chronological or a psychological sense, but in a logical sense. We must make a distinction here. There is the type of answer one would give to particular questions like, 'Why does my faith exist now?' – or better, as we shall see later, 'Why am I now a believer?', 'Why do I go on believing?', 'How does this unbeliever pass from not having faith to having faith?'. These questions can have perfectly good answers which contain elements of psychology and chronology (an account of a series of events and experiences) which are relevant to the particular cases. 'I am now a believer because I was brought up as one and my subsequent experiences have confirmed rather than undermined my faith'; 'X became a believer because Y, an authorized minister of the church, so authoritatively expounded certain passages of the Bible that X felt obliged to make a serious response to that which was so expounded and this has led him into a way of life in which he takes it for granted that the Bible is or can be a source of authoritative insight into God and his purposes.' In this whole range of particular questions and instances it would not be true to say, for instance, that *my* faith has no other basis than my *faith*. My faith can clearly be said to be in some sense based on the faith of those who brought me up and on my own subsequent experience. Similarly, it would be true to say that X's faith is based on the Bible and the church or on the Bible set forth by the church, or on the church expounding the Bible and so on. At any rate, that X is a believer does not depend upon, is not based upon, the fact that X is a believer. We are not therefore arguing that particular cases of faith are based on nothing but the faith of the particular believer or believers concerned. Indeed, it will be a later stage of the argument that faith is neither unreasoning nor unreasonable, precisely because grounds can and should be given for holding particular beliefs or for taking particular decisions which commit one to 'faithful' ways of living and acting.

The question at issue is not a generalized form of questions about why particular believers believe or why particular beliefs should or should not be part of the mental furniture of those who are believers. These questions are, of course, related to the present inquiry and come later. The question at present is about the ultimate validity of faith as such. The church may persuade me to faith. The Bible, through

expositors or through my own reading, may compel me to
faith. My own experience, as I seek to face life 'faithfully' and
to live as a member of the community of believers, may cause
me to grow in faith. But supposing I ask myself or I am asked
the question whether this faith is an ultimately valid response
to 'reality as it really is' or, 'What are the grounds for holding
that this faith is somehow or other true, laying hold of truth,
related to truth . . ?'? It is an accurate description of present
facts that I am encouraged in a faithful attitude by church,
Bible, fellow believers and experience, and, indeed, the
faithful attitudes 'work', i.e. are 'life-enhancing', in a way
which believers and unbelievers might agree to recognize.
But are they grounded in objective truth? To put it crudely
and bluntly, 'What is the basis for maintaining that faith is
true?'.

It is in connection with this type of logical question that
faith is, from the human end, the ultimate basis, and,
ultimately, there is no basis for faith – from the human end.
There are many what might be called 'mediate' arguments
for faith. That is to say, there are many reasons (as I shall
maintain, validly and reasonably called 'reasons') which
persuade people to commit themselves to belief and which
justify the holding of particular beliefs. Moreover, it may very
well be the case that it is right and proper that most believers
for most of the time should be convinced by and remain
contented with the 'mediate' arguments only. But when and
where the ultimate question of faith is raised it is necessary
to be clear that there is no 'final' argument. To appeal to
church or Bible as ultimate logical *guarantees* of the truth of
the faith which is proclaimed is patently circular. This
patent circularity could be ignored as long as church or Bible
enjoyed an unquestioned prestige. But once external changes
and internal divisions and questionings remove this prestige,
then the question of what is the *final* authority, the *ultimate*
argument has to be faced in its starkness. The present thesis
is that there is no ultimate *argument*, only mediate arguments,
and the final authority comes from faith – but it is none the
less authoritative faith, nor any the less connected with truth.
From the human end there is only one way out of the logical

circle which arises whenever an attempt is made to find a
basis for Christian faith, e.g. 'Why do you believe so and so?
Because it is true. How do you know it is true? Because the
church teaches it. How does the church know it is true?
Because she believes it and has always believed it.' The only
way out of this circle is not the authority of the church and
the authority of the Bible refurbished by either being brought
up to date or being restored to its old weightiness. The only
way out is the authority of faith.

To clarify and support this thesis further and as a step
towards the clarification of the concept of faith to which we
must eventually come, we must now pass from the consideration of 'ultimate' to the consideration of 'from the human end'
in the thesis 'faith is, from the human end, the ultimate basis'.
It is necessary to insert a phrase of this nature to draw
attention to the fact that all who have faith would presumably
admit that the decisive and absolute basis of their faith does
not lie in the human end at all but in God. Since God is the
'object' of faith, since the truth to which faith is related is
God, it follows that God and God alone is the ground of
faith. The only adequate, decisive and irrefutable establishing
of faith beyond all denial is God. But the only 'verification'
of God is God. This is so because even if we allow God to be
spoken of as an 'object' of thought at all, he will by definition
be greater than and not commensurable with any other
objects of thought whatever. Hence he cannot be established
by means of arguments using other objects of thought. (It
might be that such arguments tend to show that he probably
exists or do persuade some people that he does exist or raise
questions which appear to demand an answer which 'goes
beyond' the other objects of thought, but the God who is the
'object' of faith is not a hypothesis, a probability or the
answer possibly required by a dimly conceived cosmic
question.) 'From the human end', therefore, the position is
that either there is no God or he cannot be known or he
makes himself known. This last is, of course, the assertion of
the biblical and Christian tradition, and it is that tradition's
'faith' that we are discussing.

It might be thought unnecessary to draw attention to so

obvious a point and absurd to attempt to traverse so vast a field as proofs of the existence of God and questions concerning our knowledge of God in a paragraph. But the necessity of at least stating a position in that field cannot be avoided because the authority of faith is clearly related to the connection of faith with truth; furthermore, since faith is faith in God, faith's connection with truth is equally clearly related to knowledge of God. Faith may happen to be truth, but if it is not assuredly known as such it cannot be validly authoritative. Hence we must face the fact that the ultimate and decisive assurance about God cannot be based on any 'mediate' authorities like church or Bible, nor in any 'mediate' arguments drawn from the language and tradition of the community of believers or the experience of oneself, but can rest firmly and finally only on God himself. If God is and if he is God, he cannot 'be established'. He can only 'establish himself'.

Indeed, in this matter of seeking to 'establish God' and to state a basis for faith on which men may rely for the truth and authority of the believing which is demanded, there would seem in both Catholic and Protestant circles to be some grave forgetfulness of the doctrine of justification by faith. It might be proper and salutary to see parallels between an attempted relationship with God which relies upon 'faith' expressed in accepting certain propositions guaranteed by the church or by the Bible and also expressed in performing certain activities required by the church or the Bible on the one hand, and, on the other, an attempted relationship with God which relies on acceptance of the Law of Moses as the very Word of God and an attempt to live according to this Law. It might be argued that in both cases the real object of faith or ground of the believer's life was not God but religion, that the believing practitioner really relied on his orthodoxy and orthopraxy to 'keep him right' with God and that consequently the possibility of his being truly and totally centred upon God and upon God alone was gravely imperilled. Such a line of thought would further suggest that the God who does not abandon his people, however often they may turn back from him to their own ways, is even now

thrusting upon his church the further reformation which is
needed by removing further and further from us the possibility
of once again finding plausible any out and out reliance upon
an infallible church or an infallible Bible and by leaving open
only the possibility of reliance upon and faith in him.
Certainly the near-panic which seems to develop in many
quarters in the church when old authorities seem to be
resolutely questioned does suggest that faith *in God* is not a
very dominating element in the life of the church. It seems to
be feared, and very strongly feared, that doubts about
historicity in the Gospels, or compromising the inerrancy of
Scripture, or the possible undermining of the whole concept
of the validity of Orders, if worked out to the end, may well
destroy our faith in God. This sort of thing would seem to
evidence not faith but faithlessness. Indeed, it is the argument,
explicit or implicit, of this whole book, that from a proper
understanding of the nature of faith there arises a demand for
the constant questioning of mediate authorities and that it is
in such questioning that faith lives and again and again
renews its authoritativeness.

To place the basis and validation of faith anywhere else
than in God himself is to attempt to go back to a non-
Christian position wherein it is implied that men have some
standing-ground of their own from which they can control
and validate their knowledge of God, independently of God.
They think that they can accept the authority of the church
and *thus* be sure of God or that they can be satisfied that the
Bible is a guaranteed source of guaranteed truth and *thus* be
sure of God. But to be sure of God on any other grounds than
God himself is to set those grounds above God and oneself
above both the grounds and God. So it is that the only
ultimate basis of faith is God. And so it is therefore that *from
the human end* there is, ultimately, no basis for faith. For faith
is precisely that activity or response of the human being
wherein God is sought and known. The core of faith *is* being
sure of God. So to look for any basis for faith is to display
faithlessness, and to require an authority which guarantees
faith is to border on the verge of blasphemy, for it is requiring
guarantees for God.

We have, therefore, come to the point where we have
started on the clarification of the concept of faith and this we
must now pursue further. When we are talking about faith,
what are we talking about? There is no specific 'what' that
we are talking about, for faith is an abstraction; it is an
abstraction from the life and experience of believers,
believers, that is, who stand in the biblical and Christian
tradition. We are not concerned with all and every sort of
belief and believing. Faith, then, is an abstraction from the
life of believers and refers to the quality or activity or response
which is found in each and every believer and which constitutes him as a believer. Faith cannot be pointed to, but
believers can, and they are recognizable by their being
disposed to do and say certain things and so on. Faith is
what lies behind or what is expressed in these doings and
sayings. When I speak of 'my faith', the primary reference is
not to *what* I believe, but to the fact *that* I believe; although
what I believe is certainly bound up with, related to and
derived from the fact that I believe.

But when I 'believe', what am I doing? It will seem to the
'outsider', i.e. to the non-believer, that I am taking up or
expressing an *attitude*. I am looking at the world in a certain
way. I am understanding things or making decisions (or
think I am) in a certain context, and so on. 'Believing' is
being in a certain state of mind which I have either grown
into for reasons of environment and upbringing and never
cast off, or else which I have chosen to adopt. Hence faith is
a matter of 'mere' belief. It is 'just an' attitude. So faith will
seem to the unbeliever (and so it *must* appear). But this is not
what faith is.

It certainly involves an attitude, a way of looking at the
world, the understanding of a context within which decisions
are or ought to be made and the constant reiterating of
choices to remain faithful and to adopt faithful responses to
and interpretations of situations. But the believer knows that
all this arises from the fact that faith is at its heart a response,
an awareness of and an enjoyment of a relationship – a
relationship with God, a response to God. However we
formulate this point, we must be careful. We may be allowed

to say (it *is* said!) that we are related to God *by* faith, we respond to God in faith. But faith is not something different from the awareness of the relationship or the making of the response. Faith *is* awareness of God, this responding to God. This is most important, for it is the crucial point about knowledge of God and the truth or validity of faith.

For faith is the normal mode of human knowledge of God. (I say 'normal' because I do not wish either to discuss or exclude the question of a peculiar mystical way of knowing God.) And it is a knowledge of God, not in the sense of a descriptive knowledge of objects but in the sense of a responsive knowledge of another person. A great deal of descriptive knowledge about God has been built up, can be discussed, assessed and conveyed, and is of use in helping individuals towards the knowing of God himself. But the authoritative pivot of all knowledge about God is that faith in God which is, at heart, awareness of God. There is some 'point' or 'focus' in a believer's range of experiences and assembly of dispositions at which he does not *claim* that in faith he has knowledge of God and does not *believe* that in faith he is responding to God. At this 'point' he *is* knowing God, he *is* responding to God. He may translate his personal knowledge of God into all sorts of confusing and conflicting propositions, most (or even all) of which he may eventually hold to be incorrect. (We shall discuss this matter of 'propositional translation' later.) He may conclude later that the modes and methods of his responses may very well have been misconceived – certainly imperfect. Moreover, this 'point' or 'focus' may be a very dim or elusive one, not to be chronologically pinned down and almost certainly never to be self-consciously apprehended at any given *present* moment. But if he attends carefully to his position as a believer he will find that it is not sufficient to say that the sum total of his position taken in its history of experiences and its present deposit of dispositions and character is covered by a claim to know God or a belief that he responds to God. There is some core of faith which does not have either this affective tone or the sort of epistemological consequences which flow from mere claims and beliefs. The core of faith is neither affectively nor

epistemologically hypothetical. It is, in whatever fear and
trembling, and with however much unsureness in application
and action, unquestionably *indicative*. God is here and here
God is known. Because God is God, in the moment in which
I dare to say 'here' I know also that I must say not 'here'
but 'there', for no 'here' can contain God. None the less, I
must say at least that he was 'there', which was a 'here' in
which I then was, and I cannot now deny that I have known
him. To accept this as just a claim or as merely a belief
would simply be to perpetuate a falsehood. I knew and I
know I knew and the *truth* is that God is and can be known.

What is being pointed to here is surely what is also being
pointed to, although in a form which has much greater
vividness and also much more content, by all the great
encounter narratives of the Bible: Moses and the Burning
Bush, Elijah and the 'still small voice', Isaiah in the Temple,
Paul on the Damascus road. Or perhaps such narratives as
these highlight in a peculiar way the more 'routine' (!)
encounter with God which after a 'call' sustained and
informed a Jeremiah or a Paul in their respective missions.
And surely one is also referring to pathetically dim and spora-
dic examples of that awareness of God which seems to have
been so strong (and – at any rate up to the cry of dereliction
on the cross? – so unbroken) a feature of the life of Jesus.

I rather hesitatingly thus compare small things with great
because I wish to point out that the whole of the biblical
tradition concerning God and the truth of God finds its
ultimate authoritative anchorage and guarantee in this type
of personal encounter and awareness. We have therefore, as
Christians, neither any right nor any grounds for looking
elsewhere for the ultimate basis of our authority. Moreover,
we have no reason at all for any panic or despondency when
we are thrust back on this type of ultimate authority. That
we are so upset shows simply that we have forgotten or
misunderstood the tradition in which we stand and the faith
in which we live. God never has been verifiable. He has
always taken steps to make himself known, and those who
have encountered him have known this. They have not 'just
believed'.

We are saying that knowledge of God normally comes by faith and that faith is the normal mode of human knowledge of God. It would seem, therefore, that we have neither explained nor explicated anything and that we are back in that circle from which it was alleged that the only way out was the authority of faith! It is to be hoped that this is not so, but that rather attention has been drawn to the fact that the ultimate authority for and validity of knowledge of God and statements about him must lie in the realm of personal relations. If anyone is asked 'How do you know you know God?', the answer must, by however devious a route, finally end up in the reply 'Because I know God'. This is so because the God with whom we have to do (as the Christian must say) or the God with whom we claim to have to do (as the non-believer must say) is a personal God – that is to say, he is a God who is known *as* a God who takes the initiative in evoking personal responses from human persons and who is known *because* he is such a God. Thus it is not only reasonable but inevitable that the decisive answer to the question 'How do you know you know God?' should be 'Because I know God', for this is very similar to answering the question 'How do you know you know your wife?' by answering in the end 'Because I know my wife'. In a relationship between persons, awareness of that relationship is ultimate and not to be established on any other grounds. And this is not affected by the philosophical difficulties over knowledge of other selves nor by such possibilities as that if my wife dies before me I may in my dotage have hallucinations about my wife's presence. Personal knowledge of persons is an ultimate epistemological category, and no person can possibly get outside it or 'do better' than it.

Such knowledge may be said to be self-authenticating and to carry its own intrinsic and decisive authority. It is true, as has been indicated, that it is possible for individuals to be mistaken or deluded about particular experiences which are taken to be encounters with another person (e.g. the hallucination concerning a dead wife), but the knowledge of another person of which I am speaking is a matter of reciprocal relationships built up over a period and such knowledge is its own direct authentication. I know this other person because of the relationship I have established and enjoy. The other person establishes his or her existence by 'being there' to be related to. In a similar way, God 'establishes' himself by 'being there' and anyone who has encountered him can neither doubt his existence nor doubt that he has *knowledge* of this existent God. Consequently he is bound to maintain and entitled to maintain that his knowledge has connections with truth, validity, reality (which is the same thing as maintaining that it *is* knowledge).

All the complications arise because, although God is known, he is not known as objects are known. He does not share in an object-like nature as human persons do, and therefore he is not 'there' to be pointed at. Consequently, I cannot have any simple 'drill' or assured technique whereby I can put you assuredly and rapidly in a position where it can be practically guaranteed that you will enter on a personal relationship of knowledge which will straightway persuade *you* that the personal God is indeed available and knowable. Indeed, I cannot do it for myself. Therefore we are obliged to speak of knowing God by faith. And therefore, also, the non-believer quite understandably and inevitably says that we are simply making a subjective claim and we are concerned *not* with knowledge *but* with faith ('mere belief'). But it may now, perhaps, be clear why a believer must both understand that the demand of the non-believer will be 'Establish your claim' and also be aware that he cannot, and indeed must not, attempt to meet that demand directly. (The way in which this understandable, and from the standpoint of the questioner, reasonable demand can be reasonably met will, it is hoped, appear in the sequel.) For the demand amounts to requiring us to 'establish' or 'point to' God, and God must be left to establish and reveal himself. And this occurs only in faith. Hence it is that faith is the only ultimate basis for authoritatively establishing the relationship of Christian affirmations about God, the world and the self to truth and reality. Faith, in fact, is the only ultimate human ground for asserting that there is objective truth and reality involved at all.

I have thus far sought to show why it is that any attempt
to find the ultimate basis of authority in Christianity is bound
to be thrust back upon faith, and that this means being
thrust back upon the biographies of particular believers and
also upon the autobiography of oneself as a believer. The
reason lies in the being and personal nature of God. If God is
as he is understood to be in the biblical and Christian
tradition, then no other position with regard to authority
could reasonably be looked for or sustained.

It is now necessary to go on to attempt two things. First,
to show how this recent argument getting back to individual
biographies and an individual autobiography is to be related
to the earlier contention that we were not 'arguing that
particular cases of faith are based on nothing but the faith of
the particular believer or believers concerned'. That is to say,
there must be a consideration of the interaction between the
individual impact of faith and the corporate context of faith.
This will provide us with material for the second attempt.
This must be to sketch out the lines along which the basic
authoritativeness of faith, as I have attempted to describe it,
is to be related to and, up to a point, transferred to, the vast
complex of propositions in the forms of theological statements,
ecclesiastical instructions, pastoral advice and so on in which
and about which so much debate and controversy rage. For
it is in these fields that the problem of authority is so acutely
and practically felt.

First, therefore, some thoughts concerning the authenticating faith of individuals and the corporate context of faith. All
individuals come to faith, or faith develops in them, in the
context of a community. The direct encounters which
constitute the ultimate authentication of faith (i.e. which
provide the authentication which faith gives) occur in connection with the individual's relationship to the (up-to-a-
point) believing community and take the form either in
which they are experienced, or at least in which the experience
is remembered and conveyed, from symbols, images and
sentences which are 'current coin' in the life of that community. Moses is portrayed as receiving the revelation of the
'new name' of God in the incident of the Burning Bush, but

it is the God of the fathers, the God of Abraham, the God of
Isaac and the God of Jacob who reveals himself. Isaiah's
vision is actually in the Temple and is clothed in images of
Temple liturgy and Temple sculpture. Saul was actually
engaged in persecuting the community whose Lord he was
sure he had encountered. And lesser believers have their (not
always lesser?) assurances in connection with praying or
worshipping or reading the Bible or the fitting together of
ideas drawn from such sources in connection with some
problem or excitement with which their lives present them.
Faith is thus neither absolutely arbitrary nor completely
incoherent but related to an already existing pattern of
community belief and life which may be said to be, from the
human end, the *causal* ground, although not, as has been
argued above, the ultimately *justifying* ground of faith itself.

Further, as I have also tried to indicate above, very many
believers cannot point back to actual identifiable 'moments'
of authenticating encounter. It is only that a survey of the
believer's total position arising out of his history of experiences
and present disposition and character leaves him with an
impression equivalent to or parallel to the highlighted impact
of such an encounter. He is able to recognize and unable to
deny that he in his dim way is really related to this same
Reality of which the tradition speaks with so much more
confidence and (symbolic) clarity. Thus it is in all probability
the case for many believers most of the time (and surely all
believers some of the time) that not only would there be no
question of their ever having come to faith without the
believing community, its tradition and its life, but that further
they would scarcely recognize that they had faith at all if it
were not for their part in the life of that community. The
vivid and convincing personal encounter clearly enjoyed by
some believers and able to be recognized by all has an
essential role in the understanding and justification of faith,
but it is not sufficient of itself psychologically and in actual
practice to sustain faithful living.

Moreover, the isolated and individual personal encounter
would not be 'sufficient of itself' to allow one reasonably to
assert for faith the objectivity and authority which is the

burden of the first part of this essay. It remains true (how can it be otherwise?) that only God can establish the reality of himself, that he does this in personal encounter, and that consequently the ultimate assurance of the reality of God can be based only upon the encountering of him by persons. Such encounter will necessarily be inter-personal and, therefore, from the human end by human individuals. Consequently, the absolute and ultimate basis for our understanding of God and for our assertions about him must lie in the faith-experience of individuals. Further, *any* individual who really does encounter God could neither doubt nor argue with such an encounter. He will be absolutely sure of his objective knowledge and he will be right to be sure about it. But, if he is taken as an isolated individual, he may as reasonably be taken for a completely deluded man as for a witness to the one true God. Strength of conviction may be reasonably persuasive grounds for investigating that conviction, but it is no logical ground at all for accepting that conviction and sharing it. But the situation is worse than this.

As every believer must be painfully aware, the strength of one's convictions notoriously fluctuates. Any reader who has got thus far must have asked again and again what right I had to talk with such reiterated assurance of the assurance of faith, of 'knowing' and 'knowing that one knew' and so on. Certainly, if I were talking of isolated and individual encounters I would have no such right. For just as the isolated individual may as reasonably be concluded to be deceived as inspired, so the reflective individual may himself subsequently conclude that any isolated and individual experience of assurance or knowledge he had was at least as likely to be a mere subjective disturbance as an actual objective encounter. Yet both our present difficulties and our previous assertions arise out of an attempt to describe *all* the aspects of the 'faith-situation' from the inside. The excuse for so temerarious an attempt is that nothing else can be done. Belief in God is something abstracted from believers' believing. And whatever may be the role of the community of believers (it is surely immense), descriptive analysis is bound to fix on where belief 'resides', i.e. the individual believer. And since belief in God is a personal relationship with a personal Being, one is forced back upon the only person of whom one has 'inside' knowledge, viz. oneself.

I am obliged, therefore, to hazard an attempt both to describe the epistemological assurance perceived in faith (faith is not the *grounds* for 'being sure' but *is* being sure – of God) and at the same time to do justice to the fact that faith is no guaranteed disposition to enjoy constant assurance at the forefront of one's thinking and experiencing. I wish, at this stage in the argument, first to give some account of why faith should have this double, even ambiguous, nature and then to indicate what grounds there are (beyond the fact that no other procedure is possible!) which justify the offering of an account of faith based on a particular believer's experience of faith (viz. my own) as a general account of the nature of the faith which can be reasonably offered for general acceptance and illumination.

Faith has this ambiguous nature of assurance and diffidence because it is a relationship between a human being such as myself and God. All inter-personal relationships clearly take their quality from the characters and natures of the persons in relationship. As has already been pointed out, human beings do partake of the nature of 'objects', i.e. they have a recognizable purely physical existence which can be pointed to – although it is perfectly possible to know 'who X is' without 'really knowing X' at all. Only by entering into some reciprocal personal relation with him can this latter knowing begin. But God is a personal Being who is not object-like at all. This is a consequence of his transcendence and sovereignty. He cannot be observed impersonally like an object wherein the knower has the initiative and the 'object' is purely passive. He can be known only as the Supremely Personal, and in this knowing, the initiative and the primary activity is always and inevitably his. Consequently, knowledge of God can never be a taken-for-granted 'possession' of the knower over which he, the knower, has more or less complete control. It must always be 'there' and 'not there' – until God pleases 'in the End' to give us the blessed vision of himself which is the completed enjoyment of his eternal life.

But there is not only this, as one may say, 'good' reason why faith must also involve diffidence. The quality of the relationship is contributed to not only by God but also by us, and we are both naturally underdeveloped beings and also sinfully misdeveloped beings. We have yet to grow to the stature of beings who can fully enter into the enjoyment of relationship with God, and we also perversely pursue projects and developments of our own which stunt our true development and take away even from the capacity we might have to respond to God as he makes himself known to us. We do not enjoy the awareness of, or respond to, the relationship with God as we might and could and should. Thus the diffidence which arises from the very being of God who must always remain supreme and transcendent is heavily interlaced by the fitfulness and even forgetfulness of our own imperfections and disobediences. Not only is God never our own, even intellectual and moral, 'possession', but we do not even respond to or enjoy as we might God's possession of us. Faith is therefore complicated not only by diffidence but also by faithlessness.

Thus this ambiguous nature of faith is in the nature of the case. It is both our only ultimate access to an assurance of God which, being a true relationship with him, is a guarantee of objectivity and therefore is entitled to be called knowledge, and yet it operates so differently from our other knowledge that we do need this distinct word (i.e. 'faith') and we may well understand the logicians' refusal to admit that faith is in any sense knowledge. (It might be better to drop all attempts to use the word 'knowledge', provided that such a giving up of the word was not taken to be an admission that faith *is* purely subjective and not a matter in which legitimate claims to truth can be involved.)

And yet, whatever the difficulties, it *is* the nature of faith to be not hypothetical but indicative, and the believer is bound to say at the 'intense' end of the scale of his faith 'I *do* know'. Even at the 'attenuated' end he will still find himself obliged to say 'I cannot deny that I know'. And yet, again, it must be admitted that this 'cannot' is not the obligation of logic but the obligation of will. God is a personal Being known to me whom I cannot deny (although under temptation or persecution my will may fail), not a fact which my intellectual integrity and understanding obliges me to underline on the page of life. But this again is in the nature of the case, the case of the relation between the Supreme Personal Being and his personal creatures. And the fact that there is in faith an element of decision (always, therefore, a decision of me and other individuals, for only individuals actually decide – whatever 'makes' them) does not rob it of its authoritativeness. Nor is the decision – or rather nor are the decisions – of faith to 'keep faith' unreasonable, although this reasonableness does not itself justify the *absoluteness* of both the commitment and the authority of faith.

We must, however, move towards an explanation of these last statements by going back to the question of why it is reasonable to offer a general account of faith based on the individual evaluation of an individual autobiography. In doing this we shall be moving back to the main stream of the argument, which is concerned with the authenticating faith of individuals and the corporate context of faith.

I endeavour to explicate and evaluate faith from my own understanding and experience of faith. This is inevitable because faith is a personal matter; to get to the heart of it, personal experience is required, and the only personal experience to which I have direct access is my own. But how dare I do this? Do I set myself up as a 'hero' of faith worthy to be inserted in an appendix to the eleventh chapter of the Epistle to the Hebrews? And, in any case, what is the use of such a procedure? To be so utterly and openly subjective when the whole argument is supposed to be directed to the expounding of the authoritative objectivity of faith is surely to make certain of either pity, ridicule or contempt? It might be hoped that at least some hints to the answers to these questions could be filtered out by the well-intentioned reader from what has gone before, but the argument requires a specific facing up to them.

The answer lies in the fact that I recognize in my own experience some faint echo, indeed some faint realization, of what the biblical 'heroes of faith' are exemplifying and of

what believers since biblical times, including believers alive
now, some known to me in person, are likewise speaking of
and exemplifying. I am persuaded, therefore, that I am seeing,
however dimly, what they saw or see with whatever clarity
and force. *They* 'endured as seeing him who is invisible' (cf.
Heb. 11.27), and they endure. Furthermore, although the
AV translation of the Greek verb '*karterein*' certainly suggests
too heroic a tone for my faith, I do none the less share in
something of the 'resoluteness' or 'steadfastness' of the conviction, knowledge and commitment which was and is theirs.
Moreover, this commitment of mine is both epistemologically
reasonable and morally compelling.

The whole thing arises accidentally, empirically, as a sheer
matter of fact, for no theoretical or *a priori* reasons, but just
out of the 'givenness'. (I am ignoring theological complications about prevenient grace, the Holy Spirit and the like!)
I am faced with examples of the class of believers. They are
not people of any sort of belief or faith or credulity, but they
are believers in this biblical and Christian tradition (i.e. they
'stand in' their tradition; not 'they all hold as the content of
their belief the same set of propositions called "the Christian
tradition" '. We shall come to propositional truths shortly as
the last stage in the essay.) It may be that I am confronted
with them from within their number (e.g. baptized and
brought up as a member of the church) or I may be confronted with them from without (e.g. 'Why do not those
hypocrites who talk about a God of love make a consistent
stand against the H-bomb?', or, 'What right has *he* to preach
at me?', or, 'Can there be anything in this business of
"God"?', and so on). This 'being confronted with' is purely
arbitrary, i.e. there was no theoretical necessity for it to have
happened this way or for it to have happened at all – it
would not have happened to me in this way if I had not
happened to be me. In this it is like all other experiential
data which come to us. I find myself attending to these data.
The form of this attention, at any rate to start with, may not
be reasoning (i.e. the attention has nothing analytic or self-
conscious about it) but it is not unreasonable. It is presumably never initially unreasonable to attend to something

which engages our attention. I find (causal) reasons for
continuing with this attention which may take a wide variety
of forms – attacking believers, debating with them, seeking
instruction from them, joining in (or at least being present at)
some of their characteristic activities like a service of worship
or a prayer meeting. My 'reasons' for continuing with this
attention or participation at any stage will be very various;
some of them would not seem even to myself to be really
justifying reasons if they were coolly and openly examined
and quite possibly none of them would seem sufficient to some
persons. But I can talk about and support my giving of
attention. It is certainly not a totally unreasonable and
unreasoning procedure. (There is probably a very widespread
and implicitly accepted myth current as to what are 'really
reasonable' reasons for various forms of procedure which
makes people suppose, erroneously, that 'religious' behaviour
is very much more unreasonable than other sorts of behaviour. But we cannot go into that now.)

As I proceed in my attending to and participating with
believers, I find that despite bewilderment, disagreement, lack
of clarity and inconsistency both in behaviour and argument
among believers themselves, they do have a discernible
pattern both of thought and of life which is meaningful to
them and shows signs of being meaningful to me. That is to
say, I begin to perceive and appreciate connections and
coherences between bits of their 'doctrines' or between these
and things said and done in their services, and I find that the
sense and coherence I am beginning to perceive also
occasionally makes sense of and makes sense in the conduct of
my life and in facing up to and dealing with the situations
that I find myself in. (The order of the discovery of 'meaningfulness' may very well more often be from the practical to the
intellectual than the order which I have just given.) Since I
have 'seen for myself' something of what believers say the
tradition of belief and the life of believing is about, it is
perfectly reasonable for me to suppose that they are 'on to
something' and that it is not all mere talk and attitudes.

The artificially abstracted and intellectualized 'I' who is
being used as the stalking-horse for this exposition does not

yet *know* that believers are 'on to something' (viz. in touch with God), but my supposition that they might very well be is perfectly reasonable and supported by reasoning. In actual practice, if I attended to my attending, I should doubtless find that I had imperceptibly passed into a frame of mind (or never passed out of one) in which I was taking for granted that believers are on to something, i.e. I am myself a believer of sorts. But we are not concerned here with giving an actual psychological description of the process of becoming or being a believer, but with an attempt to explicate the epistemological status of faith. So – I have reasonable grounds for committing myself further to the sympathetic understanding of the thought and the responsible sharing of the life of believers. It is reasonable, in fact, to trust my convictions as far as they go and see how far they do go!

It is at this stage in the argument that the 'jump' occurs from the reasonableness of continuing experimentally to identify myself, at any rate up to a point, with a community of believers to the absolute assurance and absolute commitment of faith. I say at this stage *in the argument*, because I do not think that there is a *corresponding* decisive jump in the actual process of development of a particular believer. Where a conscious moment or incident of 'conversion' does occur, it may seem to the particular believer that this is *the* decisive moment in which he attains to 'real' faith, and one may also be inclined to identify, or at any rate align, such a moment with the decisive epistemological 'jump' to which I am about to refer. But I am very doubtful about the precise sense in which a moment of conversion is decisive, and in any case we need not investigate this, as it is quite clear that a particular moment of conversion (even if it is a genuine encounter with God) cannot be taken as being generally epistemologically decisive (cf. the possibility, already referred to, of an isolated assured individual being deluded and of an individual deciding that an isolated experience of his own of assurance is an instance of self-delusion). Moreover, it is also clear that very many assured and committed believers do not have any awareness of a moment or incident of conversion. We are therefore concerned with the logical difference there

is between the reasonable pursuance of a tentative and
experimental policy of investigation by association with some
community of believers and the absolute assurance of faith
wherein one is convinced that the believers are, in some real
sense, 'on to' truth (indeed the Truth!), and one is further
committed to an obligation both to follow up *and propagate*
that truth.

The point at issue, then, is the passing over from being a
believer 'of a sort' (by association) to being one who *knows*, or
the passing over from an approach which is permeated by the
awareness of the possibility that the whole thing might be
untrue not merely in detail but in principle (although this is
not likely), to the knowledge that the reasonable possibility
that there is a fundamental mistake ('it remains possible that
God does not exist and that Jesus gives us no decisive clues
about him' – or the like) is not an open possibility at all.

The new and decisive position is that it is undoubtedly the
case that the God to whom this tradition bears witness does
exist, and that he is rightly, if inadequately, pointed to by
that tradition. Consequently faith is not only a possibility, *but
a necessity*. That is to say how I get to the position where my
absolute commitment to God and to continuing life in the
believing community is 'both epistemologically reasonable and
morally compelling' (see p. 221 above).

That position is reached because there is a joining together
of the reasonable type of experimental commitment (at each
stage 'up to a point'), which I have just been outlining, with
the discovery that one is in the position of faith, which I have
spent the earlier part of the essay seeking to describe. That is
to say, there is superimposed upon, mingled with, arisen out
of or imperceptibly added to my inclination to entertain
sympathetically the assertions of and tendencies to belief, the
awareness that I too stand (or at least cannot deny that I
have stood) before the God in whom believers believe. In
following my convictions as far as they go, I have been taken
far beyond them, taken to what is at least equivalent to, if it
is not the same as, a glimpse of 'him who is invisible'.
Therefore I can no longer be hypothetical and I cannot deny
him, although I cannot 'prove' him. Moreover, I know I must

not deny him because I do not need to 'prove' him. He has established himself in my knowledge – in, that is to say, my faith.

And when my faith, in intensity of awareness or conviction or control of feelings and the like, fluctuates, and I wonder once again if I do know him, or rather if it is true that he knows me, and I ask the question whether I am really drifting on a sea of subjectivity, temporarily supported, but in no way anchored, by a precarious raft of 'self-authenticating' experiences which cannot safely be distinguished from self-delusions, then I turn once again to the matrix of the community of believers out of whom and among whom my faith first grew. In their tradition, whether it be in 'church' form or in 'Bible' form, in their continuing life, whether it be in the sacraments and in formal worship or in their fellowship and their taking for granted of the Christian pattern of understanding and life, I find sufficient reasonable evidence for holding that my own conclusions and my own faith are not in fact 'mine' in the perilously undermining sense of being confined to me, subjective to me. I am thus not merely 'tided over' psychological wanings of my own faith, but I am constantly sustained and built up in this faith by the life of the community and its authorities.

But there remains a final and decisive sense in which however much my faith depends causally for its inception on the faithful community and is sustained in its fitfulness and developed out of some of its imperfections by that same community and its life, none the less the absolute assurance and absolute authority of that faith rests for me on the 'glimpsed' or 'sensed' awareness of God who is and can be the only immediate and final authority for any theological faith or truth.

I could not be absolutely assured that the tradition of church and Bible encountered in the life of the communities of believers was really in touch with, stemmed from and pointed to objective and transcendent truth (indeed I could have no assurance that there was any such 'thing'), unless I had myself been touched by the self-authentication of the supreme personal self who is the Truth. Such authentication is necessary to be assured that faith is related to knowledge and truth, not merely to opinion, attitudes and belief. But it is not sufficient. I need to be able to recognize that this faith of mine is no faith of my own, but rather the shared faith of the people of God, if I am clearly to be justified to my reflective self and at least plausible to others in my statement that I am not after all engulfed in the abyss of subjectivity. But again – and so the pendulum of argument and exposition concerning faith swings to and fro – the only unquestionable ground where the whole matter can come to any sort of rest is the assurance of faith. Here is the only certainty that one is grounded in truth and not merely searching in a flux of 'maybe's' (although one is certainly also searching in such a flux – 'living with questions', as the previous writings contained in this book seek to show).

In order to meet the demands of unbelievers for the justification of our faith or even (and quite as frequently in present practice, I suspect) to bolster up our own confidence shaken by the church's loss of prestige and our own inability to make ourselves meaningful in the cause of Christianity in one situation after another, it is quite useless to attempt to reinstate the mediate authorities (in particular church and Bible) into the position of looking like final authorities which accidents of history have allowed them to enjoy. This is to retreat from faith and therefore to retreat from God who is directly encountered only in faith. It is to retreat also from the world which is where God is to be encountered, for it is his world and the scene of his operations, into an increasingly limited and private field of religion inhabited by church-conditioned and biblically brain-washed persons who can continue to persuade *themselves* that they speak objectively and with authority because they speak to no one but themselves. But this is not the picture of the New Testament people of God, nor of the sub-apostolic age, nor of the time of an Irenaeus or an Athanasius. They wrestled in the confidence of their faith with the idiom and spirit of their time. They were not conformed to this idiom or spirit. They did much to transform them. But their understanding and expression of their faith was immensely influenced and shaped by this faithful and obedient confrontation.

Authoritativeness does not arise out of the authoritarian repetition of past solutions to the 'problem of communication'. Rather do we who have entered (as we believe, by the calling and grace of God) into the heritage and tradition of faith, have to have the courage of that faith to submit all the 'deposits' of the tradition to the double test of the most searching scrutiny and questioning by the faithful and of the most intensive exposure to the demands and pressures of the present time. We are sure, in faith, that God is and that *he* is faithful. We do not therefore have to establish for ourselves or for anyone else the basic truthfulness that lies behind and in the tradition which has come down to us. (As has been argued above, this, in any case, cannot be done.) What we must long for and strive for is that the being and relevance and application of the Truth of God may be opened up for us, and for those all around us, in whatever form we and they can lay hold on and make sense (of course, partial and not final sense) of today. Thus may we be successors of the men who in the past were men of faith and preachers of the Gospel. But we shall not be their successors by saying what they said in the terms they said it. If we confine ourselves to this, neither we who speak (and suppose we are speaking the Word of God) nor those who, unbelievers, indifferent, frustrated, ought to be given a chance of hearing the Word of God will come anywhere near to apprehending what the Faith is really about.

The authority of faith will once more become plain to us and renew its impact in the world when we cease to look for or hanker after an old authoritarianism, but are prepared in the confidence of faith to submit ourselves, our understanding of all the tradition that has come down to us, our conviction of our commission from God and the apprehension that we at present have of the Gospel that is offered to us to the questionings and searchings that arise in us and are put to us by the idiom and spirit and need of our age. Then God will give to his obedient servants such authoritativeness as is necessary to persuade men to faith. It is certain that no man, however 'heavily' authorized, can by the weight of his own authority establish another man in the faith of God. It is also certain to the eye of faith that God uses those who faithfully respond to him to be the occasioning of the waking of faith in others. And when this faith is occasioned, then they also see, as we do, the authority of faith. And, if we require it, there will be a little further reasonable evidence that we see what we see and do not imagine it. And we shall be thankful, because we need the auxiliary aid and comfort of reason. But we shall not forget that the demand of God is absolute and this absoluteness no unaided reason can justify.

But in order that these last paragraphs should not trail off into rhetoric without the rigour of an attempt at practical and specific application, it is necessary finally to make the attempt (promised earlier) to 'sketch out the lines along which the basic authoritativeness of faith . . . is to be related to, and up to a point transferred to, the vast complex of propositions in the forms of theological statements, ecclesiastical instructions, pastoral advice and so on', which constitute the 'deposit' of the tradition of faith referred to above. In other words, this is to consider a little more clearly the question of the 'mediate' authorities and to seek to reflect systematically on the investigations and questionings instanced in previous papers in this book.

Faith, as we have had occasion several times to point out, arises in the context of and in connection with the believing community. Men believe in God, humanly speaking, because men believe in God. But in fact, belief in God is not arrived at, experienced as, expressed as or sustained by belief *in God* – at any rate for the vast majority of believers for the most part of the time. I have been arguing that in the end (i.e. as the ultimate logical and authoritatively justifying basis) God must and can only establish himself, and that the heart of faith lies in this encounter with God. But although God is not himself an object, and this fact, when we come to ultimates, has consistently and continuously to be reckoned with, it is equally clear that the knowledge of him is evolved in us and recognizable by us through the medium of the ordinary 'object-like' world. Were this not so, we could not talk or think about God at all, for we can only deal in talking and thinking with concepts, and these have to be built up from the 'objects' which we perceive and experience in the world. Thus the context of faith is as necessary for the possibility of the existence of faith as the heart of faith is necessary for the assurance that faith is related to an objective reality. Both are necessary, neither is sufficient alone. The context is chronologically and causally prior. The heart is logically prior or ultimate. Now it is out of the context of faith that 'the vast complex of propositions in the forms of theological statements, ecclesiastical instructions, pastoral advice and so on' arise. Indeed, they, together with the pattern of living and particular characteristic activities of the believing community, constitute this context.

It is a context which has a long history of development behind it, and which consists at any given time of a great deal of material of very different types and of very different degrees of fixity and fluidity. There are certain elements which in the course of the history of the development of the believing community have emerged with a defined fixity. These are the elements in the whole context of belief which the believing community itself has come to regard as authoritative for its believing. They have therefore become the authorities of the believing community. It will not, I think, be a misleading summary for our present purposes, of the views which are current in the actually existing community of Christian believers today on the subject of authorities, if we say that the authorities are the Bible and the church. The Bible is defined by a sufficiently agreed canon (although there is, of course, dispute about the status of the Apocrypha). The definition of the 'fixity' of the church is, as is notorious, greatly disputed. Unless you first define the '*fideles*' there is no '*consensus fidelium*' on this. But there would seem to be a sufficiently general agreement to be discerned from practice that the ordered Christian community, whatever is held to be its proper form of ordering, does have authority and means of making that authority heard and brought to bear. Moreover, it is undeniable as a matter of history that the authoritativeness of the fixedly defined church experienced through her properly constituted authorities has, for a very great part of Christian history to date, been taken for granted as an integral and necessary part of the Christian context of faith. We are justified, then, in speaking of church and Bible as the authorities of the Christian community. (In order that it should not appear that I suppose that these generalizations are any more than rough and ready, and for the purposes of the argument, I may perhaps be allowed to say of a body like the Quakers that it seems to me that they represent and uphold a tradition which has borne a perfectly proper witness to the questionable status of the commonly received authorities by consistently and yet improperly underrating their importance.)

The Bible is, of course, the 'Scriptures', i.e. *the* authoritative writings of the believing community, so that with it we have finally reached the point of facing up to the connection between the authority of faith and sets of propositions. We are also faced with the same problem with regard to the church, as the authority of the church is likewise naturally expressed through and attached to propositions. In some church traditions, there are more 'in the highest degree' authoritative propositions than in others. The commonly received creeds would be held to be authoritative propositions by a wide range of Christian communities; the Roman church has a carefully worked out grading of authoritative propositions; confessions have some authoritative standing in some traditions and so on. There is also the whole question of authoritative pronouncements from time to time on the application of the Christian faith to particular situations as they arise. These will range from authoritative rulings by 'competent' authorities on some matter of morals or canon law or liturgical ordering and the like, through 'pronouncements' by church 'authorities' on matters of great public interest and importance, to the particularly directed guidance or instruction of the pastor and the preacher. All this and much else which could be added to the 'pattern' (!) simply draws attention to the bewildering complexity of the problem of authority. But if there is bewildering complexity, how can there be authority at all? A mentally bemused man wandering in a fog would be bemused to the point of insanity if he set himself up as an authoritative guide to strangers.

Presumably the way to stop running into such a 'fog' would normally be said to be that one should be clear about one's *primary* authorities. Naturally there are in practice very different levels of authoritativeness, and the Christian community, or individual Christians within that community, will be faced with the same or similar practical problems about coming to decisions in particular circumstances as face any group with particular responsibilities for taking particular decisions. For example, if a particularly difficult medical case arises it is the responsibility of the local 'expert' (the general practitioner) to refer it to appropriate specialists, and when the case arrives in a big hospital then the appropriate 'authorities' in the field in question who are available are, or ought to be, assembled, and they have to take the most responsible and considered decision they can. You get together the best 'authorities' or experts in and interpreters of authoritative knowledge and 'know-how' that you can. They have to make the most responsible decision or pronouncement they can. And you go on from there. Clearly 'the church' or any church organization also has to proceed in this sort of way. The present resources of understanding and training available to the community have to be called in to use, and the persons having such resources have to make use of the tradition and deposit of the community in coming to their conclusions, taking their actions, issuing their advice or instructions. In practice there is surely much in common here between responsible members of the Christian community coming to decisions in Christian matters and, say, responsible persons of the medical profession in medical matters.

No doubt there is a parallel in procedure. But is there not a distinctive difference in the type of authoritativeness of their respective primary authorities? And ought there not to be a distinctive difference in the type of authoritativeness of their respective pronouncements or instructions? A responsible medical group will, of course, rely very heavily on the 'authorities' relevant to its concerns. But its obligation to be bound by these authorities is a purely pragmatic and prudential one. Advances in medicine are made by revising the authorities, and there are certainly no 'absolute' authorities at all. Moreover, the decision they come to is not guaranteed to be 'right', and certainly would not be held to have any unquestionable right of absolute acceptance by another competent group. If such a group came to a different decision on a question of treatment, this would not necessarily discredit the authority of medical science and medical men. It would simply underline the sort of authority it is. But is not any church group *bound* by its primary authorities, and are there not at any rate some situations in which the voice of the church is somehow or other supposed to be heard saying 'Thus saith the Lord . . .'?

A preacher, for example, does not suppose (if he is sane) that there is a straightforward equivalence or identity between what he has to say and a 'word of God'. But he knows he stands in a tradition, has, indeed, been commissioned ('authorized') in a tradition of authoritative pronouncers of words which have been used as means by which men have heard what they have believed to be 'what God has to say' to them. He is very likely to feel that he cannot be the sort of authoritative preacher which it seems to him his like in the Christian tradition have been, unless he can appeal to some primary authority behind what he is trying to say. He seeks something on which he can fall back if challenged and say, 'What I was trying to put over was "this",' and 'this' will have to be able to be referred to something like 'the Bible says . . .', or '*Roma locuta, causa finita*', or 'it says in the creed . . .'. What possible use or authority can there be in an utterance like, 'If we are able to trust the majority of critics, and on balance we *probably* can, then it is quite possible Jesus said . . . although it is more than likely that we can have little more than a guess at the original context of the saying and the original meaning is therefore obscure'? The full impact of this last point is not at all mitigated if one supposes that the justifiable degree of the hypothetical mood is much less than the 'typical' ('caricatured'?) sentence I have just made up. For the fact of the matter clearly is that if hypothesis is introduced *at all* into the *primary* authorities, then there is *never* any justification for *absolute* authority to be attached to any of the propositions either contained in, or based by watertight logic upon, those contained in the primary authorities.

This fact is perceived with exemplary clarity by both Fundamentalist and Roman Catholic theologians, and it should surely be recognized by all of us. But the aim of this essay is to seek to show why it is that this position should in no way surprise us and that our way of facing up to this situation cannot and must not be that of the Fundamentalist or Roman Catholic or some other position which attempts to produce the same results by asserting that either the church or the Bible or some balanced complex of church and Bible is, *in the last resort*, an absolute authority. The historical primary authorities are in fact mediate and mediating authorities, and there is and can be no other absolute authority than God. We are left, therefore, even in the realm of Scripture and in the realm of church dogmatic, credal and moral statements (however we declare these are arrived at or wherever we find them) with our 'if's' and 'maybe's'. It is worse than useless, because one deplores the consequences or apparent consequences of this, *therefore* to assert that the position cannot be so, and we must 'believe in' the church or 'believe in' the Bible or 'believe in' the Holy Ghost's having miraculously conserved some *consensus fidelium* of a Vincentian sort which is none the less existent for being empirically quite undiscernible. It is worse than useless because it is faithless. And God can have little use for a church which refuses to trust him and him alone (what of justification by faith?), while the world will have no use for a church which claims boldly to be commissioned by him whose kingdom is supreme, and yet which cannot dare to face manifest facts.

The solution lies, surely, in facing the situation in the faith we have been given. We know that the whole tradition and life of the people of God is not built or based on a lie, for we also have faith in their God. Indeed, we must not talk of 'we' and 'they', for it is we who now are the people of God (and shall we learn any better than the old Israel that this calling is to serve the world and not to lord it over the world as wielders of superior authority and owners of a superior

guaranteed place with God?). We therefore know that we
are entitled to take with full seriousness all the deposit and
tradition of the life of the believing community as it comes
down to us, all the propositions and pronouncements and
practices. This seriousness will entail that we shall pay
particular attention to, indeed regard undoubtedly as
authorities to be carefully considered and consulted, any 'foci
or faith' which the life of the people of God has produced
and which clearly have nourished and guided that life. The
Bible and the ordering and tradition of the church will, in
particular, be the authorities to be consulted and considered.
That is to say, we shall approach our task of now being the
people of God in the world by seeing to it that we are as
prepared as we can be by as thorough a knowledge as we
can get of the Bible and of the tradition, and our technique
will be always to go to and fro between the problems posed
to our faith by the demands of our situation in the world and
the enlightenment we can get for our faith from the deposit
of the faithful through the ages. Because of our faith we are,
so to speak, 'on the same wavelength' as other believers, and
we are, therefore, able with confidence to accept what they
say or at least to be predisposed to suppose that there is
'something in it'. We do not, therefore, for example have to
establish for ourselves that the Bible has something to do with
truth before we can make any sort of use of it. We know that
our predecessors have found truth through it and in it. We
therefore faithfully scrutinize, question and search to see what
we in our turn shall be taught. The writers of the Bible are
bearing witness in their various ways to the Truth of which
we also have had some glimpse. We know as they knew (by
faith) that this Truth is Truth indeed, and therefore we
confidently interrogate their witness so that we in our turn
may receive our understanding and be able to bear our
witness.

But we do not make the mistake of supposing that all the
'deposit of the faithful' is in fact 'faithful deposit'. When we
remember that the sole and possible ultimate basis of the
truthfulness of our faith is the relationship between God and
men, and when we recall the conditions of that relationship

until 'the End' which we have discussed above, we are not
surprised to find that all the manifestations of the human end
of this relationship are inextricably 'mixed' material. The
faithful of every age are still men whose redemption is not yet
worked out in them to their completed restoration, and
taking their 'deposit' seriously will be as likely to involve
learning from it by rejecting some of the aspects of it as by
positive illumination. (Surely, e.g. the Book of Esther, is the
sort of discreditable daydream wherein the unconverted
underdog in each one of us allows the mean level of his soul
to delight in a fantasy about the vicious discomforture of his
enemies?) The faithful are justified by their faith, not yet
made perfect in perception or expression.

This situation still holds with regard to the faithful witness
to Jesus. It may be that the orthodox christology of his person
is to be taken absolutely seriously as the most adequate and
correct indication we can give of his status and reality (I shall
return briefly to this below), i.e. that in *his* case we have one
unique example of 'the human end' of things where the
situation is not 'mixed', but is a perfect unity of perfect God
and perfect man under historical conditions. But this fact is
discernible only by faith, and we are dependent for our
evidence for the fact on the portrayals of faithful witness. (If
they had not had faith they would not have bothered to
witness.) We cannot deduce *a priori* what e.g. would be the
range of the knowledge displayed by this unique figure,
because as *he* is, *ex hypothesi*, the definitive evidence for the
nature of God, we cannot argue deductively from generalizations about God which ignore him, and we cannot have any
knowledge of what the *human* situation of such a person could
be other than from what we know about him. For he is,
again *ex hypothesi*, the only such human figure. Therefore
a priori arguments are out, and we are dependent upon the
evidence of the witnesses. But the witnesses, however faithful,
are, again *ex hypothesi*, the 'ordinary' sort of faithful (for they
do not have *his* personal status) and their witness is bound to
be 'mixed' (as New Testament criticism – conducted very
largely from among the faithful! – has made so abundantly
and decisively clear that no one who did not have an immense

vested interest in 'absoluteness' would any longer attempt to deny it). We cannot, therefore, have absolute confidence in the records of the Gospels as, say, a source of 'hard' historical data which will guarantee that the faithful view of Jesus is certainly true. (As a matter of fact *no* historical data can be absolutely 'hard', for being concerned with matters of fact and particularity it can only have degrees of probability. And further what (impossibly 'hard') historical data could possibly *guarantee* the fact that 'Jesus was God'? God cannot be established or guaranteed by any historical data at all!)

But we are not therefore condemned to lack of or loss of faith. We are taking the gospels seriously now (i.e. after we have developed into self-conscious faith) because they are clearly a central part of the deposit of faith. We are identified with, or rather in, that faith and we are right so to be identified. (Our faith has the twofold support of 'heart' and 'context' referred to above.) We therefore know that that to which faith witnesses is not false. Faith is not based on a lie but on the Truth. We accept, therefore, quite rightly what the faithful witnesses say as their witness to the underlying Truth, and we confidently investigate and interrogate that witness to be taught its meaning for us. The acceptance and apprehension of this witness will take different forms among different believers and different traditions of believers, although all will be agreed in their faith that something is being said and that what is being said is related to ultimate reality, i.e. God – and that, for them, *what* they understand as being said must be able to be shown to be related to and in some way or other consistent with the witness born in the Gospels and through the life of the faithful community. Thus, for example, all will be agreed that the confession 'Jesus Christ is risen' is a faithful witness to an abiding reality. The question is not 'Is this true?' but 'What is the truth (reality) which is witnessed to here?'. We know this is true because it is so clearly at the heart of the witness of the faithful and we are one with them. But we have the faithful task of growing into an understanding of what that reality is which is here witnessed to, i.e. we have to discover how it impinges on us and on those to whom we are sent by the risen Christ simply because we are among them. (Indeed, as far as unbelievers go, while as faithful 'we' are not 'of them', none the less as denizens of the twentieth century we are certainly 'of them' – we are all 'we' together.)

There will be different ways of accepting and understanding 'the Resurrection', and this will involve differing judgments about the historical status of the resurrection narratives in the four Gospels and their connection with the faith in the Risen Christ. It is not possible to carry out investigations into such a matter as the Resurrection without much fear and trembling and the possibility of a good deal of pain. For there can be no doubt that doubts about, say, the truth of or the relevance of 'the Empty Tomb' can and do 'upset' the faith of some. But ought we not to realize that faith is not only a joyful but also a painful thing? It is certainly not a complacent disposition. It is rather a gift of God which enables us to go adventuring further and further into the heart of his revelation of himself. And this is surely done by questioning, i.e. by asking questions in faith of the faithful witness which has come to us and submitting our faith to the questioning and testing of the totality of the world in which we live.

It certainly cannot seem unreasonable to a man who has faith that God should raise the dead, but this does not settle the question of *what* he did and what his 'doing' was in connection with Jesus. It may be that the continuing intensity of New Testament study will show that the 'ultra-radical' critics, as some hold them to be, are historically mistaken. That is to say that the conclusions of a Bultmann about the rarity of historically descriptive accuracy in the gospels is not reasonable on the weighing of all the evidence and when presuppositions shared with (if not taken over from) Heidegger are less in fashion. But this is a matter for continuing historical, philosophical and theological study, and whatever position is reached (or held to have been reached by the prevailing competent opinion), it will only be (as Bultmann's position is) a reasonably probable position. If faith can be undermined to the point of disappearance by radical critics, then it cannot be restored to the point of assurance by conservative ones. Rather, the doubt of the critics is part of the dialogue of faith from which each responsible and obedient believer culls such insights as he can and which it is his duty to offer to the continuing life of the church.

I may perhaps be allowed to attempt to make the point of view which I am here advocating a little clearer by two further examples before I close. Consider the notorious and discomforting problem of the historicity of the Fourth Gospel. That Gospel has spoken powerfully to many of the glory of Christ. I would dare to say that it has so spoken in some measure to me. But if, to take an example, the famous discourses are not historical, i.e. if Jesus probably never spoke them in this form, if indeed it is more than possible that he never uttered most of the words given to him in this gospel *at all*, what becomes of the glory? Is it simply a warm and golden glow of 'affective tone' compounded out of elements which might have been produced by the enjoyment of a Brahms' symphony on the one hand and an intellectual pprehension of moral worth on the other? I do not believe hat this is the position.

'John' (and it does not ultimately matter who he is, for there is the internal evidence of his Gospel and the external evidence of that Gospel's inclusion in the new 'Scriptures' of Jhe faithful that he also is one of the faithful – cf., indeed, ohn 21.24) makes his presentation of the impact upon him of the faith which is in and through and in connection with Jesus. As one who is now conscious of the fact that I, too, am one with the faithful, I accept this witness without requiring beforehand some authentication or justification based on, say, evidence of historicity. As I have argued above, it is not unreasonable of me to do this. I have not, therefore, just plunged into religious sentiment. I seek to understand the bearing and meaning of this witness of John to Christ with all the resources at my disposal and, as I say, I dare to conclude that I see something of the glory which he has seen and sought to bear witness to. I am now satisfied that what I have seen is not unconnected with reality, is not a purely subjective experience, for two reasons. The first is that 'authentication of faith' which I have tried to explain throughout this essay. The faith of the faithful is not based on a lie, as I know for myself. The second is that there is built into the Gospel itself a statement of the objective reference *and* merely historical base of the witness which the Gospel is bearing in the prologue (turning on 'the Word was made *flesh*'), and it is also clear that the Jesus who is the 'original' of the Fourth Gospel portrayal and the Jesus of the Synoptic Gospels, where the objectively historical figure is, up to a point, clearer, are one and the same. The degree of detailed descriptive historicity and where it lies has to be left again to the debates of the critics and experts. But that there is 'historicness' is clear enough. It may be, for instance, that a combination of conclusions to be drawn from, say, a study of the Dead Sea Scrolls and recent work such as that on the Fourth Gospel will cause a revision of the estimate of what is narrowly historical in it. We shall then have more confidence that more of the Jesus of the Fourth Gospel portrait is 'as you would have seen and heard him if you had been there'. But this again will be a probabilification which will be psychologically helpful to some (very many?). It will never reach the point of guaranteeing to us that God is rightly to be understood as a reality who reaches out to us in the form of a man whose way of life was symbolized by the washing of the disciples' feet. *This* is something which demands our total commitment both in thankful submission to so gracious a God and also in an obedient desire to be taught in practice the inwardness and reality of such a way of life. (The life of him who is the way, the truth and the life.) Such things are not guaranteed by narratives, however historically undergirded. Our faith in God will take away from us anxiety about the historicity of the writers, and this sets us free to question this witness with all the intensity we can in order to hear what is to be said to us. And we shall know that what we hear we must also speak. For we believe that the witness is a faithful witness to the significance of Jesus which is rooted on the one hand in the Jesus of history (and quite possibly more than is now most commonly held), and on the other in the authentic relationship of the author to that same God whom we also have come to know through the witness rooted in Jesus. We

speak, therefore, because we know that we are on to truth
and that that truth is for all men. We shall, therefore, bear
our witness. But we shall do so in so far as we are reasonably
clear that it is not 'our' witness but *the* witness of the faithful.
The detailed form that we give to and the manner in which
we seek to bear that witness is, of course, as liable to error
and will certainly be as 'mixed' as anything in the history of
the witnessing people of God. (We may do well to fear that
it will be more so.) But our task, like that of our predecessors,
is to bear the witness, not to establish it. That lies with God,
as does the authority. Our only authority lies in the fact that
we have the confidence of faith to continue in the way in
which God has set us. We must point imperfectly to that
which we have seen imperfectly and see how, as Paul knew,
it 'is God which giveth the increase', both in our faith and in
the number of the faithful.

This procedure of initial faithful acceptance, subsequent
faithful testing and questioning and eventual faithful bearing
witness has to be applied not only to the Scriptures, but also
to all the elements in the deposit of the faithful which have
acquired historical claims to be taken with particular seriousness. Among these would be such matters as a moral tradition
concerning, say, divorce, liturgical tradition concerning the
meaning and practice of the Eucharist and dogmatic
traditions and formulations such as the Chalcedonian
Definition. In view of my earlier reference to christology I
may make this last my final example.

The Chalcedonian Definition has been, in many quarters,
'getting a bad press'. My impression is that a good deal of it
is vitiated by a failure to enter sufficiently into an understanding of the circumstances and ways of thought of those
who were responsible for this Definition and who took part in
the debates out of which it eventually grew. None the less, it
is clear that the terms in which this definition is stated are
completely foreign to us today. Even those traditions which
make much of metaphysical words like 'nature', 'substance',
etc., do not use them in the precise (if there was one!) sense of
the Definition, and many would hold that terms of this sort
cannot satisfactorily be rehabilitated today at all. Certainly,

there is no agreed metaphysical language even among
Christians for making a general statement of 'catholic'
significance about permanent truths of the Faith. Further,
there are obvious difficulties about a concept like 'nature' in
an age of post-Darwinian biology, to mention no other
complications. Do we then 'start again' with christology?
Surely this would not be a faithful procedure at all. The
Chalcedonian Definition is a vitally important 'authority' in
matters christological. Anyone who wishes to contribute to
the church's understanding of the person of Christ today must
come to terms with it. That is, he must satisfy himself that he
understands what the Fathers were 'getting at' when this
Definition emerged, and he must show that any understanding of the person of Christ which he urges the church to
accept and make use of takes account of all that the Chalcedonian Definition took account of and safeguards all that that
Definition safeguarded. He must show very weighty cause
indeed for recommending the abandonment of any element
in the Definition.

I do not think that we can exclude the possibility that in
the long run some element or other of the Definition might
drop out of our understanding of the person of Christ. This
cannot be excluded, because although we are, in faith,
questioning the truths of faith *not* in order to establish their
truth but in order to see what is the truth which they now
have to convey to us, none the less it may eventually appear
under such questioning that some things that were taken as
truths of faith are in fact not so. This is bound to be the
position because, as we have seen, there is no absolute
authority short of God. But no perceptive and would-be
obedient servant of the tradition of faith will lightly reject
anything which he perceives that tradition to have taken
seriously, and he will search the harder for an understanding
of a truth the more seriously he perceives it to have been
taken. None the less, if the tradition does not 'come alive', i.e.
if the 'truth of faith' cannot be shown to be apprehensible as
relevant truth for the living and witnessing of the church
today, then its status is clearly in dispute, and it might be
that it will not be revived, but will eventually fade out of

serious significance. If this were to happen concerning the Chalcedonian Definition (I do not say it is happening or that *I* think it will) we may be sure that the faithful process of questioning, testing and eventual rejecting to which it had been subjected would have yielded for the continuing life of the faithful all that was essential in the original 'deposit'. What is quite certain is that any 'crystallized deposit' which is treated as a sacred formula but is never put to the test either of faith's questioning or of attempted use by the faithful is assuredly not crystallized but fossilized. It has become so much archaic nonsense, and the present life of the faithful has become impoverished by a failure to realize in present belief and action the truth out of which the formula originally grew and for which it once stood. It is a faithless mistake to suppose that the repetition and passing on of the *words* of 'truth of the Faith' and the treating of them with a so-called reverential respect which forbids any coming to grips with them is 'believing' them. Faith grows out of, feeds on and is corrected by what was believed 'then'. But authoritative and lively faith is always 'now'. How could it be otherwise since it is concerned with the living God?

A false authoritarianism does not earn (or deserve) respect and belief, but ridicule and then indifference. Faithful men striving to live faithfully and seeking to address themselves to whatever situations God thrusts upon them with whatever understanding and message God has seen fit to give them will not be lacking in authority. For they will not be letting themselves and their authority stand in the way of God. And we cannot doubt that faith will continue and will grow until the End. For we know that God is and that he is a God who calls men to himself.